The REBEL and the ROSE

The REBEL and the ROSE

JAMES A. SEMPLE, JULIA GARDINER TYLER, AND THE LOST CONFEDERATE GOLD

WESLEY MILLETT AND GERALD WHITE

CUMBERLAND HOUSE
NASHVILLE, TENNESSEE

THE REBEL AND THE ROSE
PUBLISHED BY CUMBERLAND HOUSE PUBLISHING, INC.
431 Harding Industrial Drive
Nashville, Tennessee 37211

Cover design by Gore Studio, Nashville, Tennessee

Library of Congress Cataloging-in-Publication Data

Millett, Wesley, 1939–
   The Rebel and the rose : James A. Semple, Julia Gardiner Tyler, and the lost Confederate gold / Wesley Millett and Gerald White.
         p. cm.
   Includes bibliographical references.
   ISBN-13: 978-1-58182-583-1 (hardcover : alk. paper)
   ISBN-10: 1-58182-583-8 (hardcover : alk. paper)
   1. Semple, James A. (James Allen) 1819–1883. 2. Confederate States of America. Navy—Biography. 3. Tyler, Julia Gardiner, 1820–1889. 4. Presidents' spouses—United States—Biography. 5. Confederate States of America. Dept. of the Treasury—History. 6. Gold—Confederate States of America—History. 7. Richmond (Va.)—History—Siege, 1864–1865. 8. Davis, Jefferson, 1808–1889. 9. Confederate States of America—Politics and government. 10. United States—History—Civil War, 1861–1865—Underground movements. I. White, Gerald, 1944– . II. Title.

E467.1.S48M55 2007
973.7'38092—dc22   2007015512
[B]

Printed in the United States of America

1 2 3 4 5 6 7 8 9 10—10 09 08 07

To our wives,
Laurie and Susan

CONTENTS

FOREWORD

$\mathcal{T}$HIS MAY BE THE most colorful and adventurous story of the great Civil War era, and it is brought to life for the first time by two new authors and dedicated researchers, Wesley Millett and Gerald White. There is everything here: war, gold, illicit love, mysterious romance, and meticulous documentation.

Rarely does a book come along that actually adds to the vast body of knowledge on the Civil War. Most nonfiction offerings rehash existing "facts," sometimes providing a different perspective or conclusion. I am pleased to say that *The Rebel and the Rose* joins the works of authors committed to correcting long-accepted statements that are incomplete, misleading, or simply untrue. More than that, it brings to light for the first time, details about events that have eluded writers since the war ended.

What has it taken authors Wesley Millett and Gerald White to dig out the information? About twelve years of research. Obscure lines in obscure letters; the linking of events that by themselves are meaningless; an eBay listing of a note written by Stephen E. Mallory, secretary of the Confederate navy, that never made it into the public domain; and private documents stored away for years are but a few examples of their new sources of information. The culmination is undoubtedly a letter recently found in the walls of an old Virginia farmhouse. In that February 1866 letter one mystery is solved and another is revealed.

What happened to the gold in the Confederate treasury? Over the years, many have speculated on its being buried somewhere around Washington, Georgia. It isn't. A television documentary conjectured that the gold was hidden in an old mill. It wasn't. Most authors simply note that it disappeared with a bonded naval officer, James A. Semple. It didn't. *The Rebel and the Rose* will tell you what happened to it.

What about James Semple and the vivacious Julia Gardiner Tyler, wife of a former president of the United States? We will leave that for you to figure out. The evidence is here. You will learn about their mutual attraction and their symbiotic relationship. One thing is clear: Julia would have had a difficult time at the end of the war without the help of James Semple, and he would probably not have lived much beyond his forty-fifth birthday without her. The union of these two people may have been unorthodox, but they survived, and Julia's reputation remained intact.

Finally, what was Semple involved in after the war that had him constantly on the move between Savannah, New York, and Montreal . . . with other cities, such as New Orleans and Albany occasionally visited as well? Let's just say, it was his way of helping the South, or at least he thought so at the time. Of course, there was one other person involved who could do little where he was, but he was kept informed . . . Confederate president Jefferson Davis.

By the way, there are still *two* unsolved mysteries in the book, and they both involve the man who wrote and then hid the letter in the wall of his house. I wondered about them, and you will too. But perhaps that's a subject for another book. In any case, hopefully, Millett and White have only begun their Civil War saga with this fascinating and valuable story hidden in the rubbish of its aftermath.

DOUG WEAD

presidential historian,
author of *All the Presidents' Children*
Haymarket, Virginia

INTRODUCTION

*L*ATE FALL WAS UPON eastern Virginia. Through the end of October, the weather had been sunny and pleasant, and despite the war and intrusions of the enemy in parts of the state, farmers were busy seeding their fields with wheat. Gradually, the coolness of the evenings and early mornings began to pervade the days. Bleak and unseasonably cold on November 9, 1863, the transformation was complete, at least temporarily, with the first signs of snow in the air.

Seven miles below Richmond, the fortifications at Drewry's Bluff on the James River represented a formidable obstacle to efforts by the Union navy to capture the city. Here, at a steep bend in the river, the Confederates had scuttled side-wheelers and schooners to obstruct the passage of Federal gunboats, and on the bluffs, ninety feet above the James, heavy artillery had been emplaced behind a maze of earthworks. Rifle pits provided protection along the banks of the river for marine sharpshooters, hand-picked for their accuracy.

Though the cold and spitting snow were unpleasant on top of the bluff this November day, the defenders manning the batteries were comforted by the apparent willingness of Union warships to remain downriver. Another day would go by without an attack on the Confederate stronghold.

In his quarters at Drewry's Bluff, navy paymaster James A. Semple contemplated the letter he was writing to Julia Gardiner Tyler, wife of former U.S. president John Tyler. Julia had become a widow in January of the previous year and suddenly found herself alone in raising her family at Sherwood Forest, Tyler's sixteen-hundred-acre plantation in Charles City County.

Sherwood Forest was thirty-five miles east of Richmond and less than fifty miles west of the Union garrison at Fort Monroe, where the James River flows into the Chesapeake Bay at Hampton Roads. The plantation would be in the path of any thrust toward the capital from Fort Monroe, as it had been in June 1862, when the Union army threatened Richmond under Maj. Gen. George B. McClellan. With the Union army expanding its hold on the Virginia Peninsula, enemy gunboats edging up the James, and Yankee cavalry raiding ever closer to Sherwood Forest, the countryside was no longer safe, even with Confederate soldiers encamped and patrolling the area.

Julia had been thinking for weeks about the wisdom of staying where she was with her two youngest children, though neighbors such as the Willcoxs at Belle Air and the Cloptons at Selwood were only a short carriage ride away and the Seldens were a few miles upriver at Westover plantation. She might be able to seek refuge with a family close by, should Union troops invade the area again in strength. On the other hand, all of the plantations along the James River, from Sherwood Forest to Shirley, would be in jeopardy regardless of whether or not they were occupied. Berkeley plantation, the former home of two U.S. presidents and once a showpiece along the river, had been taken over by McClellan in July 1862, with his troops bivouacking on the grounds before they were forced to retreat back down the Peninsula in a series of engagements with Confederate forces in late June and early July. Berkeley, its owners having fled as McClellan approached, remained abandoned, and Evelynton, midway along the river between Sherwood Forest and Berkeley, had been burned to the ground.

With this new threat, little actual help could be expected from anyone, especially with most men of military age off fighting for the Confederacy. Property and possessions were one thing; the potential danger to her children was another matter. Charles City County would almost certainly become an intensely fought battleground, and no family would be safe. Besides, Julia was tired of the war and the hot, unhealthy summers in Virginia. Ultimately, she decided to leave, moving first to Richmond, where she formulated plans to join her mother, Juliana Gardiner, at her Castleton Hill home on Staten Island, New York. Though born and raised in the North, Julia was a vehement believer in the Southern cause. She would wait for the eventual Confederate victory while doing what she could for the South from her temporary new home. In this effort, Juliana, an ardent convert, would support her.[1]

Four of Julia's children, including fifteen-year-old Alex (John Alexander Tyler), were already staying with Juliana, the result of an earlier trip north, while seventeen-year-old Gardie (David Gardiner Tyler) was enrolled at

Washington College in Lexington, Virginia, a part of the state still relatively free from enemy intrusions. Alex and Gardie, staunch "Rebels" like their mother, would soon be pressing Julia to allow them to do their part for the Confederacy by joining up to fight the Yankees.

Refusing to take an oath of allegiance to the United States, Julia was repeatedly denied a pass from Federal authorities, which was necessary to enter the North legally and avoid the possibility of arrest or deportation. Her status as a former first lady did little for her. In frustration, she turned to Semple for help, who responded by drawing on contacts in the Navy and Ordnance departments for the necessary arrangements. Eventually, she was able to book passage for herself and her children on a blockade-runner owned by the Confederate government.[2]

The process of leaving, however, was complicated somewhat by Julia's desire to bring five bales of cotton with her; she would sell them in Bermuda. At the time, Bermuda was a neutral port where blockade-runners frequently stopped to deliver cotton and take on goods purchased by Confederate agents in England and other countries. Such goods, which typically ranged from luxury items—dresses, shoes, and hats—to blankets, arms, and munitions, were transported to Bermuda, the Bahamas, and other intermediate points on foreign-owned (usually British) ships that, under international law, could not be intercepted by the Union navy. There, the goods were transferred to lighter, faster, low-profile steamers destined for Confederate ports not yet in U.S. hands, such as Wilmington, North Carolina, and Charleston, South Carolina.[3]

Bermuda provided a safe haven to Confederate shipping while the vessels were anchored in the harbor of St. George's. Confederate and Union seamen often crossed paths, heckling one another in alleyways around King's Square and in the taverns along the waterfront. Outside the harbor was another matter. Blockade-runners were fair game for the Union navy, and in the third year of the war, the number of Federal vessels strung across the harbors of Southern ports still open made entering and leaving increasingly risky ventures.

Semple finally convinced Julia to let him handle the sale of the cotton separately, and on October 28, 1863, she and the children left from Wilmington on the CSS *Cornubia* under the command of Lt. Richard H. Gayle, who would end up in the North as well, but as a prisoner. (Gayle was captured on a return voyage to Wilmington, at the time commanding the blockade-runner *Robert E. Lee.* He was sent to Fort Warren prison and held for almost a year on Georges Island in Boston Harbor.)[4]

From Wilmington, Julia's voyage on the *Cornubia* took her safely through the blockade to Bermuda, where she arranged passage to New York. By the end of November, Julia was safely united with her mother and children at Castleton Hill. Semple kept his promise by shipping the cotton to Nassau in December and selling it to a Spanish buyer for a handsome profit.

Currently a paymaster in the Confederate navy, Semple would soon be promoted to a bureau chief in the Navy Department, equivalent in rank to a brigadier general in the army. His contacts and accomplishments were almost certainly due more to his influence and abilities than the benefits accruing to his status in the Navy Department. James Allen Semple was as much an enigma as he was competent and dependable. Adding to the mystique was the fact that he had a second legal name—Allen S. James—which he claimed, to Julia, had been granted to him by the Alabama legislature. Why he had an alias is unknown, but it may have been because of clandestine services provided to the South certainly after, and possibly during, the war. His death was erroneously reported more than once, perhaps to aid him in his activities.

Semple obviously dedicated himself to knowing people who could further his interests, despite his intent on being obscure to the public in his work and personal life. During his lifetime, he counted generals and other senior military officers, here and abroad, as friends, rubbed elbows with politicians at the highest levels of government, including Confederate president Jefferson Davis and his wife, Varina, and was highly valued by his superiors.

During the war and afterward, he operated quietly and resourcefully in the shadow of others, a role that he relished. His skill, aggressiveness, and dedication to the cause of the Confederacy ensured that he accomplished what he was asked to do without drawing attention to himself. Years later, in a letter to Julia about his responsibilities after the war, he proudly stated, "I am glad to say that even in delirium, I never spoke a word of what has happened since the war closed."[5] He remained closemouthed until the day he died—except to Julia, a woman he confided in, befriended, protected, and loved.

The facts that Semple was married and was related to Julia by marriage were apparently never an impediment to their relationship. Semple's wife, Letitia, was a daughter of John Tyler and his first wife, who had died of a stroke in 1842, while Tyler was still president. Estranged from Letitia, and with lasting bitterness between them, Semple lived as a bachelor, a lifestyle made easier by circumstances of war and the fact that he and Letitia had no children. They never divorced, never reconciled, and never lived together after the war ended.

Semple was forty-four and Julia a year younger when she steamed out of Wilmington on the *Cornubia*. Still attractive, Julia retained the alluring charm that, as a young woman, had captivated her many suitors, including the U.S. president. During the last months of the war, Semple became enamored with her, and they grew closer despite the distance between Richmond and New York and the interposition of the Union and Confederate armies between them. His willingness to help a family member, the widow of a man he respected, was sincere. At some point, however, his feelings for Julia and her family blurred the role he had assumed as her "brother."

For her part, Julia depended more and more on Semple from the safety of Staten Island. He was needed, not only for handling certain affairs and for news on the condition of Sherwood Forest in the hands of Union soldiers and former slaves, but also, and most importantly, for counseling and watching over her sons in the service of the Confederacy. In the postwar years, Julia would reciprocate Semple's affection and support, and a symbiotic bond would grow between them, each dependent on the other to meet their personal needs.

On this chilly November day, while Julia waited in the warmer climate of Bermuda for passage to New York, Semple formally addressed his letter to "My Dear Mrs. Tyler" and wrote about a number of things in which she had an interest: an upcoming marriage of people she knew, the status of her claim against the War Department for a horse and some oats confiscated from Sherwood Forest by a foraging party, his promise to let her know about the condition of Sherwood when he was able to find out anything, the favorable yield expected of her crops, and his upcoming monthlong leave. In ending, he made an offer he would frequently repeat, one that Julia would frequently accept: "Should you wish my services in any manner, I need not say to you again that you must command them in any way you desire."[6]

The odyssey of James A. Semple begins with the fall of Richmond. Chapter 1 describes the desperate straits of the final weeks faced by the Confederate soldiers in front of Richmond, protecting the capital, including Alex and Gardie, both of whom have joined the First Rockbridge Artillery.

The flight from Richmond of the Confederate government, and especially Semple, sets events in motion, inevitably linking the lives of the navy paymaster and the former first lady. The next two years for Semple would not only encompass Julia but also the missing Confederate gold, an ongoing effort to avoid capture and arrest, underground activities in New York and Canada, and ultimately, disillusionment. The name of James A. Semple has been obscured in history. This is due both to his own efforts and to an apparent cover-up by Letitia and by descendants of John Tyler, all intent on protecting the family name of an American president.

ACKNOWLEDGMENTS

*W*ITH RESEARCH ON *The Rebel and the Rose* having occurred over a period of more than a dozen years, a number of people should be thanked for their contributions of time and effort. Each of us, as authors, worked both independently and in collaboration with one another, and as a result, our contacts differed somewhat. Collectively, we wish to extend our appreciation to those providing assistance in the Special Collections Department of the Swem Library at the College of William and Mary, the primary depository of personal documents donated by the Tyler family, and at the Sterling Memorial Library of Yale University, which houses the vast collection of Gardiner-Tyler papers accumulated after the marriage of President John Tyler to Julia Gardiner.

Heather Milne at the Museum of the Confederacy and Meg Glass and Colin Woodward at the Valentine Museum in Richmond, Virginia, were especially helpful in finding photographs. Also of immense assistance at the Valentine was an unnamed research associate who spent hours poring through and providing copies of prewar and wartime newspaper articles and maps and photographs pertaining to buildings, streets, and businesses in the Confederate capital.

Sherry Tyler of the Charles City County Historical Society in Charles City, Virginia, assisted with information, insights, and photographs on the Tyler family, and Pat Cunningham of Williamsburg, Virginia, performed exceptional genealogical research for the book. Mrs. Lea Booth of Lynchburg, Virginia, went through her files of long-stored material and contributed letters and photographs of her Tyler ancestors. She is the granddaughter of Judge David Gardiner Tyler (Gardie).

Mrs. Ridgely Copeland of North Bend Plantation and Mrs. Meriweather Major of Belle Air Plantation provided helpful information about Tidewater plantations during the antebellum years. Mrs. Alice Calloway of Richmond must be thanked for information on Charles City oral history in terms of family connections with President John Tyler. T. Pat Goodman of Winchester, Virginia, owner of Linden Farm, the home that once belonged to Confederate navy clerk Edward Tidball, made a remarkable discovery, previously undocumented, that cleared up a question about the Confederate gold but created a new mystery yet to be solved.

Todd Hall has spent years investigating the kegs of Mexican silver dollars, which evidence suggests were left behind in Danville, Virginia. His input has been instrumental, not only in helping to substantiate the burying of the silver, but also in determining the location of the naval supply store from which James Semple was able to draw ample provisions for the fleeing Confederate government.

Certainly, Lynda Crist, editor in chief of the Jefferson Davis Papers project at Rice University, must be mentioned for her contributions as a mentor and for her sharing of resource material and contacts. Crist is a foremost authority on Jefferson Davis and the Davis family. She was the winner of the 2003–4 Founders Award by the Museum of the Confederacy for excellence in editing of primary-source documents on the Confederate period.

Doug Wead, who authored the foreword to this book, is greatly appreciated for his encouragement and guidance. A special assistant to President George H. W. Bush, he has been an adviser to three U.S. presidents and is a cofounder, with entertainer Pat Boone, of the relief organization Mercy Corps. He is the author of twenty-seven books, including the *New York Times* bestseller *All the President's Children: Triumph and Tragedy in the Lives of the First Families.* His books have sold more than five million copies in twenty languages.

In the early throes of research for *The Rebel and the Rose,* Robert Seager, author of the acclaimed and meticulously researched *And Tyler Too,* was a sounding board for ideas and avenues of research. He also provided leads to Tyler relatives, such as Mrs. Lea Booth, with private collections of family papers. Sadly, Seager passed away in 2004.

Personal comments by Wesley Millett: I wish to thank my daughters, Kimberly McAdams and Jennifer Millett-Barrett, and my son, Brandon Millett, for their contributions. Kimberly has encouraged the writing of the book for years and provided documents on the Fenian movement. Jennifer spent countless hours researching and digitally retouching photos and chasing down information on the Fenian leadership as well as the hotels James Semple frequented during his travels. Brandon has been a motivating force behind both the initiation and completion of the book, and he has been instrumental in developing resources and contacts for *The Rebel and the Rose*. Finally, the book would not be possible without the support, encouragement, and patience of my wife, Laurie. She, Jennifer, and Brandon also reviewed the draft editorially and offered suggestions on the content.

Personal comments by Gerald White: I am indebted in particular to my wife, Susan, for her patience in listening to seemingly endless stories about the research on James Semple and for her encouragement in this endeavor. Likewise, I wish to acknowledge the support and comments about the project provided by my mother-in-law, Louise Wimberly Hagood, of Paris, Texas, who never tired of hearing about the adventures of the mysterious navy paymaster.

The REBEL and the ROSE

1

PROLOGUE TO DEFEAT

I have received tonight your letter of this date requesting my opinion upon the military condition of the country. It must be apparent to every one that it is full of peril and requires prompt action.
—Gen. Robert E. Lee to Secretary of War
John C. Breckinridge, March 9, 1865

Sunday, April 2, 1865; 11:00 p.m. The cars lurched and rattled across the Richmond and Danville Railroad bridge spanning the James River. Billowing cinders and smoke into the rafters of the covered bridge, the engine crept along on tracks long neglected as a consequence of war and the inability of the Confederate government to allocate the iron needed to replace rails.[1]

Behind the train were the vestiges of the city that had been until only minutes ago the capital of the Confederacy. As the cars reached the south side of the James, those passengers peering back from their uncomfortable perches on the tops of the cars saw little evidence of a city in peril, the darkness of night and the unlit buildings obscuring the confusion and turmoil roiling in the streets and thoroughfares of the former capital.

Lost to view were the soldiers preparing to fire the tobacco warehouses and bridges. Also obscured were the hordes of people, many with hastily collected belongings, milling in fear and indecision. Most of these were desperately seeking transportation out of the city before the dreaded Yankees arrived. Here and there, the flickering glow of fire was visible from piles of paper and supplies burning in the streets and along the waterfront. Dark forms could be seen fleeing across Mayo's Bridge in pursuit of safety.

Inside the coaches and boxcars were the essential ingredients of a refugee government on the move: department heads, military officers, clerks, books and records, personal baggage, and even horses. Multiple trains would ultimately be required to haul offices and ordnance south to Danville, Virginia, some having left hours earlier. Calm, dignified, and lost in his thoughts, Confederate president Jefferson Davis was seated in the lead car, along with members of his cabinet and others of sufficient status or importance to the administration. Thirty people in all were wedged into the uncomfortable quarters.

Soon to follow was another train transporting wooden boxes and kegs of silver and gold, the remaining assets of the Confederate treasury. Coins, nuggets, and bullion had been loaded into an overburdened boxcar, along with foreign bills of exchange, Confederate currency and bonds—now practically worthless—and a chest filled with jewelry and precious stones. Loaded in another car were the deposits of gold coins belonging to several Richmond banks, purposely separated from the government treasury.

A pall of gloom and uncertainty hung over the occupants of the train carrying Davis and his cabinet as it jolted southward. In recent weeks, most of the fugitives had reconciled themselves to the fact that Richmond would be evacuated. When the day began, however, no one could have anticipated the events that quickly followed. Certainly, neither residents nor visitors nor reserves guarding the city expected the government to be gone and the capital to be in ruins by the time the sun rose the day after the evacuation.

Richmond's citizens had known for some time that the situation was dire. Food in the overcrowded city was in short supply. The main staple seemed to be dried beans, costing as much as $25 a quart. Flour went for $1,500 a barrel, more than double what it was two months prior, and a pound of bacon cost $20. Confederate money was so debased, notes were carried in large denominations and in large quantities. John Beauchamp Jones, a clerk in the War Department and chronicler of life in Richmond during the war years, expressed the fear in his diary that "the currency has gone beyond redemption."[2] Dallas Tucker, then a youth of fifteen, later recalled that because of the bulk of the money needed for daily use, his family kept the currency stored in a box in a closet. He wrote about going to market one day with the "inconsiderable sum of $500" to purchase a small piece of mutton and three quarts of black-eyed peas. He returned home with $175 in change.[3]

Outside of Richmond, the pressure of the enemy could be felt everywhere. Yankee cavalry severed rail lines and communications. The ominous booming of artillery was a constant reminder of how close the war had come to the doorsteps of the city.

Inexorably, a noose was tightening around the capital. In Petersburg, scarcely twenty-five miles from Richmond, Robert E. Lee's Army of Northern Virginia faced Ulysses S. Grant's Army of the Potomac. Even nearer to Richmond, Grant had positioned the smaller Army of the James, which was commanded by Maj. Gen. Godfrey Weitzel. An erratic thirty-seven-mile arc of trenches and emplacements ran from the Chickahominy River, northeast of Richmond, to Hatcher's Run, southwest of Petersburg. Over a nine-month period, Grant's more than 110,000 well-provisioned and equipped soldiers slowly extended these lines, forcing Lee to stretch his already thin forces and to hurriedly shift troops to blunt Grant's probings of his defenses.

Compounding Lee's problem were desertions. Men by the hundreds slipped away daily from the trenches to return to their wives and families in time for the spring planting. Some, driven by hunger and exhaustion, crossed over to the Union lines. By the beginning of April, fewer than forty thousand able-bodied soldiers remained. Lee's army was melting away while the enemy grew stronger with regular arrivals of reinforcements and supplies.

Lee, in fact, had known for months what the outcome would be when the roads were dry enough to accommodate the movement of an overwhelmingly powerful army on the attack. In a March 9 letter to the recently appointed secretary of war, John C. Breckinridge, Lee pointed out the impossibility of maintaining his position in the face of a far stronger enemy, especially without adequate provisions for his men and animals. Lee's conclusion was ominous. Unless his subsistence needs were met immediately, "the army cannot be kept together, and our present lines must be abandoned." He was actually less than candid with Breckinridge, for Lee knew that even with supplies, he could not protect Richmond much longer.[4]

Those in the city alert to changes in the daily routine of the government saw other signs of impending doom. For weeks, various departments had

been shipping nonessential archives out of Richmond for safekeeping farther south, followed by machinery, arms, and supplies. In late February,
signers of Confederate notes for the Treasury Department were ordered to
Lynchburg in anticipation of the paper money being produced there. And
near the end of March, a "large sum" of coins from the treasury was transported to Charlotte, North Carolina, by Southern Express. Such govern-
mental activities, while discrete, did not go unnoticed.

In mid-March, the Confederate Congress wound up its business with
little accomplishment, and legislators left the capital almost immediately,
scattering to their homes. Lee had met with a Virginia congressional delegation earlier in the month to explain the plight of his army. Something had
to be done, he urged, or Richmond would be lost. Unfortunately, Congress
either turned a deaf ear to his plea or it was simply unable to help. Whatever the reason, no action was taken. In an outburst of frustration, Lee
groused to his son Custis that while his army was starving, "They don't
seem to be able to do anything but eat peanuts and chew tobacco." Yet
Custis was more than a sympathetic son. Maj. Gen. George Washington
Custis Lee was also a military aide to President Davis who had contributed
much to the fortifications around Richmond and well knew the condition of
the army.[5]

As the end of March approached, Davis continued to cling to a hope
that Richmond could be saved. Publicly, he remained upbeat and confident
that Lee's lines would hold. He also kept a normal schedule and was often
seen riding the streets of the city as he went to and from the army camps,
his face masking the physical and mental effects of war on him. Despite the
veneer of optimism, he was growing increasingly concerned about the
safety of his own family.

Stiff in demeanor—perhaps partly because of his military training and
service—Davis was often reserved and distant in dealing with those around
him. He had once been called "cold as a lizard" by colorful Sam Houston of
Tennessee and Texas fame. His wife, Varina, and close associates, however,
saw another side: a warm, devoted husband and father.

Worries about his family finally stirred Davis into action. He decided to
send Varina and the children to Charlotte, a clear indicator to observers that
Richmond was in trouble. Presaging this event had been the appearance in
store windows weeks before of Varina's old gowns, gloves, feathers, silks,
and other apparel she had decided to sell. More valuable items had gone to

an auction house, including various antiques, furniture, cabinet glasses, silver, china, and paintings. Most, if not all of it, must have sold, for the president ended up with a check for $28,444 (that is, Confederate dollars).

On the rainy evening of March 31, much against her wishes, Varina boarded a dilapidated passenger car at the Richmond and Danville depot, along with her four children: Maggie, Jefferson Jr., Willie, and Varina Anne, ranging in age from nine months to nine years. The trip south would be fraught with danger, as the track might be cut at any time by Union cavalry. At the very least, the countryside would be crawling with deserters and bands of riffraff.

Embracing his family, Davis almost changed his mind about their going, especially when the children clung to him in tears and begged to stay. He had no idea when and where he would see them again, and the separation would be almost more than he could bear. As Varina later recalled, "It was evident he thought he was looking his last upon us."[6] He gave her a pistol and ammunition for protection and a small stack of gold, all that he had, except for a single five-dollar piece he kept for himself. Neither was adequate for the difficulties that would lie ahead.

Varina at least had a place to stay in Charlotte, a house having been rented earlier by telegraph; Davis comforted himself with the knowledge that she was being escorted by Burton Harrison, a trusted personal secretary. Also, traveling with Varina were her sister, Maggie Howell; the daughters of Secretary of the Treasury George A. Trenholm; three servants; and midshipman James Morris Morgan, who was charged with guarding the party. Morgan was pleased with the assignment, because he was engaged to one of the Trenholm daughters, Helen. As Davis watched from the platform, the train jerked into motion and slowly snorted and swayed its way into the rainy night.[7]

The most astute of Richmond's citizens had begun to make plans to leave the city themselves. Jones, writing daily in his diary, noted on March 21, "There are many red flags displayed this morning in Clay Street for sales of furniture and renting of houses to the highest bidders."[8]

Still, though the threat to the city was real, many believed that Richmond would somehow survive Grant's armies. The Confederacy had Lee— "Marse Robert," as he was affectionately called—and that brought a certain peace of mind. Lee was beloved by his men. And though desertions occurred regularly, primarily out of concern for home and family as Union armies penetrated the South, the core of his army was committed to fight to the end. In a letter home, an Alabama private wrote, "We are not a frade of the yankees while we have old General Lee to lead us in the fites."[9] "God bless him!" exclaimed a soldier in Richmond headed back to his unit on a Sunday morning.[10] The feeling was widespread among the populace as well as the military, and tintypes or engravings of Lee were prominently displayed in many Richmond homes.

The capital had faced such threats in the past, most notably in the spring and early summer of 1862. Union Gen. George B. McClellan had led an impressively equipped and trained army up the Peninsula between the James and York rivers southeast of Richmond. Overly cautious and with wagons often mired in mud, McClellan eventually approached close enough for his lead regiments to see the church spires in Capitol Square. The battle of Fair Oaks soon changed the course of events. During that battle, Confederate Gen. Joseph E. Johnston was seriously wounded, and the next day, Lee was named to command the Army of Northern Virginia. Though he had little more than half the number of soldiers of his opponent, Lee seized the offensive and fiercely attacked McClellan, driving him down the Peninsula in a series of hard-fought battles over a period of seven days. Richmond was saved, and Lee was instantly revered for rescuing the capital and the Confederacy.

Despite the inequities in ordnance and the superior numbers arrayed against him, there was an element of expectation that Lee would somehow stop Grant in '65 as he had done McClellan in '62. With the end of winter, spirits had improved somewhat in Richmond, "starvation parties" (parties without refreshments) flourished, and people on the streets ignored the obvious to reassure one another.

Weddings abounded, perhaps in defiance of the Damocles sword hanging over the city, or more likely because of the uncertainties of the future. According to diarist Judith Brockenbrough McGuire, "There seems to be a perfect mania on the subject of matrimony. Some of the churches may be seen open and lighted almost every night for bridals, and whenever I turn I hear of marriages in prospect."[11] The wife of an Episcopalian minister, McGuire and her husband were forced to leave Alexandria when the Union army took over the city. She eventually ended up in Richmond, along with thousands of other refugees, where she took a job as a clerk in the Commissary Department.

Richmonders were left to form their own opinions, the government having censured the publishing of war news. Often the rumors that floated on the streets and in gathering places were those that put a positive spin on events: overestimates of military strength, enemy assaults being repulsed, treaties with France and Mexico, etc. Reality was less in demand than hope and good news.

Contributing to the delusion was Edward Pollard, the normally vitriolic editor of the *Richmond Examiner.* Pollard relayed to his readers the rumor that Gen. Joseph E. Johnston, now commanding an army in North Carolina, no longer opposed the Union forces under Maj. Gen. William T. Sherman and was headed north to link up with Lee. Together, Pollard reported, Lee and Johnston would defeat Grant and then turn back to deal with Sherman, apparently giving little weight to the fact that Grant would still have more than twice as many men as the combined armies of Lee and Johnston.[12]

Nothing could be further from the truth.

Johnston had his hands full trying to stall the Sherman juggernaut, which had already cut the state of Georgia in two with a swath of devastation. Given full rein to do so by Grant, who had instructed him to "create havoc and destruction of all resources that would be beneficial to the enemy," Sherman, with almost one hundred thousand men and three armies, burned barns, homes, and even towns, laid waste to fields, and destroyed or confiscated whatever harvests, stored food, cotton, and livestock his foragers could find.[13]

Sherman had begun his march through the heart of the Confederacy in the mountainous country of northern Georgia. Opposing him was the Army of Tennessee, commanded in early 1864 by Johnston. With half as many men, the Confederate general sought to block Sherman behind strongly fortified positions, but Sherman repeatedly outflanked his army in a relentless surge toward Atlanta. With Johnston pushed back to the entrenchments around Atlanta, Davis finally had enough of his reluctant warrior and replaced Johnston with Lt. Gen. John B. Hood, who immediately took the offensive in a series of attacks and was soundly defeated by Sherman.

Atlanta fell on September 2, 1864, and much of the city was burned to the ground. Sherman then organized his army into two divisions of two corps each, totaling some sixty thousand seasoned veterans. With the separate armies traveling more or less parallel routes some twenty to forty miles apart,

Sherman commenced his trek toward the Georgia seacoast, brushing aside local resistance and creating a wasteland through the state up to sixty miles wide. Ranging even farther afield were the cavalry screens for the two wings.

Savannah fell to Sherman on December 21, and the Union commander gleefully telegraphed the Abraham Lincoln, "I beg to present you as a Christmas gift the City of Savannah, with one hundred and fifty guns and plenty of ammunition, also about twenty-five thousand bales of cotton."[14] After a few weeks of waiting for soaking rains to end, Sherman pointed his armies north to South Carolina, capturing and burning Columbia, the capital, before advancing into North Carolina.

Sherman had to be stopped. The devastation wrought by his armies was stripping the Confederacy of an essential food basket, not to mention the loss of homes and businesses, as well as manufacturing capability. Pressured to do so by Lee, Davis restored Johnston to command, replacing Hood, who had all but decimated his army in a campaign to reclaim Tennessee. Johnston's prospects were slim, however, as he faced his nemesis with a hodgepodge force assembled from the battle-weary remnants of his former Army of Tennessee. Adding to his numbers were a small army of around ten thousand men under Lt. Gen. William J. Hardee, originally assigned to defend Savannah; Maj. Gen. Robert F. Hoke's division, sent south by Lee to protect Wilmington, North Carolina, and now commanded by Gen. Braxton Bragg; and some cavalry under Lt. Gen. Wade Hampton . . . in total, somewhat more than twenty thousand men. Johnston was hopelessly outnumbered and could only exercise his old strategy of slowly falling back in front of the invaders while looking for a weakness he could exploit.

Finally, at Bentonville, North Carolina, Johnston saw an opportunity and struck. With Sherman's army temporarily divided and advancing toward Goldsboro along three different routes, Johnston saw that the Union left wing, under Maj. Gen. Henry W. Slocum, was separated some ten miles from the column closest to him. On the morning of March 19, Johnston attacked Slocum with some success, driving the Union lines back and capturing some artillery. Success, however, gradually turned to stalemate as the Union positions stiffened and the Confederate troops were battered by Slocum's remaining batteries. The day ended with the Confederates pulling back at night to their original positions; though the battle raged for two more days, the element of surprise was spent, and Johnston's opportunity was lost, while Sherman brought up reinforcements. Technically, the battle was a draw, but Johnston was forced to retreat northward, and the last major engagement south of Virginia was over.

For Gen. William J. Hardee, the battle had been especially tragic. Pestered for months by his sixteen-year-old son, Willie, Hardee finally allowed him to join the Eighth Texas Cavalry, a unit under his command. On the morning of the last day of fighting, the general came upon litter-bearers carrying his mortally wounded son to the rear.[15]

The situation for Johnston was as desperate in the pine country of North Carolina as it was for the Army of Northern Virginia at Petersburg. In reporting to Lee about Bentonville, Johnston stated the obvious: "Sherman's course cannot be altered by the small force I have. I can do no more than annoy him." Thus Johnston would be of no help to Lee.[16]

Near the end of March, Lee knew he had to do something to relieve the pressure on his lines. With his situation growing more desperate each day, only the rainy weather and the muddy condition of the roads and fields were holding the enemy back from punching through the Confederate defenses. If Lee could force Grant to "curtail his lines" by seizing one of his fortifications, perhaps he could hold the position with a portion of his troops and stop the encirclement of his army.

In the predawn of Saturday, March 25, Lee launched a surprise attack against Fort Stedman on Hare's Hill, a salient in the Union fortifications on the south bank of the James River and about a mile east of Petersburg. A combined force of infantry and cavalry under Lt. Gen. John B. Gordon took the fort and three adjacent batteries without difficulty, but then lost them in a heavily reinforced counterattack. What brought momentary hope to Lee ended in another disaster, with nearly four thousand casualties, soldiers Lee could ill afford to lose. The Confederate army settled back into its entrenchments, waiting for Grant to make the next move—which was soon to come.

On Wednesday, March 29, Union Maj. Gen. Philip H. Sheridan was in motion with three divisions of cavalry and two corps of infantry. Grant had ordered him to outflank the extreme right of the Confederate lines and cut the South Side Railroad, an essential link for supplying Petersburg. To blunt Sheridan's advance, Lee hurriedly patched together a force under Maj. Gen. George E. Pickett of Gettysburg fame, along with cavalry units under Maj. Gen. William Henry Fitzhugh "Fitz" Lee. Skirmishing occurred on March 29 and 30; on March 31, at a crossroads called Five Forks, Pickett was able to push back Sheridan's attempt to outflank him.

With night coming on, Pickett ordered a halt to the action, and his troops withdrew to a defensive position. The next morning, not seeing any Union soldiers across from him, Pickett convinced himself that Sheridan was not going to attack that day. The general and some of his officers then accepted an invitation from Maj. Gen. Thomas Rosser to attend a fish fry. In their absence, and while they savored whiskey and picked at grilled shad, Sheridan attacked in the late afternoon, overwhelming the defenses and scattering or capturing Pickett's men. Pickett had been fooled on April Fools' Day.

The loss to Lee was unexpected and devastating: more than four thousand killed, wounded, or captured. It was a disaster from which Lee could not, and would not, recover. Several days later, he ordered that Pickett be relieved of command, partly in anger and partly because Pickett had so few soldiers left to command. For some reason, however, either because he did not receive the order or because he refused to obey it, Pickett remained with the Army of Northern Virginia. Lee never forgave Pickett, even years after the war was over, for leaving his post for a picnic.

Thick fog cloaked the terrain between the opposing lines in the predawn of Sunday, April 2. Silently at first, Union soldiers advanced through the fog and pines; then with a cacophony of yells, rifle fire, and cannonading, Grant's men assaulted the defenses around Petersburg, breaking through the sparsely manned lines in a number of places. About the time the attack began, Confederate Lt. Gen. James Longstreet, commander of the First Corps, arrived at Edge Hill, the home of William Turnbull, which was being used as Lee's headquarters. Lee awoke and the two generals discussed the loss at Five Forks the day before. As they talked, a staff officer informed Lee that the lines had been broken. "You'll have to go," he said. Lee pulled his robe around him and walked with Longstreet to the door. What they saw must have been a shock: a long line of blue skirmishers spread out across the field "in quiet march toward us."[17]

Lee was dressed within moments. Calmly belting on his sword, he mounted his horse, Traveller, and rode from his headquarters, accompanied by members of his staff. Behind him in the house, a telegraph operator was sending off the first of Lee's messages, notifying Davis and Breckinridge of the immediate need to evacuate Richmond.

Lee would try to buy several hours of time, but from this point on, the Confederate government was on its own. He had one objective in mind: to somehow save his army. With units spread along the front between Richmond and Petersburg, organizing their removal while holding Grant at bay would require both skill and luck . . . and the cover of night. He had to slow the Union onslaught for most of the day. If he could do that, and if he could somehow pull his forces back during the night without alerting the Union pickets along the lines, Grant would be looking out at empty trenches when the sun rose the next morning.

* * *

The First Rockbridge Artillery was camped on the north side of the James River, about a mile inside the outer defenses of Richmond. In March, the First Virginia Artillery, which included the First Rockbridge, had been relieved at the front, and as the month ended, most of the battalion was stationed along the New Market Road, south of the city and near the Laurel Hill Church. The battery had been on reduced rations for months, a "dirty corn meal resembling horse chop," according to one soldier.[18] Unlike some of the other companies, though ragged and underfed, the men of the First Rockbridge remained strong in their conviction that Lee would eventually defeat Grant. Desertions had been few.

The morning of April 2 began peacefully for the First Rockbridge and Pvts. John Alexander Tyler and David Gardiner Tyler, disturbed only by the sounds of an awaking camp and the tocsin clanging at daybreak in the city. The young sons of former President John Tyler and his second wife, Julia Gardiner Tyler, Alex and Gardie had exchanged the tedium and comparatively sedate life of studying the classics in a college classroom for one of hauling artillery through rain and mud, picking lice from clothing, and standing guard in the cold of the night. The First Rockbridge was a renowned artillery unit that had fought under Thomas J. "Stonewall" Jackson at Manassas in July 1861 and earned glory on the battlefields of Fredericksburg, Gettysburg, and Cold Harbor. The president's sons had missed all that, however, as they were relatively recent additions to the battery. Gardie enlisted with the First Rockbridge in September 1864 at eighteen, and Alex, at sixteen, signed up about six months later.

Though Alex was new to war with the First Rockbridge, Gardie had his first taste of army life while attending Washington College (renamed Washington and Lee University with the death of college president Robert E. Lee in 1870). There he joined a reserve infantry company of old men and young boys attached to the Virginia Home Guard. In May 1864, with a Union force under Maj. Gen. David Hunter threatening to sack homes and towns in the Shenandoah Valley, the reserve unit was activated and assigned to support an outnumbered army under Confederate Brig. Gen. William E. Jones. During late spring and early summer, Gardie spent much of his time marching and countermarching up and down the Valley between Lynchburg and Staunton. His first chance to shoot at Yankee soldiers occurred during an assault on the trenches at Lynchburg by Hunter. The victorious Confederates, now under Brig. Gen. John C. Vaughan after Jones's death, repulsed the Union attack, forcing Hunter to withdraw. With the Valley free of the enemy for a time, the reserves were disbanded.

Going back to school, however, was not an option for Gardie, for Washington College had to close for the semester. After burning the Virginia Military Institute in Lexington, Hunter had sacked the college as well, causing extensive damage to buildings, books, and equipment. As tragic as the loss was, it was the excuse Gardie needed to become more than a part-time soldier for the Confederacy. "You must get over the notion that I am only a child for indeed I feel I am fully able to take care of myself," he wrote to his mother.[19] He joined the Virginia Home Guard in late July, only to find himself with the unexciting job of guarding prisoners at Libby Prison in Richmond. Bored and anxious to see action, Gardie concluded that service with the First Rockbridge would be more noble and rewarding.

As sons of a former president, Alex and Gardie were pleased they had enlisted with a unit that contained "gentlemen of the best standing," some of whom had been classmates with Gardie at Washington College. Their father would have been proud of them, staunch "Rebels" fighting for the South and particularly for their home state of Virginia. After his single term as president had concluded in 1846, John Tyler had retired to his plantation, Sherwood Forest, in Charles City County. There he assumed the leisurely life of a gentleman farmer until elected as a member of the Confederate Congress. On January 18, 1862, shortly before the first session of the Congress, Tyler passed away in a room in the Exchange Hotel in Richmond, dying at age seventy-one of an apparent stroke. He never knew, and probably could not have imagined, the hardships that his family and millions of other Southerners would be facing three years later.

The responsibility for running the plantation fell entirely on his wife's shoulders, and overcoming her grief, she accepted the responsibility with determination. The former first lady, in fact, continued as mistress of Sherwood Forest even as the plantation fell within Union lines in June 1862. Fortunately, with Lee driving the invaders back down the Peninsula, her home was again on Confederate soil.

A year later, however, the situation was more foreboding. With her move back to Castleton Hill, the home of her mother, Juliana, on Staten Island, Sherwood Forest was essentially abandoned, except for the slaves who remained and a couple of farm laborers. Julia was unable to sell the plantation and hired her husband's nephew John C. Tyler as manager to oversee the planting and harvesting.

Alex, isolated from the war with his mother, was uncomfortable living in the midst of Yankees. He had to get back to Virginia. How could he study Homer in the North when the property and the lives of his family and neighbors were being threatened in the South? With Gardie at Washington College and later with the Virginia Home Guard, Alex nagged his mother for months about enlisting. At one point, he ran away, getting as far as Baltimore, Maryland, before being brought back to Staten Island. In the end, Julia had no choice but to let him go. She would soon have two young sons serving the crumbling Confederacy, and despite their assurances, she feared for their health and safety. For a brief time, she even thought about returning to Virginia with Alex. That way, she would be closer to them, should they need her, and she could see for herself what was going on at Sherwood Forest. She eventually discounted the idea.

In July 1864, Alex left New York for Halifax, Nova Scotia, and from there, he caught a steamer to Bermuda, where he arranged passage on the CSS *Mary Celestia*, a sleek and fast blockade-runner. The *Mary Celestia* slipped safely into Wilmington, North Carolina, and near the end of August, Alex casually strolled into Gardie's camp, much to the surprise of his brother.[20] Alex had made one concession to his mother as a condition of being able to go: he had promised her that he would try to enlist in the Confederate navy, which she believed had a lower casualty rate.

Julia's property in Virginia, her financial affairs, and her two sons were competently watched over by James A. Semple, whom Alex and Gardie adored and whom Julia completely trusted. In April 1864, Semple had been promoted to head the Bureau of Provisions and Clothing for the Confederate Navy Department under Secretary Stephen R. Mallory, and moved from his quarters at Drewry's Bluff to an apartment in Richmond, only a short walk from the War Department building, where he worked. As mentor, guardian, and friend of Alex and Gardie, Semple accommodated them in his apartment during the time between college and enlistments.

In the case of Alex, his stay with Semple lasted for several weeks, while he waited in vain for an appointment in the navy. Semple arranged interviews for him with President and Varina Davis and with Mallory. Unfortunately, even such influences were of no help. Openings were simply nonexistent as the Confederate navy became reduced to a few aging vessels locked within blockaded harbors. Finally, Semple sent Alex to Washington College, which had reopened for the fall semester. In December, the college closed again, due to lack of students, and Alex returned to Semple's apartment. By the following February, he decided not to wait any longer. If the navy could not take him, the army certainly would, and he joined his brother in the First Rockbridge.

On the bright and cloudless April 2, with the sun shining down on services being conducted by the chaplain of the First Virginia, the Reverend Henry M. White, neither Alex nor Gardie had any idea of how their lives and those of their mother and "Brother James" were about to change. Before the war, all four had known a degree of wealth and leisure that would escape them in subsequent years. There would be no going back. For the young Tylers, the impact would mean being sent to school in Europe, away from the turmoil following the surrender of the Confederate armies. There they could temper their anger and frustration at the subjugation of the South. For Julia, it would mean remaining in the North years longer than she had anticipated and an ongoing struggle to pay bills. For Semple, however, the war was not yet over.

As the word quickly spread in the capital and to Alex and Gardie camped a few miles away that Lee's lines had been broken, the immediate objective of the army under Lee and the government under Davis was the same: to escape, regroup, and continue the fight. Subsequent events, however, took Semple in a different direction from that of the Tyler brothers.

FINAL HOURS IN RICHMOND

I think it is absolutely necessary that we should abandon our position to-night.
—Gen. Robert. E. Lee in a dispatch to President
Jefferson Davis, April 2, 1865

𝒯HE TRAIN CARRYING THE fugitive Confederate government lurched and belched its way through the suburb of Manchester on the south side of the James River; the locomotive's whistle screeched into the night. Inside the car carrying the president and his cabinet, Jefferson Davis paid no attention to the snippets of solemn conversation around him and the passing of "old peach" brandy bottles, which gradually lightened the mood of the other occupants.[1]

With his first opportunity to reflect on the tumultuous events of the day, Davis maintained an unshakable faith in the ultimate ability of the Confederacy to win its independence. He had been willing to give up Richmond, to free Lee from the yoke of needing to defend the city. In his mind, however, the end had come too soon and too suddenly.

In a way, Davis bore responsibility for the chaos in the streets, though he was incapable of admitting, even to himself, that he had made a grave mistake in waiting as long as he did to evacuate the capital. The government was now forced to flee, and the residents of the city, uninformed and unprotected, had been left to fend for themselves.

Despite the warnings and advice of Lee, perhaps the president had been lulled by the tranquility of the Sunday morning. After days of rain, heavy at times, the clearing on Saturday had been a harbinger of a bright and beautiful day to come. The sun rose on Richmond in a cloudless sky, the peacefulness of the Sabbath broken only by the repeated ringing of the tocsin at dawn—three quick taps, a brief pause, then three more quick taps. Government and munitions workers who made up the Home Guard were being summoned to their posts. The clanging of the bell was an all too familiar interruption to Richmonders, who, after four years of siege and attack, had become jaded by the frequent call to arms and the often false alarms.

In this case, the call was real. The local defense force was needed to replace James Longstreet's troops in the defenses protecting Richmond north of the James River. Maj. Gen. Charles W. Field's skeleton force, one of the divisions making up Longstreet's corps, had been ordered to Petersburg to help stem, if possible, the overrunning of the Confederate lines. Along with the city militia and three battalions of convalescing patients and staff workers from Chimborazo Hospital, Virginia Military Institute cadets formed ranks and marched out of the city to fill the gap left by the absence of Field's veterans. The cadets had been housed in the City Alms House on Shockoe Hill after the burning of VMI in Lexington by Union Gen. David Hunter.

Ignorant of the true state of affairs, churchgoers emerged from their homes for a leisurely walk along streets now mostly dry and dusty after the rain. Greetings were exchanged with friends as parishioners gravitated toward their places of worship, drawn by the peals of church bells. For observer Mary Fontaine, it was a day "when delicate silks, that look too fine at other times, seem just to suit."[2] Even Navy Secretary Mallory thought that "the old city had never, during the war, worn an aspect more serene & quiet."[3] Contributing to the bright and clear morning was the fact that the Tredegar Iron Works no longer spewed black smoke into the air. The furnaces were now cold, and removable machinery had been sent south, both due to the lack of raw materials and the enemy threat to Richmond. The crystal blue sky was thus but a small compensation for the loss of the foundry, machine shops, and rolling mills to the Confederacy.

While pockets of people hung around the War Department and the Spotswood Hotel for news, as they had for months, no particular threat was apparent. If anything, the early signs of spring masked the grim realities facing Richmond. Maple and tulip trees were budding in yards and along the streets, as were the majestic lindens on Capitol Hill. A haze of yellow green lined the banks and islands of the James River. Crocuses with purple and white blossoms had popped up through the soil in gardens, and daffodils were in full bloom. The freshness of the mild and breezy April morning, tinged in parts of the city with the pleasant aroma of tobacco emanating from warehouses, diverted attention from the war-worn appearance of the city and brought renewed feelings of hope. Johnston had surely escaped from Sherman and was about to pounce on Grant and help Lee drive him from his positions around Petersburg. Soon the worst would be over, perhaps in a matter of days.

John Beauchamp Jones, however, was focused on signs more ominous than the weather. Hearing a rumor of "bloody fighting" and a "fearful loss" by Pickett the previous day, the War Department clerk was bothered by the absence of dispatches, especially given the hurried movement of Longstreet's troops through the city.[4] At the War Department, housed in the former home of the Virginia Mechanics' Institute on Ninth Street, he found he was not alone. Head of the Bureau of War, Col. Robert G. H. Kean, had been there since 8:00 a.m. Postmaster General John H. Reagan had stayed late the night before and returned early Sunday morning. Both were waiting for further news from the Petersburg front. Jones, who had reason to worry, was apparently not privy to a telegram from Lee to Secretary of War Breckinridge that arrived around 9:30 a.m. In it, Lee warned, "I see no prospect of doing more than holding our position here till night. I am not certain I can do that. . . . I advise that all preparation be made for leaving Richmond tonight."[5] Breckinridge, who had been keeping vigil with Reagan on Saturday night, was notified at the Broad Street Methodist Church, and he quickly returned to the War Department.

In a follow-up message to the secretary of war, Lee indicated that he believed the Danville road—the only track not yet controlled or destroyed by the enemy—"will be safe until tomorrow."[6] Reagan went looking for President Davis to deliver the news. Intercepted as he and his aide, Col. Francis R. Lubbock, strolled to St. Paul's Episcopal Church on Grace Street, Davis evidently believed the situation was not yet critical. In Reagan's opinion, the president appeared distracted, seemingly unmoved by the news. Quite possibly, he was confident that Lee would somehow reestablish his lines as he had done so many times in the past. In any case, Davis decided to continue on to church. His absence at St. Paul's on Communion Sunday would only cause the rumors to fly. He was hoping for a miracle and perhaps planning to pray for one.

For a short time, the illusion of normalcy prevailed. Almost certainly, no one on the street before church, other than those officials aware of the dispatches from Lee, had any idea that Sunday would be the last full day the Confederate "Stars and Bars" would fly over Capitol Square. Though Davis had to know that panic and despair would prevail once the government left the city, even he could not have imagined the devastation ahead. In less than twenty-four hours, more than seven hundred buildings—all or part of fifty-four city blocks—would be burned to the ground, leaving only chimneys and partial walls of brick as sentinels mocking the recent defenders of the capital. The total destruction of property, the vast loss of homes and businesses—including hotels, flour mills, restaurants, newspaper offices, and all the banks in the city—would not be caused by the enemy.

Reaching St. Paul's, Davis climbed the steps with Lubbock and entered the sanctuary through the two large center doors, removed his wide-brimmed hat, and took his place in his family pew. His face was drawn and expressionless. Shafts of light pierced the windows on the east-facing Ninth-Street side of the church and splashed in patches on the worshipers, brightening the interior. Those who had arrived ahead of him discretely turned to scrutinize the president, attempting to penetrate the solemn mask for any sign of his state of mind.

Permitted to sit in the gallery—a distinct privilege for a boy of fifteen—Dallas Tucker looked out at the throng from his seat in the front row and saw the president directly below him. Seventeen-year-old Emmie Crump, daughter of the assistant secretary of the treasury, Judge William Wood Crump, was in church as well. Judge Crump had been sent on a mission for the government a few days earlier. Anticipating the worst for Richmond and his family, he had left his wife with a quantity of gold coins, since Confederate money would be of no use once the city fell. He had also arranged for an old friend who lived with him for many years as his body servant, a free black man, to help them when the city fell to the enemy. For both young people, the events of the next several hours would become etched in their minds, so much so, they were able to clearly recall and write about them years later.[7]

As might be expected, the congregation was mostly women and children, many of the wives in mourning for husbands and other relatives lost in battle.

The few men in attendance were either government officials, soldiers in uniform convalescing from injuries, or "old" men beyond draft age (fifty years and older) and of little interest to the Home Guard. Rector of the church was Charles F. E. Minnigerode, a German immigrant who was widely respected by parishioners and Confederate leaders. Recollections of events during the service vary in the postwar accounts, but at some point before communion, Minnigerode reportedly read what would prove to be a prophetic verse from Psalm 46:9: "He maketh wars to cease unto the end of the earth; he breaketh the bow, and cutteth the spear in sunder; he burneth the chariot in the fire."[8]

At 10:40 a.m. another dispatch arrived at the War Department. This time it was for Davis instead of Breckinridge. Lee was taking no chances; he wanted to make sure the president understood the urgency of leaving Richmond that night. A courier was immediately sent to St. Paul's with the telegram. Not wishing to interrupt Minnigerode as he began Communion, the messenger caught the attention of sexton William Irving, an elderly, somewhat pompous usher and guardian of decorum in the church. Filled with the importance of his mission, the sexton stiffly made his way down the aisle to Davis's pew, a curious figure in a faded blue suit with brass buttons and a shirt replete with ruffles. Touching the president lightly on the shoulder, Irving handed Davis the sealed note, an "uneasy whisper" rippling through the congregation as the rector paused momentarily in his Communion sermon. Glancing at the message, the president calmly rose from his seat. Erect and dignified, he quietly exited the church, his face perhaps a shade grayer but still impassive.

The dispatch finally convinced Davis that Lee was not going to pull off the impossible by keeping Grant out of Richmond. The message to the president was blunt and clear: "I think it is absolutely necessary that we should abandon our position to-night. I have given all the necessary orders on the subject to the troops, and the operation, though difficult, I hope will be performed successfully. I have directed General Stevens to send an officer to your excellency to explain the routes to you by which the troops will be moved to Amelia Court House, and furnish you with a guide and any assistance that you may require for yourself."[9]

Davis might protest about not having enough time to complete the evacuation by nightfall, but he could do little about it. The wheels would soon be in motion, literally, as artillery pieces became harnessed to horses and rolled out of position and supply wagons were prepared for the trek

along routes both north and south of the James River. Resigned to the inevitable and spurred to motion himself, the president went directly to his
office in the Treasury Building on Bank Street, a short walk from St. Paul's.
The granite structure, formerly known as the old Customs House, had been
converted into executive offices shortly after the Confederate Congress
voted to relocate the capital from Montgomery, Alabama, to Richmond in
May 1861. The first floor of the building held the Treasury Department,
while the Department of State and the cabinet room took up the second.
The offices for the president, his private secretary, Burton N. Harrison, and
his aides were on the top floor.

Around the city, cabinet members and key officials were being summoned from church services, their departures being noted in some instances with increasing apprehension. At St. Paul's, four trips down the aisle
by the sexton were too much for those in attendance. Murmurs and rest-
lessness turned to a general stirring, and the Reverend Minnigerode realized
that he was about to lose his congregation. Notified in the vestry room that
Lee's lines had been broken and the army was in retreat, the rector returned
to the chancel and pleaded with the people headed for the doors to stay, his
Teutonic accent perhaps more pronounced, as he emotionally reminded
them of where they were. In what might be regarded as adding to the alarm
of his audience, however, he also announced that Lt. Gen. Richard S. Ewell,
in charge of the city defenses, was ordering the Home Guard to gather at the
Capitol at 3:00 p.m.

Apparently, most of the congregation remained through Communion
and the weekly offering. With the ending of the service, anxious parishioners
spilled out into the bright sunlight on Grace Street and mingled with worshipers leaving St. Peter's Cathedral, on the other side of the street, a half
block away. News and rumors were soon being exchanged and excitement
grew. Most disturbing of all, according to Dallas Tucker, were the piles of
documents being burned in the street as workers emptied nonessential
records from the auditor and comptroller offices in the former Monumental
Hotel building directly across from St. Paul's.[10] The people's worst fears were
confirmed in the flickering flames and ashes swirling skyward.

At the Second Presbyterian Church, a few blocks west of St. Paul's on
Main Street, the Reverend Moses D. Hoge was also informed during the
service about the contents of the note and chose to pass the tidings on to his
congregation. An impassioned, thundering defender of the Confederacy,

Hoge had run the blockade months earlier to arrange the donation of Bibles by church groups in England. Some ten thousand Bibles and fifty thousand New Testaments had been handed out to soldiers in the Confederate armies. Renowned for his beliefs and hospitality, Hoge was often prevailed upon by military officers, lawmakers, and government officials needing a place to sleep while visiting the city. Accepting defeat would not be easy. With sadness, he acknowledged to those in church that morning that they may never meet there again, and he "bade them farewell."[11]

The service at the First African Baptist Church, on the corner of College and Broad streets, a block north of Capitol Square, was comparatively more subdued. The congregation, which consisted of both slaves and free blacks, had been listening to a sermon by Dr. Robert Ryland. The Reverend Ryland was widely respected as a Baptist minister and as president of Richmond College (present-day University of Richmond). Closed for the duration of the war, the school buildings were being used as a hospital. Ryland also met the basic tenant of Virginia law for being the pastor of the church: he was white. Though the service had not been interrupted by a call for a government official to leave, no doubt, word spread quietly as the worshipers exited the church onto Broad Street, hope rising as events at the other churches became known. The news and the conclusion were almost unbelievable: "The government is leaving. The Yankees will soon be here and free us all." They could only wait and watch the escalating confusion on the streets, however, afraid to express their joy beyond cautious smiles and handshakes. The rumor might be wrong. Or if by some miracle the news were true, they could end up bearing the brunt of frustration and anger by panicking citizens.

In his office on the third floor of the Treasury Building, Davis faced the difficult challenge of expediting the evacuation of the government, and he immediately sent out runners to find his cabinet officers for a noon meeting. Invited also were Gov. William "Extra Billy" Smith, former governor John Letcher, and Mayor Joseph C. Mayo. Navy Secretary Mallory was already there, having arrived from St. Peter's ahead of the president; he was soon joined by Judah P. Benjamin. Sporting a gold-headed cane and blithely puffing on a Havana cigar, the secretary of state had been reached at his home on Main Street. With all in attendance, except for Attorney General George Davis, who could not be located in time, the president began the meeting by "calmly and solemnly" reviewing the contents of the telegrams from Lee and stating his views on what had to be accomplished, by whom, and when. The urgency of the situation and the need for immediate action were underscored by the concluding lines in Lee's most recent warning: "I think every hour adds to our difficulties. . . . I am in the presence of the enemy."[12]

At this point, Davis could no longer worry about alarming people. Within hours, the city, and all who remained in it, would be under Yankee rule. Nothing was going to change that fact. Most important was survival of the Confederacy. The relocated government would be set up in Danville, Virginia, a small tobacco community 160 miles southwest of Richmond, just north of the North Carolina border. All documents essential for the continued functioning of the government had to be transported to the Richmond and Danville Railroad depot that afternoon. Papers not considered to be essential were to be destroyed so they would not fall into the hands of the enemy. Burning them in the streets seemed to be the most effective way to do this, a process that had already begun. Davis also made clear that all who were being asked to go—namely, the cabinet, department heads, chief assistants, and certain dignitaries—had to be ready that evening and at the depot with their personal baggage.

Secretary of War Breckinridge was given the responsibility of ensuring that enough engines and cars were standing by at the station. One train would be for Davis and his cabinet while a second train would contain the remainder of the treasury. A total of eight trains would be made up, a task especially difficult on a Sunday. Rounding up train crews would be as much a challenge as locating adequate rolling stock and engines that could hold a head of steam. The problem was quickly assigned to Capt. Peter Helms Mayo, a quartermaster with Lt. Gen. A. P. Hill's Third Corps. Mayo had previously been in charge of the movement of soldiers on trains running between Richmond and Petersburg. He was no longer needed for that purpose.

The most impossible responsibility belonged to Gen. Richard S. Ewell, "Old Baldie" as he was known by his troops when he led a division and then a corps under Lee. He had been badly wounded in the knee at the battle of Groveton on August 28, 1862, just before Second Manassas. After a long recovery of about nine months, he returned to field command, outfitted with a wooden leg. With the death of the irreplaceable Stonewall Jackson at Chancellorsville in May 1863, Lee assigned Ewell to lead Jackson's Second Corps. Ultimately, however, he was placed in charge of the Department of Richmond, and was thus responsible for defending the city. It was not a promotion. Lee had come to have little confidence in his eccentric, abrasive subordinate who had difficulty staying on a horse during battle because of his leg and whose field performance had been erratic. Obviously, Lee was not counting on Ewell's Home Guard and a small force of fewer than five thousand regular troops to fend off the Union army. Ewell would be expected, though, to maintain order in the city, and when evacuation was eminent, to destroy the cotton and tobacco in the warehouses without setting fire to the city. He failed at both.

On the fourth floor of the building housing the War Department, Paymaster James A. Semple surveyed the job before him. As head of the Bureau of Provisions and Clothing for the navy, he was responsible for cleaning out the records of his department, deciding what was essential and had to be transported with the government and what was to be destroyed. Formerly a technology school, the brick building was known as Mechanics' Hall, or more popularly, the Mechanics' Institute. The lecture rooms had been renovated by the Confederate government to serve the purposes of the various military departments; the large hall on the third floor, which had been used for meetings, lectures to large groups, and community services before the war, was occupied by the Patent Office. At the moment, this particular floor was the least frenetic part of the building. Patents and applications in various stages of review somehow seemed less of an immediate concern to the fleeing departments.

Down the hallway from Semple, John M. Brooke in the Office of Ordnance and Hydrography and W. A. W. Spotswood in Medicine and Surgery were also hurriedly sorting through records not yet packed, as were the heads of other bureaus on the floor. Throughout the building, the stairs and wooden floors of the building creaked and echoed with the heavy footsteps of government clerks, aides, and slaves hauling boxes and packets of documents to the street. Each box and packet was intended for either the flaming piles of paper on Ninth Street or wagons commandeered for transporting essential records to the railroad station. The wide corridor of the first floor was filled with humanity, and workers on the four floors converged as they repeatedly passed in and out of the building.

With all that he had to do, Semple had little time to dwell on others. His wife, Letitia, he knew, was safely with friends, not far from Danville, coincidently, the destination of the Confederate government. He and Letitia had almost nothing to do with each other these days, but she was still his wife, and he felt some responsibility for her welfare.

On Staten Island, Julia Gardiner Tyler was a long way from Sherwood
Forest and the war. A notorious Rebel among Yankees, despite her Northern
upbringing, Julia was criticized and slandered from time to time—especially
since she actively participated in Copperhead activities—but she was at least
free from physical harm.[13] Semple looked forward to her letters. Julia was
warm, gracious, and exciting; in those respects, she was the polar opposite of
Letitia. Unfortunately, he was not likely to hear from her for a while.

Then there were the boys, Alex and Gardie. They were now caught up
in the mass withdrawal of men and animals as Lee began to extricate his
army from the overrun defenses and unite it south of the James River. The
movement of troops toward Amelia Court House was motivated by logistics
and by the expectation of finding much-needed supplies waiting for him
there.[14] Regrettably, Semple could do little more for Julia's sons than pack
their belongings in his apartment, along with his own, and take their trunks
with him. For the time being, he had to put those concerns aside. His personal survival and that of the Confederacy were at stake.

Along with his chief clerk, Assistant Paymaster Thomas J. DeLeon,
Semple did the final sorting and bundling of records—applications and recent communications—and saw to the carrying of the boxes downstairs.
Fortunately, he was well prepared for the inevitable loss of Richmond to
Grant. He had written to Julia on March 25, only days earlier, that he was
still "working hard" to get Alex an appointment as a midshipman in the
Confederate navy. He also reported that Gardie was well and needed "reading" matter. Despite the casual, routine tone of the letter, Semple had
known for some time that evacuation of the city was eminent. Until it actually happened, however, there had been no need to upset Julia, since neither could do anything about it.[15]

Besides packing up his office ahead of time, Semple had made arrangements to send surplus navy supplies out of Richmond—probably to his
naval store in Danville—where the likelihood of loss to the enemy would be
less, at least for the time being. Other than the James River Squadron, commanded by Rear Adm. Raphael H. Semmes, the Confederate navy had essentially ceased to exist. What was left consisted of three ironclads
("chained and sulky bulldogs," Mallory called them) and five wooden gunboats, with several hundred sailors and officers either onboard the vessels or
assigned to batteries at Drewry's Bluff.[16] Included in the skeleton squadron
was the school ship CSS *Patrick Henry* with sixty or so midshipmen, boys as

young as fourteen. Only the Confederate raider CSS *Shenandoah* remained at sea as a fighting warship.

The navy thus had little need for the supplies, but they could be a welcome resource farther south. Semple reasoned that if Lee had to give up the capital, he would probably try to link up with Johnston. Clearly, the provisions would be of more help to the army in Danville, through which Lee would likely pass, than the nonexistent navy in Richmond. When informed of Semple's intention, however, Mallory directed him to keep the supplies in the city. As late as March 23, the navy secretary must have still believed that Richmond could be held.[17]

Semple had also been thinking about Julia's silver, which remained behind when she left Sherwood Forest for the North. Since then, the silver and other personal effects of the Tyler family had been stored in the vault of a local Richmond bank. He and Gardie, who was particularly worried about the safety of her possessions, both believed that once the Yankees entered the city, the banks were certain to be stripped of their assets. In his letter to Julia, Semple let her know that he would like to transfer the silver, along with family photographs and papers, to the warehouse of Dunlop, Moncure, and Company, on the corner of Eleventh and Cary streets, only a block from his apartment. Not waiting for a response, he had the silver moved and the boxes hooped with iron straps to strengthen them and make them more difficult to break open.[18]

Soon, during the afternoon, most of Richmond knew its fate. Word spread across the city like the fire to follow. Trunks, bundles, and luggage of every size and description appeared on sidewalks, and the streets became crowded with horses pulling carriages, carts, wagons—anything with wheels—as people sought to move their possessions to comparative safety, wherever that might be . . . a warehouse, the home of a friend or relative, or preferably outside of the city. Anxious women, many without men to help them, filled doorways in the residential areas of the city and stood on the steps to their homes, calling out to passersby for the latest news.

Emmie Crump was not yet ready to accept that her day and routine were going to change drastically. In the early afternoon, she set out on a walk of several blocks to St. Philips Church, where she taught Sunday school to the small black congregation. She had not gone far, however, before she met friends who told her to go back home. There would be no school that day. Returning through streets that were becoming increasingly chaotic, she found her mother packing the silver and her father's papers in preparation for their removal to her aunt's house on Seventh Street. Living as they did on the edge of Capitol Square, soon to be the ganglion of Yankee occupation, Mary Crump had been advised to leave her home. Her sister's house would be less convenient to the "incoming enemy."[19]

Clattering over the cobblestones of the commercial district, personal conveyances merged with the government wagons filled with archives as the masses of vehicles and people gravitated toward Mayo's Bridge and the Richmond and Danville Railroad. By midafternoon, the station was thronged with people attempting to arrange transportation on the trains being loaded and sent south with the politicians and the remnants of the government. Some, giving up hope of leaving Richmond by rail, trudged the towpath of the James River and Kanawha Canal toward Lynchburg, probably with no clear destination in mind, while others sought to escape by boat, using either the canal or the river to float out of the city. Blocks away from the depot, inmates from Libby Prison were being marched to the two flag-of-truce steamers at Rocketts Landing for a final exchange downriver, the captured Union soldiers no doubt wondering about the growing excitement and traffic along the waterfront. For the most part, however, panic and desperation had not yet set in, despite the anxiety and confusion and the jostling of crowds.

To ensure that depositors would not lose their money after the Union army took over the city, banks opened at 2:00 p.m. and encouraged customers to close their accounts. While many did that, at the end of day, the banks were left with assets that needed to be shipped to Danville, along with the treasury. The total amount of funds can only be surmised. The contents of the kegs shipped by the individual banks were known only to the bank and the agent assigned by the bank to accompany the specie until the funds could be returned. Estimates range from $230,000 to as much as $450,000 in gold and silver coin.[20]

While the situation was grim, Davis's focus and instructions during the cabinet meeting had to do with moving the government to Danville; there was no talk of the war's being over. If anything, the president's resolve was stiffened, and he would not have accepted any hint of capitulation from the cabinet. There was much to be done, however, in transporting the machinery of government, and they had only a few hours to do it.

Either during or shortly after leaving the cabinet meeting, Mallory sent a brief directive to Capt. William H. Parker, superintendent of the Confederate

Naval Academy. At the request of Treasury Secretary George A. Trenholm, the midshipmen of the *Patrick Henry* were to be given the most important mission of their short careers: they were to guard the gold and silver of the treasury and the bank deposits during the loading and transit of the specie on the railway cars. Normally quartered on the school ship, the midshipmen had recently been moved to a tobacco factory on the corner of Twenty-fourth and Franklin streets. Foul-smelling bilge water in the aging ship had caused health concerns, and a number of the midshipmen suffered from dysentery, a few even being hospitalized. Parker was ordered to assemble the corps of students and instructors at the Richmond and Danville station by 6:00 p.m.

During the afternoon, a courier from the Navy Department arrived as Rear Adm. Raphael Semmes was sitting down to dinner onboard the *Virginia II,* one of the three remaining Confederate ironclads. The steel-eyed Semmes was known, North and South, for his exploits in eluding vastly superior Union naval forces while captain of the CSS *Alabama.* During a twenty-two-month reign, the *Alabama* had captured more than sixty merchant ships flying the U.S. flag before it was finally sunk by the USS *Kearsarge* in a battle off the coast of Cherbourg, France. Picked up by the British yacht *Deerhound,* Semmes was able to escape to England. On returning to Richmond, he found that Mallory had no ship to offer him; his adventures on the high seas for the Confederacy were over. The secretary of the navy appointed him to what he had available: command of the makeshift James River Squadron. At some point, Semmes must have reflected on how far the fortunes of the Confederate navy, and his own career, had fallen in recent months.[21]

Annoyed at the interruption of his dinner, Semmes opened the sealed envelope to find a cryptic message from Mallory that included the directive: "Upon you is devolved the duty of destroying your ships, this night."[22] He had known the city would ultimately need to be given up, but such an eventuality was far from his mind on this bright spring day. Contrary to Mallory's assumption, Semmes had not heard anything from Lee. Ensconced belowdecks on his flagship, he had no idea the defenses had collapsed and that Richmond was in the process of being evacuated. Mallory's note was a complete surprise.

With his small flotilla anchored near Drewry's Bluff to guard the city from Yankee gunboats moving upriver, waiting until after dark made sense. Otherwise, Semmes might alert the enemy, only a few miles downstream, too soon to the destruction of the Confederate naval defenses protecting

Richmond. Without the Confederate ironclads to oppose it, the Union navy could steam around the obstructions in the river and shell the city before the evacuation was completed. As Semmes waited for the day to expire, he watched the flag-of-truce boats return upriver with exchanged Confederate soldiers, who were celebrating their release from Northern prisons. "Sick at heart," he could only imagine their shock and dismay when the boat docked at Rocketts Landing. Though Semmes had also been ordered by Mallory to join Lee after destroying his ships, he decided that he would pay "no further attention to the movements of the army." Instead, he would attempt to escape from the city with his men, and if he could, he would follow the government. He knew from Mallory's note where it was going. Danville was far inland from the nearest port, and the only naval facility there was Semple's warehouse and store, but Davis could almost certainly use the help and advice of a senior officer.[23]

By 4:00 p.m., fifty of the midshipmen had been supplied with three days' rations, outfitted as infantry, and were double-quick marching toward the Danville depot under the command of Capt. James H. Rochelle. William H. Parker headed for the Navy Department and conferred with Mallory before joining Rochelle a couple of hours later. The remaining ten midshipmen were left with Lt. James W. Billups to set fire to the *Patrick Henry*. Before the night was over, the last of the Confederate warships would be burning or sitting on the bottom of the James River.

At the Treasury Department on the first floor of the Treasury Building, the atmosphere had taken on a sense of urgency. A number of the department's employees had gone home, and some had already departed for Danville on one of the trains. Still working were Mann S. Quarles, the youngest teller at age nineteen, senior teller Walter H. Philbrook, and a few others. Anticipating the need to evacuate the city, the clerks had ordered the construction of boxes weeks ahead for transporting papers of value to the department. The process of packing had been underway for days. One hundred forty barrels of papers had already been sent south on March 27. With the packing of essential papers completed, they began to burn the papers they would not be taking with them.

More important than the papers were the assets of the treasury. With Philbrook supervising the process, Quarles and the others turned their attention to the task of boxing the silver and gold, which consisted of U.S. silver coins and bullion, U.S. double eagle gold coins, gold sovereigns

(British pounds), and gold ingots and nuggets. Mexican silver dollars, already contained in wooden kegs about the size of a nail keg, made up the bulk of the treasury in both weight and value. Each of the fifty kegs was filled with four thousand of the eight reales coins, also known as "pieces of eight," for a total value of two hundred thousand dollars. The U.S. silver coins consisted of half dimes, dimes, quarters, half dollars, and dollars in sacks, which were then packed in boxes. The U.S. gold coins, in sacks with a value of five thousand dollars each, were packed five sacks to a box, the boxes then being bound with iron straps. There was also a keg of copper pennies.

In all, although never officially counted, the treasury was later estimated by Philbrook to have been "less than $600,000." The U.S. silver coins contributed possibly as much $157,253 in value, while the silver bullion, Mexican coins, and the gold (coins, nuggets, and bullion) may have added another $369,770 for a total of $527,023.[24] Realizing that the money was not being counted as it was boxed, Quarles folded a number of sheets of brown paper into a booklet about six-by-eight inches in size and proceeded to record the contents of each box and the markings on the outside of the boxes. When a box became filled, he then sealed the box with a Treasury Department seal. After the packing was completed, he put the seal in his pants pocket for safekeeping.

There were also five safes in the Treasury Department office. Quarles apparently removed the contents from each of the safes, then locked them and secured the keys in a newer yellow safe with a combination lock. The reason he did this is not clear, since all six safes were found to be empty when they were opened by Micajah H. Clark after the war was over and he had returned to Richmond.[25]

In addition to the silver and gold, the treasury contained "Liverpool Acceptances," worth about sixteen thousand to eighteen thousand British pounds sterling, and a white oak chest filled with jewelry donated by Southern women to buy a warship for the Confederacy. Millions of dollars in Confederate notes and bonds were also stored there. As they were already essentially worthless, and transporting them would be a cumbersome and useless effort, the decision was made to burn them, along with the treasury papers that were to be destroyed. During the packing of the specie and bullion, the furnace in the basement of the building was kept "red hot," the fiscal promises of the nation disintegrating in flames and smoke.

By 3:00 p.m., the packing of the papers and the metal assets had been completed, and the extremely heavy load of Treasury Department boxes was on its way to the Richmond and Danville railway station in wagons drawn by teams of four horses; eight wagonloads were required to transport it all. Guarding the procession to the station were the clerks. The midshipmen ordered to protect the treasury by Mallory reached the depot sometime after 4:00 p.m. By then, the cars making up the "treasure train" were being loaded.

With the bureau records cleaned out, James A. Semple left his office in the Mechanics Building to pack some personal things for the trip to Danville. Noticing the streets were now filled with people, he wended his way past the piles of burning paper in front of the Treasury Building to his apartment in a building across from the American Hotel on the corner of Eleventh and Main. With the Exchange, Ballard, and Powhatan hotels converted into lodging houses, the American was one of only two hotels of any prominence still operating in the city, the Spotswood being the other. Stripped of carpeting, long ago contributed to the war effort for blankets for the troops, and lacking furniture, the American Hotel showed the effects of four years of war and months of deprivation. The Union blockade and Grant's stranglehold on Richmond had been devastating to businesses in the city, but the hotel had managed to stay open.

As Semple approached his apartment building, he undoubtedly noted the carriages and wagons queued up to the hotel and the commotion around the entrance.[26] Remaining guests were hurriedly abandoning the building for what they hoped would be safer quarters elsewhere in Richmond. Any "Rebels" in the hotel would almost certainly be evicted to provide accommodations for Union officers and officials occupying the city. As later events proved, they were wise to do so, but not because of the enemy. Within hours, the hotel would be consumed in the fire that swept through the city's commercial district. One guest would die, an elderly resident who could not be convinced to leave his room.

Semple's apartment, though small, was large enough for his needs, as well as Alex and Gardie when they stayed with him. He had also set up a makeshift office there. In recent months, his job as bureau chief had become increasingly more difficult, and his hours had been long and exhausting. Since he had replaced his older predecessor, John DeBree, who had been depending heavily on Semple for months, the Confederacy had been rapidly shrinking in size, with Union forces capturing ports and pushing inland throughout the South. Despite the loss of farmland, Semple's civilian agents continued to scour the countryside of what remained of the Confederacy for food and other supplies.

Fortunately, DeBree had enlisted the help of a particularly resourceful agent, William F. Howell, brother of Varina Davis, the president's wife. Early in the war, Howell had operated out of New Orleans, traveling throughout the South to purchase goods from farmers and manufacturers. When the city fell to Union Adm. David G. Farragut and Gen. Benjamin F. Butler in late August 1862, Howell left New Orleans and eventually moved his family to Augusta, Georgia. There he concentrated on developing a network of suppliers for wheat, vegetables, and fruit, and he was remarkably successful in this endeavor. Large quantities of produce were dried and processed, while the wheat was ground at private mills and baked into bread. He also contracted for beef, which he had butchered, cured, and packed. Howell also became adept at bartering tea, molasses, flour, and textiles—items he had less trouble obtaining—for bacon, beef, and pork. He was even able to supply quantities of whiskey, though not on a regular basis. Semple had come to rely on his industrious agent, as DeBree had done before him, and a bond of trust grew between them, which Semple later came to regret.[27]

Food was only one of Semple's problems. With the loss of the ports and the increasing effectiveness of the blockade, few shipments of clothing and shoes were getting through from Great Britain. For a time, local shops. which had been set up in Richmond, Savannah, and Mobile, met the navy's needs for woolens, blankets, and shoes, but with the growing lack of raw materials and with the loss of Savannah, Semple faced the possibility of severe shortages. Yet, somehow, he had kept the Confederate navy well supplied and the warehouses stockpiled with food and clothing right to the end. Confederate sailors may not have had pay in their pockets, but they were well fed, wore decent uniforms, and were properly equipped. They also had a coat to wear in the cold weather, and when quantities of shoes became scarce after the army took over the navy shoe factory and the blockage tightened, Howell found a British cutting machine that enabled the mass production of both uppers and soles, substantially easing the shoe problem.[28]

Upon reaching his apartment, Semple packed clothing and other belongings, probably lightly. He would not be coming back to his apartment, so personal items, such as Julia's letters, would have been important, but he knew he could requisition shirts and pants in Danville and whatever else he might need to wear. What he had to do, though, was to go through the bureau papers in his apartment office. Any reports, letters, account information, applications, etc., would have needed checking, most of which probably ended up in a burning pile. At some point during the afternoon, Alex and Gardie left the camp of the First Rockbridge Artillery for a time, as many were doing while waiting for marching orders, and rode into the city to say good-bye to their friend and benefactor. Since Danville seemed to be the destination of both the Confederate government and Lee's army, Semple told the boys he would have their trunks shipped with his on the train.[29] It would be a wasted effort, for Alex and Gardie never saw their clothes and personal effects again.

For much of the afternoon, President Davis remained in his office, calmly making last-minute arrangements for the departure, as people and events swirled around him inside the Treasury Building offices and on the streets. While Mayor Joseph C. Mayo met with his city council to figure out what to do next to save the city, and Secretary of War Breckinridge conferred with General Ewell on keeping the military stores—food, tobacco, cotton, and other supplies—out of the enemy's hands, Davis's thoughts were focused on the task of transferring his government to Danville. Certain departments, such as the Treasury and War departments, would need to function again as soon as they arrived.

At no time since Lee first broached giving up the city did Davis entertain the possibility of ultimate defeat for the Confederacy. In early February, he had authorized an attempt to negotiate a peace with Lincoln at Hampton Roads, Virginia. But Lincoln's conditions were simple and blunt: the Rebel armies had to lay down their arms and the seceded states must return to the Union. In other words, after four years of war and tens of thousands of dead on hundreds of battlefields for a cause they believed in, there would be no Southern independence. While his enemies at home would point out that his stubbornness and narrow-mindedness made him, and the South, a martyr to an ideology that could no longer be defended, trading liberty for peace was unacceptable. Davis truly believed that should the Confederacy lose the war, subjugation by the North would lead to punishment, the loss of fundamental rights, and immense suffering for the Southern people. There was no alternative but to continue the fight.

Certainly, the situation was bleak, but it was not hopeless. He could even see a positive side to the evacuation. Lee might be on the run for the moment, but he now had the ability to attack and move . . . like a prize fighter. Johnston's army still confronted Sherman in North Carolina. Confederate troops were resisting Union advances in Georgia and Florida, and Lt. Gen. Richard Taylor's army, along with the hard-fighting cavalry of Lt. Gen. Nathan Bedford Forrest, remained in the field in Alabama and Mississippi. West of the Mississippi River, an army of some thirty-six thousand soldiers under Lt. Gen. Edmund Kirby Smith operated independently and was essentially unscathed by war. Smith's Trans-Mississippi Department could form the core around which a substantial force might be rallied for defending the region. Finally, there was Brig. Gen. Stand Watie, chief of the Cherokee nation, who commanded a brigade in Indian Territory consisting of Cherokees, Choctaws, Creeks, Osages, and Seminoles, enough to harass the enemy.

Then, too, the armies would begin to increase again, now that winter was over. Letters from home had devastated the ranks, many soldiers leaving for a time to hunt food, make repairs, and plow fields for their families and to take care of other needs. Desertions from Lee's army alone had amounted to about sixty thousand when last tallied a month ago, and some would return . . . or so Davis thought. If Lee and the other armies could hold out longer, an outcry for peace would begin in the North, as it had the previous year, before Sherman captured Atlanta and quieted the protests. The Confederacy might survive, or at least the South might be able to sue for terms that would allow it to control its own affairs and destiny. At this point, he was willing to accept the smallest sliver of hope, as unrealistic as it may be, over the reality of living under Northern rule.

Despite his rationalizing that Lee's Army of Northern Virginia would now be free to unite with Johnston's Army of Tennessee, Davis made a final effort to buy more time, protesting in a message to Lee about the short notice he had to prepare for the evacuation. Lee, immersed in trying to save his army, was frustrated by Davis's inability, or unwillingness, to accept the inevitable. He had no time for coddling, and there was no way he could hold off the onslaught. Nevertheless, declining to remind the president that he had warned him for weeks that Richmond could not be held, Lee chose to reaffirm the fact that the army was pulling out: "Your telegram received. I think it will be necessary to move tonight. I shall camp the troops here north of the Appomattox. The enemy is so strong that they will cross above us & close us in between the James and Appomattox rivers, if we remain."[30] Davis had no choice but to leave that night; otherwise, he would be captured.

While chief clerk Micajah H. Clark saw to the removal of official records from the executive office to the depot, Davis's aides—Francis R. Lubbock, Col. William Preston Johnston, and eventually, Col. John Taylor Wood, the president's nephew—moved some of his more important personal papers to the executive mansion to be packed there, along with papers in his home.[31] The process would have been supervised by Davis's secretary, Burton N. Harrison, but he was shepherding Varina, who was still two days away by train from her destination of Charlotte. Attorney General George Davis, missing from the noon meeting, came by for a briefing before leaving to attend to personal matters. Around 5:00 p.m., the president, composed and dignified, walked to his home on East Clay Street. To those along the way who anxiously inquired if what they were hearing was true, that the government and army were leaving Richmond, he admitted they were. He assured them, though, that the setback was only temporary and the cause would ultimately be helped by the evacuation.

In reaching the executive mansion, Davis could see that the sorting of papers was well underway, and he began to pack clothing, toiletries, and other personal items in a trunk, including pistols, photographs, spectacles, and a quantity of cigars. He also included a key to the code used in government and military communications. In the middle of the packing, Clement C. Clay showed up, having returned from a failed peace mission to Canada for Davis. His appearance was a surprise; most people were leaving Richmond, not arriving. Davis asked his old friend and fellow senator from the prewar days to travel with him in the executive car reserved for the president and his cabinet. Clay agreed, as he wanted to catch up with his wife, Virginia, who had left Richmond and had been staying with various friends and relatives since the summer of 1862. The last he knew, she was in Washington, Georgia.

His personal packing completed, Davis arranged for the disposition of certain family possessions he would need to leave behind. He also sent a treasury clerk off with the $28,444 check he had received from the sale of furnishings to see if it could be cashed at one of the banks. Taking a last look around the mansion, he recalled the moments of happiness and sadness during the past three years he and his family lived there. In addition to birthdays and Christmases, the highlights had been the victories on the battlefield and the hope they had offered for an end to the war. The lowest point, without question, had been the tragic death of his son Joseph, "Little

Joe," who, at the age of five, fell from the east portico of the mansion to the brick walkway below.

The clerk returned to tell the president that the bank refused to honor the check. Perhaps recognizing that the banks were packing up whatever assets remained in the vaults, Davis asked the clerk to take the check along with him to Danville, thinking that perhaps he could cash it there.[32] For a while, the president sat and talked casually with his aides. Around 7:00 p.m., he lit a cigar and stepped into the carriage that had arrived to take him to the depot.

At the train station, the crowd was growing in number and becoming agitated, as hordes of people clamored to be included on one of the trains. Though it would be Grant entering the city, Richmond's citizens knew full well the path of destruction wrought by Sherman's army through Georgia and the Carolinas, and the same fate could befall the capital of the Confederacy. Yankees were Yankees. As rumor bred rumor, fear and anger mounted, as did the desperation to get out of the city. For many people, their attempt would be in vain. Some had managed to finagle their way onboard one of the earlier trains, and others were hanging "by their eyelids" on the outside of the trains left in the yard. As soon as Capt. William H. Parker arrived at the station, around 6:00 p.m., he placed sentinels at the doors of the depot to restrict access to the cars.

Arriving at the depot with his aides, Davis had to wedge his way through the press of humanity. Confronting him also was a maze of horses, wagons, drays, carriages, and a conglomeration of trunks and boxes, along with household articles. Quartermaster Peter Helms Mayo had done his job well. Summoning the train crews to the depot with blasts from a shift-engine steam whistle, he had somehow found the cars and engines to make up the trains he needed, and the fireboxes of the cabinet and treasury trains were glowing with hot coals. Secretary of War Breckinridge, who had arrived on horseback ahead of the president and the other cabinet officers, was a commanding presence in overseeing the departure preparations.

Under the watchful eye of senior teller Walter H. Philbrook and guarded by Parker's midshipmen, the specie and bullion were being transferred from the wagons to the treasury train. The lead boxcars were designated for the gold and silver and other government assets, while additional cars were to be loaded separately, as necessary, with the funds of the six Richmond banks. Given the poor condition of the cars and rails and the massive weight of the coin and bullion—the treasury specie alone weighing almost ten tons—care was taken not to overload the cars. Standing on the platform and ready to accompany the funds south were the agents assigned by the banks and their wives.

Also being packed were the boxes of archives transported to the station from the War and Treasury departments and other offices. During the afternoon, several trains had already left with papers, ordnance, and government employees. While the intent was to keep the papers out of enemy hands, as events turned out, their removal from Richmond saved them from the conflagration that followed. Their eventual recovery would provide a comprehensive record of the Confederacy for posterity.

Semple, as a bureau chief, was assured of a spot on the president's train, though he would be riding in a different railway car. The executive car would transport Davis and his cabinet as well as select individuals, including the president's aides, the Reverend Moses D. Hoge, Clement C. Clay, and a number of others, thirty people in all. Semple had to know, though, that his status with the administration was one of importance and dependence, especially with Mallory, who recognized his abilities and accomplishments. With his trunks and those of Alex and Gardie stowed onboard, Semple had time to reflect on how this day had begun and was ending. The train was not going anywhere for a while. As he watched the bustle of activity around him—the hurried loading, the jostling for seats among those fortunate enough to be passengers, the vying of soldiers for a spot on the tops of boxcars, etc.—there must have been some satisfaction in knowing that most of them, including the president and the cabinet, would be depending on the supplies he had had the foresight to store in a Danville warehouse.

At the camp of the First Rockbridge Artillery near Laurel Hill Church, south of Richmond, rumors abounded as the afternoon dragged on, fed by soldiers returning from the city, where they had attended church and visited friends and relatives. What was in store for them and where they would be going, no one knew for certain. Returning from their brief foray into Richmond to see Semple, Alex and Gardie pulled their things together and waited to move out. Around dusk, orders were finally passed from captains to lieutenants to sergeants, and the quiet, suspenseful lull was replaced with yelling of commands, cursing of soldiers, and the tramping of earth by men and animals as the camp came to life and began to move toward Richmond, hauling two of the four artillery pieces assigned to the battery. The other two had been given to another battery; with the Tredegar Iron Works closed, there was no way to replace the guns. As with most units in the Army of Northern Virginia, the First Rockbridge had been depleted in both men and equipment. With a lack of horses to pull the commissary, each man took as much as he could carry for rations. Food would likely be scarce over the coming days.[33]

By early evening, Alex and Gardie were once again inside the city, headed for Mayo's Bridge and Manchester on the other side of the James River. They could see the commotion building in the streets, the burning and smoldering piles of papers, and the flow of people and vehicles toward the Danville depot. Somewhere in the confluence of citizens, sailors, and the Home Guard in and around the station were Semple and their trunks. As they trudged down Fourteenth Street and onto the bridge, they would have been able to look over at the train standing at the platform, embers spewing from the engine funnel into the darkening sky. At that point, they must have wondered when they would next see their former roommate and mentor . . . perhaps in Danville. They could not know that six months would pass before they knew where he was and what had happened to him.

Eighty-thirty p.m., the intended departure time for the president's train, came and went. The cars were fully loaded and the cabinet officers, except for Breckinridge, were aboard, anxious to be off. If anything happened to the railroad bridge over the James, they would all be prisoners in the morning. Davis, however, was reluctant to leave. Hoping for more favorable news from Lee, he and Breckinridge remained close to the telegraph office, joining railroad president Lewis Harvie for a time in his office. Around 11:00 p.m., when no further messages had come, the president returned to his seat in the executive car, as did Harvie. Breckinridge would not be accompanying Davis; instead, he would ride out of Richmond in the morning after Ewell's troops had left the city to try to catch up with Lee. He would no doubt carry instructions from Davis, but he would also provide Lee with some authority in making decisions in the coming days, as the general attempted to reach Johnston and meld their armies. He might or might not get that far, depending on Grant's ability to maneuver around him.

As Breckinridge watched, the "government on wheels" jerked forward, the drivers of the engine catching hold on the worn rails. Slowly, the train labored away, into the night. Next was the treasury train, ringed with midshipmen, each armed with two revolvers. Inexplicably, the train lingered for another hour, and William H. Parker grew increasingly nervous. Fires were now breaking out in the city. He could see the streets filling with drunken mobs—thieves and deserters, he supposed—and he worried about the cars containing the gold and silver. Could his young sailors hold off an unruly crowd? His own son, Clifton, was one of those guarding the train, as was a son of Breckinridge. Fortunately, they were never tested; around midnight, the train inched its way out of the station and across the railroad bridge, the midshipmen having moved to the interior of the cars. Behind them, the fires in Richmond would grow as the tobacco in the warehouses was ignited by Ewell's men; vessels and ammunition magazines began to blow sky high, shaking the city. The rabble would control the night; Armageddon had come to Richmond.

* * *

Somewhere in or near Richmond, a free black man must have been smiling. Sylvanius Tyler Brown had done his part for the North, escorting a Union scout to where he could view Confederate positions, carrying messages as a runner for spymaster Col. George H. Sharpe, and helping "white and colored people" in Richmond escape to the Union lines. The war, in many instances, had tragically pitted family members against one another, but for Sylvanius, the circumstances were somewhat more unusual. In his case—at least as far as many believed—his father was supposedly white and also a prominent Virginian, the head of a distinguished family who had led both his state and his country.[34] Former President John Tyler may have been turning over in his grave.

3

THE FUGITIVE
AND THE
FIRST LADY

The kindness of Brother James we will never be able to repay. He is the best man that ever lived without any exception. I love him next to yourself and the children.

—John Alexander Tyler to Julia Gardiner Tyler,
August 27, 1864

*J*ULIA GARDINER TYLER HAD every reason to be worried. She knew within days about the collapse of the Confederate lines around Richmond, and she realized that Alex and Gardie were now in more danger than they had been since they entered the war, as Lee attempted to extricate the remnants of his army from the overrun defenses. She could imagine the hardships and the constant threat of enemy fire they were facing, with Yankee soldiers swarming around the flanks of the retreating Confederate columns. The brothers' days of monotonous guard duty and sitting around campfires during the stalemate of winter had suddenly come to a cataclysmic end, and she had no idea where they were and or whether they were even together.[1]

With telegraphs busily chattering between Virginia and the War Department in Washington and in newspaper offices around the country, the *New York Times* of April 4 reported the fall of Richmond and the fact that Lee's army was being pursued as it retreated toward Amelia Court House, cut off from supplies and harassed by Union cavalry. No doubt, Julia wondered if the boys had been captured, or worse, if they had been wounded or lay dead in a field or along the route traveled by their artillery unit. Wherever they were, they could no longer look to Semple for help, and neither could Julia. She could only wonder what had happened to him. The person they had all grown to depend on so much would be missed during the most trying of times and circumstances for the South and for the family of John Tyler.

Despite her concerns, Julia must have been comforted by the fact that her sons were self-reliant and capable of taking care of themselves. Such qualities she readily acknowledged in herself; she could recall times that her individualism had exasperated her proper, socially conscious mother, Juliana, and her father, former New York state senator David Gardiner. With the family living in East Hampton, New York, fifteen-year-old Julia was sent to a finishing school in New York City for young ladies of wealthy, socially prominent families. Even there, at Madame N. D. Chagaray's Institute, and only in her middle teens, her freethinking, extroverted personality must have been evident, for she was soon counseled by her mother: "You must be more cautious in expressing your opinions so freely as it will certainly give you trouble."[2] By age nineteen, Julia had grown into a beautiful, sophisticated young woman with a trim, hourglass figure. Her jet black hair, usually parted in the middle, framed a round face with expressive gray eyes, full lips, and a straight nose. Fully aware of her looks and charms, she had become particularly adept at attracting male admirers. That fact, and an incident causing embarrassment for her parents in the stuffy East Hampton community, led the senator to expedite plans for an extended trip to Europe for himself, Juliana, and their two daughters.[3]

The actual reasons for the incident are unclear. Perhaps Julia was talked into it, but more likely, she became aware of the opportunity and thought it might be fun. She was also probably enticed by the attention she knew she would receive. In any case, the nineteen-year-old allowed her image to be used in an advertisement by Bogert and Mecamly, a New York clothing and dry goods store. The circular, which was distributed widely in the city, featured an illustration of Julia in front of the store, carrying a small sign stating, "I'll purchase at Bogert and Mecamly's, No. 86 Ninth Avenue. Their goods are beautiful and astonishingly cheap." Dressed in a fashionable winter coat, she was accompanied in the picture by an older man—a dandy, some would say—wearing a top hat and topcoat and holding a cane. The advertisement displayed the caption, "Rose of Long Island."[4]

Julia's association with the advertisement (she may have even posed for it), the fact that she was shown with a man (suggesting a relationship with someone older), and the epithet she inherited as a result of the circular underscored a lack of good judgment on her part. Her parents were both shocked and mortified, an understandable reaction, considering the public mores of genteel society in the mid-1800s. To their further humiliation, additional unwanted publicity occurred with the introduction of a poem a few months later, entitled "Julia—The Rose of Long Island." Supposedly penned by a "Romeo Ringdove," the poem appeared on the front page of the *Brooklyn Daily News* on May 11, 1840.[5] Though not particularly inspiring or well written, it nevertheless reminded readers about the circular and, in a sense, perpetuated the scandal. The trip to Europe, set for September, could not happen soon enough.

Julia's independent, headstrong nature and her determination to do things her way were almost certainly enabled by the fact that the Gardiners of New York were wealthy—much more so, in fact, than the Tylers of Virginia—and they were as socially prominent. Also, quite possibly, such traits of Julia, including her unbounded energy and love of adventure, did not originate with her, but instead could be traced back to an ancestor, Lion Gardiner, a professional soldier who came to America from Holland in 1635. The first of the Gardiner line in the new country, he had been hired to build "forts of defense" in Connecticut to protect colonists living in the area from attacks by the Pequot Indians and from possible incursions by the Dutch. The first was a blockhouse with living quarters for individuals and families in what became Saybrook, Connecticut. The town was named after Viscount Saye and Lord Brooke, two of the "Warwick Patentees" hiring Gardiner's services. Though not in favor of war with the Pequots—mainly because fields of corn planted by the colony would be jeopardized and a shortage of food would likely result—Gardiner ended up being drawn into the Pequot War of 1636–37, killing a number of Indians in protection of the community and receiving both gunshot and arrow wounds in return.[6]

From his description of events, Gardiner clearly found the Pequots to be a hostile, brutal enemy, unwilling to live in peace with the colonists (perhaps, in part, because they had been stirred up as directed by leaders of the Massachusetts Bay Colony—"Bay men," Gardiner called them). Other tribes, however, were less resentful of what most Indians saw as an intrusion on their land and sought to trade with the colonists. As the Pequot War came to an end, Gardiner became close friends with Waiandance, a Montauk chief from the eastern part of Long Island. Through Waiandance, Gardiner was able to purchase Manchonake Island from the Montauks. The price for the 3,375-acre island, situated between the two forks of land that form the eastern end of Long Island, was reportedly a quantity of trading cloth. Another account from that period differed somewhat, claiming that Manchonake was exchanged for Dutch blankets, a gun, and a black dog. Whichever is right, the purchase was a bargain. Fortunately, Gardiner had the wisdom to also obtain a deed to the property from the Earl of Sterling, who had been granted Long Island and other islands along the southern coast of New England by Charles I of England.

After his four-year fort-building contract expired, Gardiner left Saybrook and settled down for a time on Manchonake Island with his wife and two children before trading the beauty and isolation of the island for the more social climes of East Hampton, New York. With considerable foresight, Lion Gardiner continued to acquire land, by purchase and by outright gift from the Montauks, to the point that, when he died in 1663, he had laid a foundation of wealth for his descendants. Three years before he died, the soldier, engineer, Indian fighter, and visionary wrote of his adventures in a frank account, which he titled *Relation of the Pequot Warres*.

Manchonake Island became known as Gardiners Island, and it has remained in the continuous possession of the Gardiner family since 1839. It is, even today, the symbolic center of the Gardiner empire, a vast estate passed down through the centuries from eldest son to eldest son, to the extent possible. When not possible, due to the young age of the eligible son, or for another reason, temporary arrangements have been made within the family until such time as the line of inheritance can continue and an eligible son is ready and able to take possession. It was under such a temporary arrangement that Julia Tyler Gardiner was born on the island.

Julia's father was David Gardiner. Though he was the great-grandson of the fourth proprietor of Gardiner Island—also named David Gardiner—he was not in line himself to become a proprietor, or "Lord of the Isle," as they were called. He was educated at Yale University and practiced law in New York City until he met and, in 1815, married Juliana McLachlan, the daughter of a wealthy Scotsman who had invested wisely in real estate in the lower Manhattan section of the city. When her father, Michael McLachlan, died in 1819, Juliana inherited the properties, which provided sufficient rental income for her and her new husband to enjoy the full benefits of material comfort. As a result, David Gardiner soon left his law practice to take over the full-time management of the Manhattan real estate.

In 1816, John Lyon Gardiner, the seventh proprietor of Gardiner Island, died. His widow, Sarah Griswold Gardiner, offered to lease the island to David Gardiner, who was her cousin. The term of the lease would only be until her son, David Johnson Gardiner, reached eighteen, at which time he would take over as "Lord." Pleased at the opportunity to reside, at least for a time, on the island he had explored as a boy and had always been fascinated with, David Gardiner moved with Juliana from East Hampton, where they had been staying temporarily, across the bay (now known as Gardiner Bay) to the island. There they lived for six years, and there Julia Gardiner was born on May 4, 1820, preceded by her brothers, David Lyon in 1816 and Alexander in 1818.

Thus, for the first two years of her life, Julia was raised in a genteel agrarian society with hundreds of acres of farmland, extensive livestock, and slaves, much like she would later experience as mistress of Sherwood Forest. In 1822, David Gardiner moved back to East Hampton with his wife and children into a new home. That same year, Julia's younger sister, Margaret, was born, and the family was complete. Gardiner soon took up politics, spending four successive one-year terms in the New York state senate before losing to an opponent in his fifth attempt. Though his formal career as a politician was short—four years—he permanently adopted the mantle of "Senator Gardiner" and essentially remained an unemployed aristocrat throughout the remainder of his life. Still interested in politics, and after running unsuccessfully for office one more time, he abandoned both his attempt at being a senator again and the practice of law.

As Julia Gardiner grew older, the impetuous behavior of her early and teenage years were complemented by her poise and growing skills at captivating the opposite sex, a combination that had already begun to worry her parents when the incident occurred. The trip to Europe was thus designed to cool the attentions of the increasing number of suitors at their East Hampton home as well as to separate themselves from the publicity and resulting embarrassment caused by Julia's indiscretion. Out of sight, out of mind on both counts was the fervent hope of Juliana and the senator. With the two sons of the family remaining in New York to continue their study of law, the Gardiner family sailed for London, England, in late September 1840, the beginning of an adventure eagerly anticipated by Julia and Margaret. The leisurely yearlong tour took in several countries, the highlights no doubt being their presentation at the court of Louis Philippe of France and an audience with Pope Gregory XVI.

Unfortunately, in some respects, the trip was a failure. Instead of being insulated from encounters with eligible males, which would have pleased her parents, Julia found the time and opportunity to hone her craft with various prospects, including a passenger on a steamer crossing the English Channel, a German nobleman, a Belgian count, and finally, an employee of the War Ministry after the Gardiners had arrived back in London from side trips to Scotland and Ireland.

While the Gardiners were away in Europe, the political scene in the United States changed dramatically. On April 4, 1841, President William Henry Harrison died suddenly from pneumonia, after only thirty days in office. Notified at his home in Williamsburg, Virginia, Vice President John Tyler hurried to Washington to take the oath of office and assume the presidency. Despite years of service as a member of the U.S. Congress, both in the House of Representatives and in the Senate, Tyler's political tenets and positions on issues beyond a strong commitment to states' rights and an aversion to a national bank were generally unknown. His speeches and voting record had shown him to be politically independent instead of a constant follower of any party line.

By the time the Gardiners returned to U.S. soil six months later, Tyler had become less of an enigma and was embroiled in controversy. Originally nominated by the Whig Party for vice president, he vetoed two successive Whig-sponsored bills. As a consequence, he found himself in the midst of a furor and temporarily without a cabinet. Tyler had unwisely retained the original members of the Harrison cabinet, and with the veto of the second bill, all resigned, with the single exception of Secretary of State Daniel Webster. Though Congress quickly confirmed his nominations for a new cabinet, his hands were effectively tied by a vengeful Congress. Tyler was formally repudiated by the Whigs, and in the words of Henry Clay, the president's political nemesis, he was a "president without a party."

With events in Washington becoming more interesting from a political standpoint, and with his daughters now well versed in etiquette after the trip to Europe, Senator Gardiner believed the time was right to introduce his family (again minus the sons) to the nation's capital. A visit of three months, beginning in January 1842, exposed the Gardiners to the elite inner circles of Washington society and gave Julia another opportunity to add to her collection of admirers.

The culmination of their social activities occurred on the evening of January 20. The Gardiner family was invited to the White House to meet the president, who cordially greeted Julia with a "thousand compliments" when she was introduced to him. Undoubtedly burdened with his political problems, the president rose to the occasion and was both gracious and charming. Missing from the reception was First Lady Letitia Christian Tyler, who was almost never seen in public, especially after a stroke had left her partially paralyzed three years prior. Tyler's reclusive wife of twenty-nine years was, by all accounts, lovely, selfless, and devoted to her husband and children. To the president's deep and crushing grief, Letitia died in September of that year.

In December 1842, the Gardiner family returned to Washington for another social season and was invited to spend Christmas Eve at the White House. By early February 1843, the widower of five months had become smitten with Julia and relentlessly courted her, despite their age difference of some thirty years. Pursued by a number of eligible men, most of whom were wealthy, cultured, and much younger than the president, Julia emphatically rejected his first of five proposals of marriage. Over the next several weeks, the prospect of marrying the president became more appealing, and by the time the family returned to East Hampton at the end of the social season in late March, Julia was giving his subsequent proposals serious thought.

In mid-February 1844, the senator and his two daughters returned again to Washington, Juliana this time staying behind with her two sons. On February 27, the senator and his daughters were among a throng of people invited aboard the steam frigate *Princeton* for a cruise down the Potomac. An attraction of the voyage was to be the firing of the "Peacemaker," a 12-inch naval gun, the world's largest. During the afternoon, the gun was fired twice without a problem. The third time, it exploded. Fortunately, the president, as well as Julia and Margaret, were safely belowdecks having a glass of champagne, but the senator was not. He and others, including Tyler's secretary of state and secretary of the navy, were killed instantly and several people were severely wounded. Julia reportedly fainted into the arms of the president, who gently carried her off the ship.

Back in East Hampton, traumatized by the loss of her father, Julia felt herself drawn inexplicably closer to Tyler. "After I lost my father I felt differently toward the President," she would recall years later.[7] Perhaps she sought comfort with a father figure, or the maturity of a relationship that a younger man could not provide. (Tyler, a month shy of fifty-four, was six years younger than David Gardiner.) In any case, her mind was made up, and in less than two months after the *Princeton* tragedy, Julia informed the president that she would marry him. They were secretly wed on June 26, 1844, in a small, quiet ceremony held at the Church of the Ascension on Fifth Avenue in New York City.

Though first lady for less than eight months, Julia Gardiner Tyler brought a touch of elegance and royalty to the White House unlike any other administration before or after. She often greeted guests on a raised platform surrounded by twelve attendants, ladies in waiting dressed in white. At appropriate moments, she would leave the dais to lead the dancing on the arm of her husband. Julia brought style, color, and energy to staid White House receptions. She introduced both the polka and waltz to balls held in the East Room of the "Presidential Mansion," and she is responsible for the playing of "Hail to the Chief" to honor the president at state occasions.

The Tylers' marriage, by all accounts, was happy, and Julia unquestionably grew to love her husband. Prolific as a father, John Tyler had eight children with his first wife and seven more with Julia. Gradually, she won over her stepchildren with her warmth and charm—with the notable exception of Tyler's daughter, Letitia. Apparently unable to accept someone only a year older than she was as a replacement for her natural mother, Letitia had no use for the new first lady. For a while, Julia tried to be friendly for the sake of the president. Repeatedly rebuffed, however, she finally gave up, and they remained hostile toward one another throughout their lives. Of course, the fact that Letitia's husband was James A. Semple undoubtedly gave Letitia a reason other than their relative ages to despise her stepmother, at least eventually.

Lacking a depth of understanding—and very likely, genuine interest—in national politics, Julia used her talents to champion her husband and his political views. In general, Tyler's years as president, however, were unremarkable, which is understandable, considering the constant opposition from the Whig and Democratic members in the House and Senate. The most notable achievement of his presidency was undoubtedly the annexation of Texas, the congressional resolution being formally signed by Tyler three days before he left office.

Deciding against running for a second term, the former president retired to his Virginia plantation on the north bank of the James River in Charles City County. Situated less than three miles from Greenway, the home in which Tyler had been born, the sixteen-hundred-acre estate had been purchased by Tyler in 1842. Originally called Walnut Grove, the president had renamed it Sherwood Forest, a tongue-in-cheek reference to his considered status as an outlaw—much like Robin Hood—though he is not known to have robbed the rich to give to the poor. In his case, instead of the sheriff of Nottingham, his archenemy had been the U.S. Congress.

The Tylers' years of retirement were relatively tranquil, though strained at times by financial concerns, up until the early days of the Civil War. While she missed the hustle and bustle of Washington and undoubtedly the social life and glamour, Julia threw herself into redecorating and refurnishing the home. She also became immediately involved in performing the duties of a plantation mistress, which included coordinating the activities of the household servants and overseeing the needs of some seventy slaves.

The institution of slavery was not foreign to Julia, nor did it offend her. In her mind, the slaves at Sherwood Forest were well cared for and happy. She would refer to their loud and merry singing while working in the fields in justifying her viewpoint, and until the war appeared on the Tyler doorstep, only one slave ran away in a period of eighteen years. As idyllic as plantation life may have been portrayed, however, the Tyler slaves were certainly not free, and when given the opportunity of freedom during the war, practically all of them quickly abandoned the plantation.

Julia's contentment with slavery was matched by her ambivalence toward the less-than-monogamous lifestyle that went on between cabins. The family bond did not seem to be all that strong, at least with regard to children, who were shuffled about and at times raised by someone other than their birth mothers. Unfortunately, no record exists as to Julia's feelings about her husband's own reported dalliances with "free blacks." If such incidents occurred—and there is no documented evidence they did—they are likely to have happened during the years of Tyler's marriage to Letitia Christian Tyler, whom he had wed in 1813. According to an oral tradition among some black residents in Charles City County, the president claimed on more than one occasion that he had fathered fifty-two children. That would have meant that thirty-seven of them were illegitimate, an unrealistic number, even for John Tyler.

Yet the legend quietly survives among both blacks and whites in the environs of Charles City and links the president with two women in particular: Polly Brown (ca. 1800), a neighbor of Tyler's, and Martha "Patsy" Boasman Brown (1812), who reportedly worked for the president before she was married. Patsy was the mother of Sylvanius Tyler Brown, who secretly provided aid to the Union army, a fact that would have infuriated Tyler had he been alive at the time.

Quite possibly, Julia either knew nothing about her husband's indiscretions, or she chose to ignore the rumors. Then, too, another Tyler—John Tyler Jr., for instance—could have been the cause of the gossip instead of the president. In any case, whoever was involved with Polly and Patsy, if anyone, the subject was not likely to have been dinner-table conversation.[8]

As the country inevitably edged toward sectional strife and civil war, Tyler became a voice for calm and deliberation in resolving the deep-felt issues that were splitting the nation. In February 1861, the former president, a month shy of seventy-one, returned briefly to public life as president of a peace conference posed by him and called by the Virginia legislature to avert war. Convened in Washington and consisting of delegates from twenty-one states, the conference represented a last-gasp attempt at peace. Resolutions hammered out and adopted by the convention, however, were unacceptable to the Congress, and the conference failed. Anticipating such a result before formal submittal of the proposed constitutional amendment, Tyler took his seat in a Virginia state convention called to consider secession, and he voted for withdrawal of the state from the Union. In the fall of that year, after a stint in the Provisional Congress of the Confederate States of America, he was elected to the House of Representatives for the Confederate Congress. With the House scheduled to begin its first session, Tyler arrived at the Exchange Hotel from Richmond in early January 1862. A few days later, he suddenly became ill, and just after midnight on January 18, as Julia and a doctor desperately tended to him, Tyler passed away from what was later judged to have been either a stroke or vascular thrombosis.

Julia became a widow at forty-one. The sole administrator of a vast plantation with hundreds of acres of fields to be planted, seven children at home, a vast number of slaves to be watched over, and enemy soldiers threatening her property and the safety of her family, Julia had her hands full. More than ever before, she would need to draw upon the inner strength, determination, and independence that had come down to her from her ancestor, Lion Gardiner. And she would need James A. Semple.

* * *

The growing-up years of James Allen Semple had been much different. He, too, was born into wealth, but there the similarities ended. His father was Col. George Semple, who was descended from a line stretching back to Robert deSempill in Scotland that included lords and baronesses and even a knight or two. The colonel was the son of the Reverend James Semple, who emigrated from Scotland to New Kent County, Virginia, in 1755.[9]

Unfortunately, New Kent is a "burned records county," which means most of the records at the time were destroyed during the Civil War with the burning of the county courthouse. In the case of New Kent, records were actually destroyed twice, first by a fire in 1787, set by a man who was subsequently hanged for his misdeed. In 1864, the county records that had accumulated after the first fire were either burned or carried off by Union troops. Information is thus somewhat sparse on the lives and dealings of the planter families who settled in the area.

What is known is that the Reverend Semple was an eminent pastor of St. Peter's Parish for some twenty years. He was also a wealthy landowner, having purchased almost fourteen hundred acres in New Kent County. George Semple, the youngest son of the revered minister, had three brothers and six sisters. With the death of his father, he inherited a tract of land, which he added to significantly in 1817 when he married a neighbor, Elizabeth A. Holt, who was a widow at the time. By combining Elizabeth Holt's land—which was called Cedar Hill—with his, George Semple amassed a respectable plantation of some 972 acres. Retaining the Cedar Hill name, he became a successful planter, probably of corn and wheat, for such staples were typically grown in the productive New Kent region of the Tidewater country.[10]

Into this world of privilege and planter social class, James Allen Semple was born on February 19, 1819. He would be their only child, for Elizabeth died that same year. How he was raised as an infant is uncertain, since no white females were living on the plantation, and of the thirty-six slaves, none were women. The most credible answer would seem to be that his mother was alive during his critical early months. Even at that, caring for a baby after Elizabeth died must have been challenging for the all-male household.

Two years after the birth of his son, George Semple died at age forty-five. Responsibility for the young child fell on the shoulders of the colonel's oldest living brother, Judge James Semple, who lived in Williamsburg, Virginia, a quiet college town about thirty miles away. Once the capital of the Virginia colony, Williamsburg had lost the mantle to Richmond in 1780, and the town of some fifteen hundred farmers, merchants, and craftsmen slowly slumbered into obscurity, distinguished solely by the presence of William and Mary College. Judge Semple was both a judge of the general court of Virginia and a professor of law at the college, which was down the street from the Semple house. At the time he brought his nephew into the Williamsburg home, the judge was married to his second wife, Joanna. She died, however, when the boy was five, and he had little memory of her. He was, however, surrounded by cousins, at least three of whom were still living at home. One other cousin, Henry Churchill Semple, was born the following year, and they were close companions in the judge's household.[11]

Cedar Hill remained in the Semple family and was operated as a business. Apparently, the judge made the decision to keep the farm—as plantations were commonly called in Tidewater Virginia, irrespective of acreage and grandeur—until his ward became old enough to take it over. Why he did this is not certain, but a portion of the land had been owned by three generations of Semples, and his nephew's mother and father were buried there, along with Mammy Sarah, a devoted servant. And land was wealth. Few planters were cash-rich. Income earned off the land was turned into livestock, seed, and other farm supplies, hired or purchased labor when needed, and purchased clothing, food, and comforts to support the wants of the family. The cycle was never ending, and depending on the season, red ink was as common as black in plantation ledgers. The judge knew, though, that by holding on to Cedar Hill and another inherited property, Scotland Neck, he was keeping watch over an investment that would bring his nephew a degree of self-sufficiency and security in the years ahead.

In 1834, the judge died, and responsibility for fifteen-year-old James Semple shifted to John Tyler Semple, the next oldest living brother of George. The boy had thus lost his mother, father, aunt, and uncle as caretakers and was then being guided by still another relative acting as his parent.

Little is known about these teenage years other than the fact that Semple was a student at William and Mary for a year. He also attended Randolph-Macon College, a Methodist school founded only a few years prior in Boydton, Virginia. (It later moved to Ashland, Virginia.) He evidently spent a total of two sessions in college, never graduating from either.[12]

Plantation families, as well as political and professional people of wealth and status in New Kent and neighboring counties, all knew each other and socialized frequently. Over the generations, marriage between these families was common, most likely in an effort to ensure the continued purity of the blood that ran in the veins of Tidewater aristocrats. Almost inevitably, James Semple began to court Letitia Tyler, the sixteen-year-old daughter of John Tyler. Though a member of the Virginia legislature at the time, Tyler was enjoying a peaceful interlude at his Williamsburg home before being thrust into the tempest of Washington politics and into the unexpected role of president of the United States. The Tylers and the Semples were actually already linked; Judge Semple's first wife had been Ann Contesse Tyler, John Tyler's sister, and his second wife, Joanna McKenzie, was Tyler's first cousin.[13]

The marriage of James Semple and Letitia Tyler on February 21, 1839, at Bruton Parish Church in Williamsburg was no doubt a happy occasion, and the couple soon retired to Cedar Hill, where Semple assumed direct responsibility for the plantation after eighteen years of stewardship. Letty, as she was called by her family and by Semple, busied herself in setting up the household and overseeing the servants.

Bearing a striking resemblance to her father, with a long narrow face and prominent straight nose, Letitia, at seventeen, would not have been considered beautiful. Her eyes were a little too large, and her mouth was a little too small. Perhaps kindly, she was described by sister-in-law Priscilla Cooper Tyler as "very handsome." (Priscilla, then in the glow of her marriage a few months prior to Robert Tyler, John Tyler's oldest son, tended to look favorably on all of his sisters.) Enhancing Letitia's looks and, to some extent, drawing attention away from any deficiencies in natural beauty was a spirited, "full-of-life," take-charge personality.[14] Unfortunately, the energy, enthusiasm, and drive of her youth would, in a few short years, be supplanted by anger and bitterness toward her estranged husband and toward her stepmother, Julia Gardiner Tyler, whom she disliked intensely.

Semple's career as a hands-on planter was relatively short, for in October 1844, he received a commission from President Tyler as a purser in the

U.S. Navy. Assigned to the sloop USS *Jamestown*, he was soon patrolling the waters off the western coast of Africa, intercepting ships engaged in the then-illegal slave trade. Semple was at sea for almost two years.

Before he joined the navy, Semple and Letitia had already been apart for a few months while she temporarily took over as White House hostess. With Letitia Christian Tyler incapacitated by a stroke, the role of hostess had at first fallen on Priscilla. The two oldest daughters of the president, Mary Tyler Jones and Letitia Tyler Semple, both had husbands and homes more than thirty miles away in Virginia. Priscilla, a former actress, was the logical choice, since Robert Tyler had been given a position in the Land Office, close to the White House. In March 1844, however, Robert moved his family back to Philadelphia to begin his law practice, and Letitia was called upon to fill the vacancy at the White House. Her days in the receiving line did not last long. In the summer of 1844, much to Letitia's displeasure, the role was taken over by Julia Gardiner Tyler when she returned from her honeymoon with the president.

After a year stationed at Hampton Roads, Virginia, on the USS *Alleghany*, an iron-hulled gunboat, Semple was assigned to the frigate USS *John Adams*, which took part in the Mexican War as a blockading ship.[15] Not long after the war was over, Semple showed up at Sherwood Forest with a full beard and mustache, bearing gifts—souvenirs of the war—for the Tylers. Somehow, for some reason, he had obtained a suit of armor for the president (minus the helmet, which had been lost overboard in transit). Despite her contentious dealings with Letitia, Julia Tyler received him warmly. He "behaved so well and complimented me so highly . . . I was not sorry I consented to see him," Julia wrote to her mother at Staten Island. She would not blame him for his wife's ill behavior, and the seeds were sown for a relationship that would blossom fifteen years later, when another war came to an end.[16]

Semple had little time for socializing, for he soon found himself in Boston, on a sloop of war, the USS *Yorktown*, which sailed for the African coast. On patrol for slave traders, the vessel struck an uncharted reef and quickly broke up off the Cape Verde Islands. Miraculously, no lives were lost, and six months after the sinking, Semple was assigned to the USS *Preble*, a sloop docked at the New York Navy Yard as a practice ship for midshipmen.[17] He was there for almost four years, and however shaky the Semple marriage may have been at the time, Letitia joined him there. As he was allowed to live off ship, they rented a house in Brooklyn. Letitia hired help both for the household and to assist her in caring for her two-year-old niece, Elizabeth. Bessie, as she was most often called, lived with Letitia until she became an adult and married.

Semple's career in the U.S. Navy was comprised of two more assignments, the USS *Congress*, which toured in the Mediterranean before being decommissioned, and the USS *North Carolina*, a huge old frigate rotting in the East River at New York.[18] Semple would encounter the *Congress* again much later—as an enemy. During the Civil War, the *Congress* was brought out of retirement to join the Union blockage at Hampton Roads; the frigate was destroyed by the CSS *Virginia* in March 1862. In charge of the powder division on the Confederate ironclad during the battle, Semple must have had mixed feelings as the *Congress* was consumed in flames. Fortunately, the ship struck its colors and was abandoned before it blew up. Of the 434 crewmen on the *Congress*, some of them possibly old comrades, 218 survived.

Semple's assignment to the USS *North Carolina* lasted for almost three years, and Letitia joined him again in New York. By late spring 1861, the nation was disintegrating below the Mason-Dixon Line. Seven states—Alabama, Florida, Georgia, Louisiana, Mississippi, South Carolina, and Texas—had already left the Union to form the Confederate States of America, and Semple was ready to shift allegiance to the new nation and seek a role in the embryonic navy. Detached from the *North Carolina* and ordered to the USS *Niagara*, Semple decided he had waited long enough and resigned his commission in May 1861. He, Letitia, and Bessie headed south, and on June 10, 1861, he was commissioned as a paymaster in the Confederate navy, where he was first assigned to the CSS *McRae*, which was docked in New Orleans.[19]

Unwilling to sit out the war, Letitia returned to Williamsburg, where she lived before her marriage. (Cedar Hill had been sold by Semple after he gave up farming for his commission in the U.S. Navy.) There she established and operated the first hospital in the South for sick and wounded Confederate soldiers. Initially occupying the Female Seminary, the hospital soon spilled over to the courthouse, local churches, and buildings on the grounds of William and Mary College.

Semple spent much of the war as a paymaster. On board the CSS *McRae* only a few months, in November 1861, he was assigned to the *Merrimack*, a burned and scuttled hulk left behind when Union sailors abandoned the Gosport Navy Yard in Portsmouth, Virginia. The *Merrimack* had been raised from the shallow bottom of the Elizabeth River and was being reconstructed into a formidable warship with bolted-on layers of two-inch iron plating.

In March 1862, renamed the CSS *Virginia*, the ironclad was ready to do battle. The day after destroying the *Congress* (as well as ramming and sinking the USS *Cumberland*), the *Virginia* engaged the USS *Monitor*, a strange-looking ironclad with a single revolving turret amidships and a deck only a foot above the water, waves washing over it with every maneuver. Looking as though it might sink at any time, the *Monitor* was deceivingly formidable, and fortunately for the Union naval force, which expected a renewed attack by the Confederate ironclad, it had arrived in Hampton Roads in time to place itself between the *Virginia* and the wooden frigates of the Union blockading fleet. For more than four hours, the two ships pounded each other from a distance of less than one hundred yards, shells bouncing off the armor of both vessels. In the end, the battle was inconclusive, each ship withdrawing from the engagement relatively unscathed.

The *Virginia* would never fight again. Two months after the battle, as Union forces advanced up the Peninsula, an attempt was made to move the *Virginia* up the James River to the protection of the Confederate capital. Unfortunately, the draft of the ironclad was too deep, and the ship had to be blown up by the crew to keep it from falling into the hands of the enemy. The officers and men, including Semple, were reassigned to Drewry's Bluff. There, Semple's resourcefulness and his skills at organization attracted the attention of Stephen R. Mallory, secretary of the navy. Ordered to Richmond to assist Paymaster John DeBree, chief of the Bureau of Provisions and Clothing, Semple's remarkable competence led to his replacing DeBree in April 1864 (officially from October 1864).[20]

As bureau chief, Semple was without equal. In October 1864, only six months before Lee's surrender to Grant, he was able to report to Mallory, "I have now in the storehouses at Rocketts [the Richmond Navy Yard] a supply of bread and flour for eight months; beef and pork, six months; rice and beans, six months; sugar and molasses, five months; and tea and coffee for eight months. . . . The cloth which was imported is now being made up as rapidly as possible, and will be sufficient to furnish each man in the navy with one suit."[21] Most of the supplies would be lost to the enemy with the fall of Richmond, but as the president and his cabinet would soon find out,

Semple's proficiencies would become apparent in Danville and Charlotte
. . . and in the village of Washington, Georgia.

At some point during the war, at the request of a friend, James Allen Semple reflected on his life, already exceedingly full for someone in his forties.

I have fished at Nahant, bathed at Newport, danced at Cape May, drank Congress water at Saratoga & laid in the shadow of "Sharon," have spent a day or
two in gazing on the seething waters of Niagara & its wonderful whirlpool,
have glided through the thousand Isles of the St. Lawrence, have whiffed my
segar on the heights of Quebec, have been frozen up in the middle of summer in the White Mountains & have also been burned by the heat of summer
in December at Pascagoula & Bay St. Louis. Have stood on the lofty Peaks of
Otter in Va. overlooking the garden lands of Virginia's valleys, have visited the
famous White, Blue, Red & Sweet Sulphur Springs & have applied the torch
to the burning springs in the Kanawha Valley—steamed in & around
Arkansas & had a good time there generally in "bunking," along with my
friend Senator G. Have passed up the steep ascent of the Hawksnest on the
New River, Va., and looked over where the clear descent was over one thousand feet. In Kentucky, have tasted the sweet waters of the Blue Lick, been up
Salt River, and explored, at that time, all the known recesses of the wonderful
cave. Have eaten oysters in Va. & Boston, clams at Coney Island, Pompano &
crawfish at New Orleans, crabs at Galveston, catfish at Cairo, Frogs at St.
Louis, Sweet Breads at Solario's (No. 33 University Place). Have visited Cash-
mere & a fair young girl had a shawl which now occasionally bedecks the
shoulders of a matronly lady. Have seen Naples, but cannot agree with the
Italian proverb "See Naples & die"—have wintered at Genoa, visited Turin,
Milan, Venice, Triest, Vienna, Prague, Dresden & Brussels, tried the "Holy
Week" at Rome, crossed the plains of Sharon, slept at the ancient Aramatha,
reached Jerusalem & for days have been engaged in viewing the Holy places
of Scripture. Have seen the Pyramids, ascended Cheops & on its summit
carved in large letters J.T. & J.G.T., eaten the watermelons, six months
plucked, but fresh, at Grand Cairo & Bonlack, made a stretch from thence up
the Bosphorus & sea of Marmora & enjoyed the splendid view as you ap-
proach the Golden Horn, with Constantinople on one side & Scutaro, on the
Asiatic Shore, on the other. The "Sweet Waters" on the European side, bright
with all the hues of the rainbow, from the dresses of the Odalisques. Have
seen the coast of Africa (west side) from Cape Verdi to the Cape of Good

Hope—entered the Senegambia River & seen the elephant in its native state. Saw the "Waltz" of the combined French & English fleets at Sebastopol. Have danced at Lisbon, Cadiz, Leville, Barcelona & Malaga.

The Rock of Gibraltar is an old acquaintance & thanks to the British officers, have always had a pleasant time. Have visited the "Alhambra," looked over the quarters of Hon. Washington Irving, conversed with the Senora, who waited on him. All honor to John Tyler, who sent & kept him there in opposition to his almost entire Cabinet; paraded the "Rambla" with its towering elms and seen the beauty of Grenada, sporting their delicate figures & graceful Mantillos to gladden the eyes & heart of the wayworn Mariner. At "Cape Coast Castle," the Poetess, L.E.L., then the wife of Govr, McLean, gave us a delightful recitation & on our return nothing was left to tell of her, but the flat tomb stone in the court yard of the castle. Passed through the Mozambique Channel, after visiting the Cape of Good Hope & the settlements in a radius of sixty miles, touched at Point de Galle, island of Ceylon, made Hong Kong, from thence to Japan in the fleet of Commo. M. C. Perry—touched at San Francisco, rounded Cape Horn, stopping a while at Valpariso and Rio de Janiero; the old homestead of New York was reached. Have been up in a balloon, down in a diving bell. Have been Hostler, carver, & holder of gentlemen's teams in a German establishment on the Vernon River, Georgia, U.S. I have seen the "Elephant" in all its phases & have yet to make up my mind, whether this life with all its varieties is not a failure. But as old Mrs. Pintard used to tell me when I was cruising around with Bill Hunter, "Jim, keep your heart, my boy, in your hand, & don't open it for every girl" & I have followed her advice.[22]

Little did Semple realize when he left Richmond with the fleeing Confederate government that he was embarking on his most challenging adventure yet, one that not only would test his energy and resourcefulness, but also his ability to keep his heart in an unopened hand. Mrs. Pintard would have approved of Julia Gardiner Tyler.

4

THE NEW CAPITAL

Please give me any reliable information you have as to movements of enemy, and dispositions to protect the Piedmont R. R. I have no communication from General Lee since Sunday.
—President Jefferson Davis to
Gen. P. G. T. Beauregard, April 4, 1865

S THE TRAIN WITH Jefferson Davis and his cabinet crawled through the night toward Danville, the somber mood continued, each passenger in the official party overcome with depression and shock at the day's turn of events. In the words of Secretary of the Navy Stephen R. Mallory, "Silence reigned over the fugitives."[1]

The capital of the Confederacy, the symbol and essence of the Southern spirit, was now gone, and the indomitable Lee, who had staved off the enemy for four years despite the overwhelming odds against him, was fleeing west in an attempt to elude Grant and secure provisions for his starving army. "The terrible reverses of the last twenty-four hours," reported Mallory, "were impressed upon the minds and hearts of all as fatal to the cause."[2] Reality was settling in.

Of immediate concern was the danger that the rail line to Danville might be cut at any time by Union cavalry, and those on board could even be captured and arrested. As officials of the Confederate government, they would almost certainly face imprisonment, perhaps even the gallows. The frequent stops long the way, to allow workmen to repair the poorly built and badly worn narrow-gauge tracks, only added to the concern and nervousness. For some, an exhausted sleep brought a measure of relief, as the *Charles Seddon* puffed along at about ten miles an hour.[3]

To pass the time, Secretary of the Navy Mallory looked around the car at the men who once made the decisions for a nation. The former admiralty lawyer and senator from Florida had been chairman of the Committee on Naval Affairs before the war. His qualifications led to an early appointment by President Davis, and he was one of only two cabinet secretaries to have held the same position in the administration for the four years of the war, the other being Postmaster General John Reagan.

As Mallory studied the faces of the other cabinet officers, he reflected on "the bloody sacrifices of the South, all fruitless now."[4] He undoubtedly regretted his own failure to build a navy sufficient to lift the blockade of Southern ports. As a result, an essential lifeline from Europe through which munitions, food, and clothing might flow had been choked off with the tightening of the blockade and the loss of ports to the enemy.

Critical shortages had, without question, undermined the ability of the South to conduct the war. Yet, of all the cabinet members, Mallory had perhaps accomplished the most with the least amount of resources. With executive skills that distinguished him from some of the other cabinet members, he had created a Navy Department "from scratch" and staffed it with competent bureau chiefs.

Two of the appointments—both replacements—had perhaps the most impact on the operation and successes of the Navy Department: Cmdr. John M. Brooke, head of the Bureau of Ordnance and Hydrography, and James A. Semple. The latter's Bureau of Provisions and Clothing had been ably run by John DeBree, a paymaster with the U.S. Navy for forty-four years. The aging DeBree, however, had drawn increasingly upon the advice and assistance of the younger Semple, who took over the bureau after DeBree's resignation in April 1864.[5]

With only a few wooden ships and only two naval yards of any note to begin with, Mallory had amassed a fleet of ironclads during the war that at times provided formidable opposition to efforts by the Union navy to penetrate Southern waterways and capture forts guarding Southern harbors. Also, thanks to the inventive minds of Brooke and naval officer Matthew

Fontaine Murray (who, early on, even Mallory doubted), underwater mines, floating gun batteries, and torpedo boats had been dire and very real threats to Union warships. The navy secretary could also claim the first sinking of an enemy vessel by a submarine, the *H. L. Hunley,* which, for reasons unknown, also went to the bottom of the bay, entombing its occupants.

At sea, Mallory was blessed with skilled and fearless commanders. The commerce raiders CSS *Alabama, Florida, Shenandoah,* and several other ships captured hundreds of enemy merchant ships and seized the cargoes for the Confederacy. For much of the war, gray blockade-runners—sleek and fast with low profiles—had run the Union gauntlet to offload supplies and return to neutral ports in Bermuda, Nassau, and Cuba. The exports, for the most part, were destined for Great Britain. But all these efforts had been in vain, of course. And as the train bumped and swayed along, Mallory took little comfort in reflecting on his accomplishments.

A glance by Mallory at Reagan "was sufficient to show his deep anxieties." The former Indian fighter, surveyor, lawyer, judge, and U.S. Congressman from Texas had created a self-sufficient postal system by taking over the routes, offices, and even employees of the U.S. postal service. A bear of a man, Reagan may have been lacking in polish as a cabinet officer and felt ill at ease in the drawing rooms of Richmond, but Mallory considered him to be a "conscientious public servant," and he had become a dependable, close friend of the president.[6]

No doubt the anxiety felt by Reagan had begun many months earlier, when he saw his postal routes disintegrating and his offices isolated with the destruction of railroads and the gobbling up of the South by the constant advances of the enemy. Deep in thought, he paid little attention to his surroundings, chewing a wad of tobacco and "whittling a stick down to the little end of nothing, without ever reaching a satisfactory point."[7]

Secretary of the Treasury George A. Trenholm was ill when he arrived at the train station in Richmond and was being cared for by his wife, Anna, the only woman traveling in the car. The distinguished banker spent most of the time prostrated across a hard bench seat, the jolting ride no doubt adding to his misery. Trenholm was suffering not only from neuralgia but also the effects of the morphine given to him by his physician before leaving Richmond. He had been appointed treasury secretary in July 1864, replacing his friend, Christopher G. Memminger, who had resigned after failing to reverse the Confederacy's failing economy.

Trenholm was the head of the Charleston shipping and trading firm John Fraser and Company, and he was believed to be the richest man in the Confederacy. The president had hoped, in making the replacement, that Trenholm's knowledge and skill in accumulating vast interests in banks, hotels, plantations, homes, railroads, steamship lines, and wharves might help in rescuing the treasury—and the country—from financial ruin.[8] The appointment, however, was too late, and with the Confederate Congress refusing to raise taxes or act on any of his proposed reforms, there was little he could accomplish, other than a direct appeal to the public for donations (specie, jewels, silver pieces, securities, etc.). The response was not substantial, considering the needs of the treasury; even his personal contribution of two hundred thousand dollars in Mexican silver dollars and a chest of jewels was more symbolic than effectual.

Of the cabinet officers, only Secretary of State Judah P. Benjamin showed any interest in conversation. A Sephardic Jew, Benjamin had been the target of anti-Semites throughout his career, especially during his four years of service to the Confederacy, which included previous positions as attorney general and a brief, turbulent tenure as secretary of war. A brilliant lawyer, the former U.S. Senator from Louisiana always seemed to be in good humor. The perpetual smile on his face (which was, apparently, his natural look) and his easygoing manner belied the seriousness of his dedication to the Southern cause. Arriving at his office every day at 8:00 a.m., he spent long hours working tirelessly in his office, often to well after midnight. Completely trusted by Davis, he was the president's most adamant supporter and closest adviser, which led to highly confidential duties. Few people in the administration, in fact, other than those directly involved, knew the details of his activities in overseeing the Confederate Secret Service and his failed attempts to orchestrate an uprising in the North.[9]

Mallory suspected that Benjamin's calm, unconcerned demeanor and his optimism this night might be something of a mask. As the secretary of state munched on a sandwich and ruminated on other great causes that had been "redeemed from far gloomier reverses than ours," the navy secretary believed that Benjamin's "deep olive complexion seemed to have become a shade or two darker."[10]

Attorney General George Davis, for some reason, went unnoticed by Mallory—at least, he failed to remark on him. Former lawyer and renowned speaker and lecturer, the North Carolinian had been generally supportive of the administration's policies while serving in the Confederate Senate. As at-

torney general, he had become a valued adviser to the president, particularly in legal interpretations. Poised and intelligent, he was considered to be
the essence of a "Southern gentleman."

The president's aides, Cols. John Taylor Wood and William Preston
Johnston, had little to say, though when asked, they "saw no reason for despair." Col. Francis R. Lubbock apparently felt a need, much like Benjamin,
to uplift the spirits of those around him. Born into a wealthy South Carolina
family, Lubbock moved west to Houston, Texas, stopping in New Orleans
long enough to become married. His subsequent career included store-
owner, rancher, and governor of Texas, all of which gave him fodder for entertaining his captive audience.[11]

Through it all, the anecdotes of Benjamin and Lubbock, and the tedious
train ride of 140 miles, Jefferson Davis remained to himself, and few saw any
reason to interrupt his thoughts. Through the four years of war, the president
had borne the brunt of blame for all that went wrong for the Confederacy,
from the defeats in the field and the loss of shipping and the ports, to the
soaring inflation and the scarcity of food and other essentials. Newspapers
throughout the South vilified him, and Congress routinely opposed him.
While most members of his cabinet admired his composure, dedication, and
even his abilities as a leader (especially Reagan, who believed Davis was "the
greatest man he had ever known"), others in the car were vehement in their
criticism of the president. Robert Kean, for instance, head of the Bureau of
War, had once noted in his diary that the president "seems to possess a most
unenviable facility for converting friends into enemies. . . . This administration could not go on a month more, in my opinion, but for the war."[12]

A degree of blame, of course, could be laid at the feet of Davis. He made
mistakes, and he was not always the best judge of military talent and ability. At
times appearing distant and aloof, he could be accused of being overly sensitive
and defensive when questioned about his opinions and decisions. Critics
pointed out that because of his successes during the Mexican War as a colonel
in leading his regiment at Monterey and Buena Vista and because of his experience as secretary of war under Franklin Pierce, Davis felt qualified to advise his
field commanders. The long hours he spent in his office, like Benjamin, could
be attributed, at least in part, to his reluctance to delegate authority.

In truth, Davis was actually gracious and caring, though few saw that
side of him, the exception being his friends and those directly benefiting
from the contact. While he could be sensitive and defensive in dealings with

his cabinet, he almost always asked for input before settling on a decision. As to interfering with his military commanders, while he may have been tempted to do so, he rarely gave orders, or even made suggestions, unless they failed to take action or update him with report. With Lee, his trust was complete, and he supported him in every way possible. Unfortunately for the president, the lack of a warm public personality increased the enmity of his detractors, and in some cases, turned friends against him. As a result, he was less effective than he might have been.

The president's personality conflicts and, in some instances, poor judgment undoubtedly contributed to the loss of Richmond and the fact that what remained of the Confederate government was now on a train to Danville. Still, his single-minded devotion to the Confederate cause, his assumption of powers necessary to support the military, his selection of Mallory as secretary of the navy, and his early recognition of the abilities of Lee no doubt contributed significantly to the ability of the Confederacy to fend off for four years an enemy vastly superior in men and materials. In any case, fugitive that he may be, Davis was not yet ready to accept defeat.

Sometime during the late morning of April 3, about twelve hours after leaving Richmond, the train stopped at Clover Station to take on wood and water. There, as at other stops along the way, people had gathered to glean the latest news from passing trains, perhaps hoping against hope that the rumors were untrue and that the enemy had not captured the capital of the Confederacy. Seeing the president, however, as he waved wanly from the car, confirmed their fears. Inside the president's car, the gloom had lifted somewhat with the rising sun and the fact that they were out of danger—for now—from being intercepted by Yankee cavalry. No doubt, Trenholm's peach brandy had helped as well.[13]

Lumbering across the Dan River, the president's train finally arrived in Danville around 4:00 p.m., where it was met by a large number of the town's residents. After seventeen hours of being bumped, jerked, swayed, and assaulted by wood smoke and the smell of burning oil lamps, the passengers were anxious to leave the cars for the platform of the Richmond and Danville Railroad depot. Official greetings were extended by a delegation that included Mayor James Walker, the town council, a special committee of ten distinguished citizens, and Maj. Edward Hutter.

Before the war, Danville had been a rural farming community with a prosperous economy based on the sale and inspection of locally grown tobacco. Four years of war, however, had taken a toll on farmers as well as merchants and townspeople. Though no battles had been fought for control of Danville, and Yankee cavalry had not yet ridden through its streets, looting and pillaging, Union soldiers had become a significant presence in town. Six of the warehouses had been converted from storing tobacco leaves to housing prisoners. Weakened by the living conditions, many had fallen victim to dysentery and the ravages of a smallpox epidemic. The three wooden buildings and tent complex that comprised the prison hospital had occasionally overflowed with patients. More than thirteen hundred died.

In April 1865, though few prisoners remained, Danville was crowded, and the population was swelling daily with refugees. Vegetables, meats, and other foodstuffs were becoming scarce, and prices were escalating. Merchants opened when they had something to sell, and of those who bought goods, many had to do so on credit or through bartering. The war had brought hardships to all.

Yet the president and his cabinet were received warmly, and the town's officials, as well as the citizenry, looked forward to Danville's becoming the new capital of the Confederacy. No one seemed to voice concern that unless Lee could stop Grant with a decisive victory, more than one hundred thousand Union soldiers would soon be descending on the town.

In a matter of a few minutes, the presidential party was headed in carriages and other conveyances for accommodations that had been arranged for them in various private homes. Davis, Mallory, and Trenholm, who was too ill to walk, were to be the guests of Maj. William T. Sutherlin. The rest of the cabinet secretaries, aides, and other members of the party were quartered elsewhere in the town. Government clerks and officials soon filled the Exchange Hotel at the bottom of Main Street and the Tunstall Hotel on Craghead Street, both only a short distance from the railroad station. Offices for the Confederate government would be set up in the vacant Benedict house on Wilson Street, which also had a kitchen, dining room, and several upstairs bedrooms.[14]

Cheered by the town's reception, Davis regained some of his vigor and confidence, at least seemingly so, and he asked if any messages had come from Lee or John C. Breckinridge. The secretary of war had left Richmond on horseback three hours after the president to catch up with the retreating army. After conferring with Lee, Breckinridge intended to make his way to Danville and provide the president with his assessment of the military situation. No messages had arrived, and for the present, Davis was in the dark as to the whereabouts of Lee and the Army of Northern Virginia.

Varina and the children were also on his mind. She could have heard about the loss of Richmond—telegraphs were buzzing between towns, North and South—but, most likely, she had not yet reached Charlotte. He would wait a day or so before writing. By then, he might have heard from Lee, and hopefully, he could relay favorable news.

Shortly after a hot meal with his cabinet around the Sutherlin dinner table, an exhausted Davis retired to an upstairs bedroom in the mansion. A former bank president and mayor of Danville, Sutherlin had grown wealthy on tobacco before the war; he was the first to employ steam for pressing tobacco leaves. When the Confederacy was forced to transfer prisoners out of Richmond due to overcrowded facilities, Sutherlin donated his tobacco factory to house the captured Union soldiers. Ill health limited his military service, and his official status was that of a quartermaster for Danville.

While the cabinet retired to its lodgings, the train was bustling with clerks and helpers, unloading the boxes of government papers. Unable to find rooms, more than a few officials and their families took up residence in the train, now parked on a siding. Such was also the fate of a bridal party, forced to arrange wedding-night accommodations for the bride and groom in an emptied boxcar. Fortunately, no one in the cars had to scrounge for food, as rations were provided from the commissary.[15]

When the treasury train with William H. Parker and the midshipmen arrived during the late afternoon, it was shifted to a siding different from that of the president's train. There at least some of the government specie—most probably the Mexican silver dollars—was removed and transferred to the Bank of Danville, with midshipmen undoubtedly being assigned to accompany the wagonloads. Trenholm had decided to allow people in Danville to exchange their Confederate money for silver at an exchange rate of seventy dollars in currency for one dollar in coin. Given the amount of Mexican coins on hand and the weight of the fifty kegs—almost twelve thousand pounds of metal—depleting the quantity of silver dollars made sense. In the view of Mallory, thinking about the difficulties in handling and transporting the kegs, the coin was "a very troublesome elephant."[16]

According to Parker, the rest of the treasury and the bank funds remained under guard in the cars, with the midshipmen bivouacking in a grove of pine trees across Linn Street from the parked train.[17] Despite the gravity of their situation and exhausted from the long journey, passengers on both trains left the cars and celebrated their safe arrival in Danville.

James Semple, after removing his trunk and those of Alex and Gardie from the train and overseeing the transporting of his department's papers to the Benedict house, almost certainly made his way over to his naval store off of Lee Street, a walk of a few minutes. He had no specific assignment at the moment. In fact, there was no Confederate navy to speak of, so his primary role, while in Danville, would be to see to the welfare of the navy refugees beginning to crowd into town. Fortunately, he had more than enough food and clothing for them and to share with others.

Unlike at Richmond, food for the Army of Northern Virginia would not be a problem. Were Lee able to reach Danville, in fact, he would find two million rations on hand to feed his Army—five hundred thousand rations of bread and one and a half million rations of meat—not including Semple's warehoused naval supplies.[18] Unfortunately, west of Richmond and many miles north of Danville, the search for food was proving disastrous for Lee.

During the long hours on the train, Semple must have wondered if Lee was able to evade Grant and how Alex and Gardie were doing with the First Rockbridge. Independent and confident as he knew them to be, they were still young—boys, really—and relatively inexperienced as soldiers. Their taste of army life had been limited to sentry duty, daily routines, and warming themselves around campfires; their indoctrination to the dark side of war was sudden. Semple had become extremely close to both of them. They lived with him; he understood their very different personalities, and he listened to their hopes and plans for the future. They were like sons to him . . . and he was worried.

About the time that Davis was headed up to bed at the Sutherlin mansion, Lee was preparing to cross the van of his army over an old railroad bridge to the south side of the Appomattox River. On the morning of April 4, the separated elements of his troops began to draw together at Amelia Court House. There he was stunned to find out the rations that were supposed to have been sent there had never arrived. Desperate to feed his weary and hungry troops, he spent the next day and a half appealing to local farmers and searching the countryside for food. The effort was doomed to failure. Very little could be found, certainly not enough to provide for his men and horses. Worse than that, the loss of time enabled Grant's infantry to close the gap and Sheridan's cavalry to block the route south to Danville. Pincers were beginning to close around Lee's disintegrating legions.[19]

For Alex and Gardie, the forced marching—more than twenty miles by the night of April 3—the utter exhaustion, the sight of equipment and animals discarded along the road and soldiers fallen out of the ranks, and the expectation of imminent attack from any direction brought a new dimension to their experience of war. It was no longer exciting. Despite their fervent commitment to the South and their burning hatred of Yankees, they could not have been blind to the fact that the end was coming for Lee's army and for the Confederacy. Even so, they would stay with the First Rockbridge to the very end.

During Monday evening, trains continued to arrive in Danville, carrying archives and government employees. Later arrivals were filled with "indiscriminate cargoes of men and things," according to Lt. John Wise, son of former Virginia Gov. Henry A. Wise. The young lieutenant observed the "incongruous debris" of the Confederacy passing by him at Clover Station. For some reason, an African parrot and a box of tame squirrels were considered essential cargo.[20]

On Tuesday morning, April 4, Davis awoke with a busy agenda. There was still no word from either Lee or Breckinridge. With Yankee cavalry cutting telegraph lines, he knew that communications would be severely limited. Touring the town's earthen fortifications on horseback with local commander Col. Robert Withers, Davis found them woefully inadequate and directed certain immediate improvements. He also assigned Col. A. C. Rives to review the defenses and make recommendations to him. Not long afterward, soldiers and slaves were laboring side by side, digging trenches and building redoubts. Davis could only hope that before long, they would accommodate Lee's army.

During the day, the president convened a meeting of his cabinet in the parlor of the Sutherlin home—probably there instead of at the Benedict house to accommodate the ailing Trenholm—and he asked those who could do so to get their departments up and running. Danville might not end up being the permanent new capital, but at this point, Davis had no idea how long the government would remain in town, and it needed to function.

With no navy, Stephen R. Mallory had little to do. George Davis had no legal matters to resolve for the government. Judah P. Benjamin constituted a department of one, with no need for foreign diplomacy. And John Reagan could have little influence on the postal system outside the limits of the town itself. Only the Treasury and War departments could be expected to function in any capacity. Still, Reagan set up an office in the Masonic Hall and sorted through the mail that had been on the various trains out of Richmond during the evacuation and the days before. If the mail was going to go anywhere, it would be going to Greensboro and possibly points in between.

Though Trenholm was confined to bed, the Treasury Department was soon open, exchanging Confederate money for silver. The War Department was in business as well, under the supervision of Robert G. H. Kean, who was temporarily running the office in Breckinridge's absence.

Davis's office was open as well, thanks to the efforts of chief clerk Micajah H. Clark. But Davis probably spent little time there, preferring to meet with his cabinet and visitors in the comfort of the Sutherlin house.

Brig. Gen. Josiah Gorgas, who had been a passenger in the president's car, attempted to organize the Ordnance Bureau, but he had little purpose or success. He had a few pieces of field artillery to emplace and almost no opportunity to obtain more. Hundreds of howitzers and cannons had to be left behind and were now in enemy hands. Gorgas could not have known that the intense flames that had consumed the Richmond arsenal had also consumed oak carriages and caissons and thousands of shells.[21]

Semple was also open for business at the naval supply warehouse. Frequently drawn there as well, Mallory reported, "The Navy people—captains, commanders, lieutenants, surgeons, engineers, et cetera—usually congregated at the naval store. . . . At any hour of the day after nine o'clock a.m., these officers . . . might be seen perched around the store upon the beef and bread barrels, some abstractedly shaping strands of cord or marline into fancy forms, which changed from running bowlines to hangmen's knots or Turk's heads, or were laid up hawser-fashion and unlaid, to be spliced and knotted or to become something else."[22]

"Others," Mallory observed, "were overhauling their trunks and bags, putting their traps in order, at intervals calling attention to some quaint cup, curious case, or odd-looking box or other strange relic of distant lands by brief allusions to its history, and to 'my first cruise in the China seas,' or to 'my cruise with old Perry to Japan.'" Many took the opportunity to write "letters upon desks improvised of provision or clothing boxes," using paper, pens, and ink no doubt borrowed from Semple. Mallory found them to be "generally grave and silent, and without ships or boats or duties, all adrift upon dry land, they presented a pretty fair illustration of 'fish out of water.'"[23]

After meeting with his cabinet, Davis composed a proclamation to the "people of the Confederate States of America" with Benjamin's assistance. The intent was to put a positive spin on the recent loss and to bolster flagging spirits. He began by admitting, "It would be unwise . . . to conceal the great moral, as well as material injury to our cause that must result from the occupation of Richmond by the enemy." Stating that "we have now entered upon a new phase of a struggle," he indicated that the Confederate army was "relieved from the necessity of guarding cities" and was "free to move from point to point" to strike at an enemy "far removed from his own base." Ultimately, he predicted that the "baffled and exhausted enemy" would "abandon in despair his endless and impossible task" of enslaving the Southern people. "Let us but will it," he wrote, "and we are free."[24]

There were two things wrong with the declaration. First, few people actually read it outside of Danville. (It appeared in the *Danville Register* and was printed as a handbill. A digest also appeared in Charlotte, where Varina read it.)[25] The second problem was that few believed it. Even members of his own cabinet, with the possible exception of Benjamin and perhaps the president's aides, had deep reservations about the future of the Confederacy.

Returning to reality and immediate concerns, Davis wrote a message to P. G. T. Beauregard, who was encamped around Greensboro, North Carolina, asking for reliable information on Sherman, where he was, what he was doing. Davis was worried about the Piedmont Railroad, which ran between Danville and Greensboro. If the government had to be moved farther south, traveling by rail would be much preferred over the dozen or more wagons that would be required to haul the specie and the archives, as well as the cabinet, department heads, and others considered essential. In acknowledging Beauregard's earlier telegram, the president noted, "The cavalry you have ordered here will be of special value at this time." He also mentioned having sent a courier to find Lee.[26]

The last train to escape Richmond arrived in Danville around midnight on April 4. On it were Adm. Raphael Semmes and four hundred to five hundred crewmen from the small fleet he had commanded. Semmes had followed Mallory's orders and set fire to the ironclads of the James River Squadron. As the flames engulfed the *Virginia II*, shells in the magazine had caused a thunderous explosion that shook the houses in town and lit the night with pyrotechnics. Mustering his band of·sailors onboard the remaining wooden gunboats, Semmes then reached the south side of the James, where he torched the boats and set them adrift.[27]

At the Manchester depot, hundreds of stranded people wandered aimlessly about, unsure of where to go and what to do. Semmes was told that the last available train had left for Danville. Not willing to follow the government on foot, he coupled a small abandoned engine to some passenger cars on a siding and stoked a fire using the remnants of a picket fence. When the locomotive and its retinue of cars were unable to navigate a slight slope, a second engine was found in the refuse of the yard and added to the first. In a matter of minutes, steam was up in the boiler, and the train puffed its way out of Manchester, the sun rising in the sky over the city. In the distance, across the river, Semmes could see the blue uniforms of Grant's army entering Richmond through the pall of smoke that enveloped the former capital.

On reaching Danville, Semmes and his command spent the remainder of the night sleeping in the cars. Early the next morning, he called on Davis and Mallory and reported for duty, no doubt updating them on his recent adventure and the condition of the city when he left. Concerned that Danville would be unable to fend off roving bands of enemy cavalry, let alone a substantial attack, the president decided to organize the contingent of sailors into a brigade of artillery and assign it to the town's defenses. Adding them to the local defense force gave Davis a total of about three thousand "soldiers." Included was Semmes's thirteen-year-old son, Cadet Raphael Semmes. Asked to take command of the expanding earthworks and act in the capacity of a brigadier general, Semmes noted that his new appointment was a step down from his former rank of rear admiral. He was about to protest but quickly realized "it was folly . . . to talk of rank," given the circumstances.[28]

For the next few days, the new "capital" was relatively peaceful, though it was rapidly swelling in size. Semmes sought help in transforming his sailors into soldiers from among the officers finding their way into town, including an old friend, Capt. Sydney Smith Lee, the assistant secretary of the navy. Fortunately, during the time they remained in the trenches, the sailors were never tested.

Wednesday was a day of attempted communications for the president. He still had not heard from Lee or Breckinridge, so he had nothing favorable to report to Varina. If he were not supremely confident in his commanding general, he might have assumed that the news was not good, that Grant had inserted a portion of his army between Lee and Danville. While anxious, he continued to maintain his veneer of confidence and control.

Davis decided, though, not to wait any longer for either Lee or Breckinridge to contact him. Instead, he arranged to send eighteen-year-old Lt.

John Wise to find Lee. The lieutenant was instructed to go by train to Burkeville Junction, Lee's probable destination since he could then use the railroad to transport his army to Danville. But the enemy might have occupied the town. Nevertheless, Wise was to locate Lee, find out his plans, and return to Danville with the information as soon as possible.[29]

Since Varina had probably reached Charlotte, the president decided to send her a brief telegram, letting her know he was in Danville. That would not be enough, of course, and he could wait no longer for a report from Lee. At some point during the day, he sat down to write her a letter describing his last hours in Richmond and the arrangements made with regard to the house and their personal effects. Davis also mentioned that he had been unable to cash the check for $28,444 received from the auction house, but he hoped to do so in Danville. He let her know that his plans were indefinite: "I do not wish to leave Va., but cannot decide on my movements until those of the army are better developed." In an uncharacteristic moment of despair, he closed the letter, "I weary of this sad recital and have nothing pleasant to tell."[30]

Before the day was over, he did get *some* news. Treasury clerk John Hendron reported that the Danville bank refused to cash the check.

In a dispatch to Joseph E. Johnston, whose army was concentrated near Smithfield, North Carolina, Davis let him know that he had not heard from Lee. No doubt, both men realized that for Lee to break away from Grant and hook up with Johnston would take a miracle. The distance was too great—almost two hundred miles between Smithfield and Amelia Court House, Lee's last known location—and with Union cavalry burning bridges and pulling up track, transportation by rail would be almost impossible.

The next day, a letter from Varina reached Davis in Danville, and he was relieved to learn that she and the children were safe and staying in a small house in Charlotte. Knowing full well the stress he was under, despite what others would see as an apparently calm demeanor, Varina offered heartfelt encouragement: "I . . . know that your strength when stirred up is great, and that you can do with a few what others have failed to do with many." In writing her back, he had little to add to what he told her the day before.[31] Mentioning that his executive office had been set up and "current business" was being transacted, he could not say where the "seat of Govt" would be in the future.

The government might be prepared to stay in Danville for a while, but Davis and Trenholm decided that the treasury would be safer if it were moved farther south. With the trenches around Danville thinly filled with local troops and inexperienced sailors, the slightest thrust at the lines by the enemy would almost certainly result in Union soldiers spilling into the town streets. Then, too, the gold and silver had to be an enticement to those who saw the Confederacy coming to an end, even to Confederate soldiers who had gone for months without pay. If the president waited too long, there might not be any specie to worry about.

The mint in Charlotte, a two-story brick building, would be far more secure than dilapidated railway cars. The mint had not produced coins since early in war, but it still had a vault and could be better protected against enemy probes and locals bent on plunder. At Davis's request, Mallory ordered Parker to have his midshipmen ready to resume their guard duty in escorting the treasury train to Charlotte. Fortunately, much of the treasury and the bank funds were already onboard. Evidence suggests that only the unopened kegs of Mexican coins had been removed, a broken keg being left with the rest of the treasury remaining on the train.[32]

Quite likely, ten kegs were returned to the train, the silver dollars, at some point, being earmarked for paying Johnston's army. Of these ten kegs, at least one keg was used to pay out silver dollars to those in Danville who wished to exchange their paper money for specie. The rest of the Mexican coins, some thirty-nine kegs, were left behind. Perhaps the plan was to pay Lee's army should he make it as far as Danville in his attempt to link up with Johnston. In any case, the thirty-nine kegs totaled more than nine thousand pounds, and the combination of bulk and weight would have severely limited travel, especially when it became necessary to transfer the treasury to wagons. With bridges being destroyed and tracks being torn up farther south, Davis and Trenholm had to have recognized that the cache of Mexican silver was a serious burden. The number of wagons that would be required to haul the coinage would certainly attract attention and could lead to their capture. Unfortunately, there is a lack of credible discussion on what happened to the coins. Where they ended up—and where they are today— remains a mystery, although the evidence is strong, due to geophysical surveys with pulse-induction instrumentation, that the coins were buried— and remain buried—in Danville.[33]

As the tents were being taken down at the camp of the midshipmen and the cars were being repacked, William H. Parker expressed to Mallory his concerns about not having a senior official from the Treasury Department on the train. Someone had to be able to make decisions about the specie; Parker's job was simply to protect it. He had nothing against Walter Philbrook, who had been given the responsibility from Richmond to Danville, but Philbrook was only a chief teller. In an obvious reference to Trenholm, Parker complained, "It was not a time to be falling sick by the wayside, as some high officials were beginning to do." While the captain would have undoubtedly preferred a more senior, perhaps more experienced officer, Treasurer John C. Hendren was evidently given responsibility for the treasury during the next leg of the journey.[34]

By nighttime, the kegs of coins that were earmarked for Johnston, camping gear, personal effects, and whatever else would be needed for the journey had been loaded in the cars. The treasury clerks and their families then boarded, followed by Parker and his midshipmen. The train slowly backed out of the siding, joined the main line, and clanked off for points south.

For Davis, the departure of the train eased his mind somewhat, but the treasury was not his main worry. He actually spent little time thinking about the funds. Perhaps not considering that the specie would be needed in order for the government to function, he was adamant that the funds could be disbursed only "for the purpose of paying men in the ranks" (other than what had been authorized by Trenholm for redeeming paper money). Yet, as Mallory noted, "the limited amount did not permit this disposition to be made of it." Thus, the treasury stayed intact as it moved on to the next destination.[35]

The larger question, of course, was whether or not the Confederate government would still exist. Of immediate concern to Davis was his lack of knowing what was happening to Lee. Where was he? And where was Breckinridge?

5

FLIGHT
SOUTH

A scout reports that General Lee surrendered the remnant of his Army near to Appomattox C. H. yesterday.

—Jefferson Davis to Gen. Joseph E. Johnston,
April 10, 1865

IN THE EARLY MORNING of April 3, John C. Breckinridge crossed the James River on horseback and rode west, away from Richmond. The trains carrying President Davis and the treasury had labored out of the depot for Danville. Breckinridge's oldest son, Cabell, and Commissary Gen. Isaac St. John were included in the small party accompanying the secretary of war. Somewhere ahead, in the direction of Amelia Court House, was Lee, and in between were roads clogged with soldiers, wagons, artillery of the Army of Northern Virginia, and assorted debris. In the effort to pull his separated forces together and stay ahead of Grant, Lee pushed on steadily through the night. A trail of exhausted soldiers was left in the wake of the army. Weak from hunger, they fell out of ranks and collapsed by the side of the road to rest before attempting to catch up with their units. Growing numbers never did.[1]

Several miles outside of Richmond, the Breckinridge party came upon the wagons loaded with food from Richmond warehouses. The vehicles

were strung out and struggling through mud and ruts north of the Appomattox River. Collecting and taking charge of the wagons, Breckinridge
looked for a way to cross the river. Passing by the abutments of the burned
Genito Bridge, Breckinridge edged farther west all day, finally crossing over
the Clemmentown Bridge on the morning of April 5. He was hoping to loop
back to Amelia Court House with the supplies before Lee moved on.

As Breckinridge soon learned, however, Lee was blocked by a strong
Union force at Jetersville, which prevented him from following a southwest
track from Amelia Court House toward Danville. Breckinridge quickly realized there was only one direction for Lee to take, and that was west toward
the town of Farmville. With the South Side Railroad from Farmville to
Lynchburg still in Confederate hands—at least as far as he knew—
Breckinridge deduced that Lee would be hoping to find that his desperately
needed supplies had been shipped there.

Driving off enemy cavalry that had attacked his rear, Breckinridge
pulled together the wagons and had them move out along the road that
would eventually take them to Farmville. He knew for certain what Davis
did not know: the Army of Northern Virginia was not going to make
Danville. Union efforts to block Lee at Jetersville would prove fatal for the
Confederate army; it meant that he had no access to the Richmond and
Danville Railroad at Burkeville Junction, which was farther south. Lee could
not possibly march his army some ninety miles with Yankee cavalry attempting to head him off and superior numbers nipping at his flanks and
heels. A rail line was essential to have any chance of escaping Grant. Still,
Breckinridge had to learn what Lee's plans were so he could report them to
the president. Cutting across country and avoiding Union patrols, he finally
caught up with the Confederate commander at dawn on April 6, just east of
Sayler's Creek.

Lee stressed to Breckinridge that his immediate concern was feeding his
army, and St. John assured the general that he would find sufficient rations
in Farmville. Unfortunately, getting there turned out to be disastrous. Due
to blunders, poor decisions, and a slow-moving wagon train, a sizable gap
occurred in the Confederate column between the lead corps of James
Longstreet and Richard H. Anderson's Fourth Corps, which was following
at a distance. As a result, Richard S. Ewell's and Anderson's commands were
cut off and surrounded by Union cavalry and infantry. Despite furious resistance and repeatedly turning back enemy assaults, more than seventy-

five hundred men—all of Ewell's corps and half of Anderson's—were ultimately overwhelmed and forced to surrender. Those who could, escaped into the woods.

During the day, Lee managed to send a brief telegram to the president from Rice's Station, a depot of the South Side Railroad. The message, his first to Davis since the evacuation of Richmond, stated simply: "I shall be tonight at Farmville. You can communicate by telegraph to Meherrin and by courier to Lynchburg."[2] In a conversation that night with Breckinridge at Farmville, Lee indicated that he still hoped to turn south and link up with Johnston. But he and Breckinridge both knew that would never happen.

The next day, the Yankees occupied Meherrin and set up camp, their tents stretched out for a mile alongside the railroad. Any messages sent there by Davis would never reach Lee. What would be worse is that an intercepted message from Davis, if not in cipher, could possibly reveal the president's plans to the enemy.

Secretary of War Breckinridge had what he needed to tell Davis (except the knowledge of the enemy's being at Meherrin), and he parted from Lee on the morning of April 7 for Danville. Skirting Yankee troops and riding into the hamlet of Red House the next morning, about thirty miles southwest of Farmville, he telegraphed the president, noting where Lee was when he left him and adding, "in afternoon met a serious reverse. . . . The straggling has been great, and the situation is not favorable. . . . We will join you as soon as possible."[3]

For Alex and Gardie Tyler, the fighting around Sayler's Creek had been especially harrowing. The First Rockbridge was part of an artillery battalion of Maj. Gen. John B. Gordon's Second Corps. In the movement of Lee's army from Amelia Court House toward Farmville, Gordon had been assigned to bring up the rear, behind Ewell. Shortly before the attack on Ewell and Anderson, the baggage train had been sent on a parallel road to Farmville, and Gordon followed to protect it. With the countryside around Sayler's Creek overrun with Yankees, Gordon fought an effective rear-guard action, finally breaking through, passing to the east of Farmville, and crossing to the north side of the Appomattox River at High Bridge. Gordon lost some fifteen hundred men, most as prisoners, but the First Rockbridge had survived the fighting unscathed.

Supported by divisions of Longstreet's First Corps on the right and left, the First Rockbridge went into position at Cumberland Church on the morning of April 7, Alex's seventeenth birthday. Little did Alex and Gardie realize that the battle in front of them would be the last victory for the Army of Northern Virginia. From early afternoon until sundown, the Confederate lines held, and the First Rockbridge pounded away at the Union positions.

Gardie wrote in his diary, "We repulsed the enemy in every attack and captured a large number of prisoners."[4] He could not have been more fortunate, though. A shell struck the ground only a foot away from him, covering him with dirt. With minié balls thick around them, there was little time to be scared. At the end of the day, what was most on the Tyler boys' minds was their hunger. In bypassing Farmville, they had missed getting rations and had to make do by sharing a few ears of corn. Alex must have thought wistfully for a moment about being home, where he would be slicing a birthday cake rather than munching on uncooked corn. The maize proved to be their last food for three days.

Sundown came none too soon, for the battery exhausted its ammunition. Soon after dark, the First Rockbridge withdrew from the field, and with the remainder of Gordon's Second Corps, the weary Confederates continued west.

The end came quickly for the Army of Northern Virginia. Lee's goal was to reach Appomattox Station, where he would find more supplies, feed his men, and then resume the march, heading farther west to Lynchburg, where a rail line would connect him to Danville. Even with a forced march, it was wishful thinking. His army was melting around him from fatigue, hunger, and constant pressure from the enemy. Still he pushed on through the afternoon and night of April 7, a light rain adding to the men's misery.

From Farmville, Grant sent a note to Lee, observing, "The result of the last week must convince you of the hopelessness of further resistance on the part of the Army of Northern Virginia," and asking Lee to surrender. In his reply, Lee disagreed with the Union commander's assessment, but a dialog began between the two men. The Confederate army was completely surrounded. On the morning of Palm Sunday, April 9, Lee tested the enemy's strength in front of him. In brief, sharp fighting, his army fought its last battle, a useless effort. Lee was trapped. His chances of cutting through, in any direction, were nil, at least without an enormous and wasteful loss of life. After further exchanges of notes and a temporary truce, Lee met with Grant at Appomattox Court House later that morning in the home of Wilmer McLean. For the Army of Northern Virginia, the war was over.

According to a later report from Lee to Davis, some eight thousand infantry, about two thousand cavalry, and sixty-three artillery pieces were all that he had to relinquish to Grant. (The official number of paroled Confederates was actually quite a bit higher.[5]) Included were the 101 officers and enlisted men of Capt. Archibald Graham's First Rockbridge.

While they camped in the woods near Appomattox Court House over the next couple of days, waiting for their printed paroles, Alex and Gardie discussed what they would do next. Their daily routine was about to change dramatically. It already had, for they no longer needed to forage for food; ample rations were provided by Grant from the captured railway cars. Eventually the brothers agreed that Gardie would return to Mrs. Compton's in Lexington and wait for classes to resume at Washington College. Alex would make his way to Richmond to inspect the family estate, Sherwood Forest.[6] He would then head north to see their mother. Both would write Julia, as they knew she would be worried about them, but it would be weeks before she saw a letter from either of them. Where James Semple was, the boys had no idea. As long as the government continued to survive, they could only imagine he was still with it.

On Sunday, while Lee and Grant parlayed at the McLean house to discuss the fate of the Army of Northern Virginia, Davis attended a nondenominational unity service at the Episcopal church in Danville. Dr. Moses Hoge, the Presbyterian minister who had fled Richmond in the same railcar as the president and the cabinet, preached the day's sermon. The peacefulness of a spring day belied the tragic events unfolding farther north for the Confederacy, though Davis and others must have wondered about the increasing numbers of soldiers drifting into town. While earlier in the war, such men might have been labeled deserters, most of them told stories of becoming separated from their company or battery during the fighting and escaping from certain capture. To some, the appearance of the soldiers was an ominous sign.

Despite Davis's anxiety over not knowing where Lee was and what was happening with his army, the first couple of days after the treasury train left had been somewhat relaxing. With the specie headed for the relative safety of Charlotte, the financial foundation of the nation was now beyond the reach of raiding Union cavalry and Grant's army, which would be close on the heels of Lee, *if* the latter were to make it to Danville. A burden had been lifted from the shoulders of George A. Trenholm and, no doubt, others in the cabinet.

The treasury train reached Greensboro the next day, where the ten kegs—something less than thirty-nine thousand dollars—in Mexican silver were offloaded to pay Johnston's army. John C. Hendren apparently removed two boxes of gold sovereigns as well, valued at thirty-five thousand dollars, to be used by Davis and the cabinet. Whether Hendren removed the specie on his own or at the suggestion of William H. Parker is unknown. No order to do so would have likely come from either Davis or Trenholm, as the president had no need for the coin in Greensboro or afterward, for that matter.[7]

The next day, April 8, the train lumbered south toward Charlotte, some ninety miles away. As it approached Salisbury, a little more than halfway to its destination, cavalry was seen descending the hills nearby, and Parker stopped the train to reconnoiter. Fortunately, the riders were Confederates, and the train passed on to Charlotte, where the treasury was unloaded and stored in the mint. Parker had been none too soon in getting through to Charlotte; four days later, Salisbury was captured by Yankee horsemen under Maj. Gen. George Stoneman, and they burned military and civilian supplies as well as parts of town. Also destroyed was the railroad bridge over which the treasury train had crossed to Charlotte.

In Danville, while waiting for news from Lee, there was little actual work for the government to do. Naval personnel continued to congregate at Semple's warehouse and exchange tales of daring deeds, adventures almost certainly growing in accomplishment with repetition and new audiences. When bored, some went fishing in the Dan River. Such opportunities for comradeship and occasional jesting were little compensation for the fact that, for them, the war was over, even if Lee and Johnston were to somehow defeat Grant and Sherman. All the ports were now in enemy hands, and just about every ship in the Confederate navy—except for the *Shenandoah*—had been either captured or destroyed. Most of the ironclads lay at the bottom of rivers and bays, including the vaunted *Virginia*. There was simply no future for the navy—and no present.

Trenholm's continued illness may have precluded his appreciation for the hospitality of the Sutherlins, but the comfortable quarters, pleasant meals, and congenial hosts were not lost on Davis. The afternoons he spent in conversation with Sutherlin in the library or over cigars on the front porch provided valuable solace. Discussions on farming and Davis's adventures during the Mexican War were therapeutic, but the realization that

Lee was in trouble nagged at the president, and inevitably, his thoughts returned to the fall of Richmond and the dim days ahead for the Confederacy. Still, he attempted to conduct his office with some degree of normalcy, and to the extent he was able to communicate by telegraph, he gave orders to generals still in the field in Alabama, Georgia, and Mississippi regarding troop deployments.

During the evening of April 8, Davis received a double dose of discouraging news. First, Breckinridge's message sent at Red House arrived. Though it said very little, clearly the secretary of war believed that Lee was not going to escape from Grant. And what was the "serious reverse" he had mentioned? Later, during a meeting of the cabinet at the Sutherlin mansion, a weary Lt. John Wise arrived with Lee's response. Passing from camp to camp, the eighteen-year-old had found the general just after midnight, north of Rice's Station. There, in a field by a campfire of burning fence rails, Lee explained to the young lieutenant that he no longer controlled the destiny of his army: "I shall be governed by each day's developments. . . . A few more Sailors' Creeks and it will be all over."[8] Lee ordered Wise to rest for a few hours, and at daybreak the lieutenant caught up with Lee at his headquarters for a message to the president. Lee wrote a few words on paper, indicating that Wise would be making a verbal report. With the enemy in front and around the army, there was a chance that the lieutenant would be captured.

Wise rode wide of the Union positions. After eluding Yankee cavalry, he took the train provided for him back through Clover Station to Danville. Standing before the seated Davis and the cabinet, he delivered Lee's bleak assessment of the situation. Queried by the president if he thought Lee might escape, Wise replied, "I regret to say, no. From what I saw and heard I am satisfied that General Lee must surrender. It may be that he has done so today." Noting the dismay on the faces of the cabinet members, he added, "It is a question of only a few days at most."[9] Later, in a more formal report to Davis and to Burton Harrison, who had returned that day from escorting Varina to Charlotte, Wise indicated that Lee was trying to hold the South Side Railroad as he retired toward Lynchburg. From there, he could still possibly reach Danville. Thus there was a sliver of hope, and Davis, as well as perhaps his cabinet, clung to that possibility.

Lee's noncommittal message of April 6, now irrelevant, finally reached Davis the next day. Choosing not to mention the ominous report by Wise, the president responded by referring to a courier line he had put in place to help Lee communicate "safely and frequently." Still hoping the armies could be joined, Davis noted, "General Johnston on the 8th telegraphs from Smithfield, asking you to inform him how he can co-operate with you." The president added, "I had hoped to have seen you at an earlier period, and trust soon to meet you."[10]

Davis apparently tried to mold events by his shear will. At that point, however, Lee was not thinking of Danville. Instead, it was the formalities he had to work out with Grant to surrender the Army of Northern Virginia. He was also thinking of his men, and asked his aide, Col. Charles Marshall, to draft a message to them. General Orders No. 9 expressed Lee's thoughts and feelings in a short, emotional farewell to the soldiers who had fought for him on dozens of battlefields, suffered without food and adequate clothing—in many cases, without shoes—and would have continued on, if he had asked. The address, delivered to his troops over a two-day period, began by stating the reality of the situation: "After four years of arduous service, marked by unsurpassed courage and fortitude, the Army of Northern Virginia has been compelled to yield to overwhelming numbers and resources."[11] Remarking that valor and devotion could accomplish nothing that would compensate for the losses that would occur by continuing the contest, and determined to avoid the useless sacrifice of his men, he ended on a personal note: "With increasing admiration of your constancy and devotion to your country, and a grateful remembrance of your kind and generous consideration for myself, I bid you all an affectionate farewell."[12]

Beginning at sunrise on April 12, Confederate soldiers marched by brigades and divisions between columns of Union soldiers and, in a formal ceremony, stacked their arms. The Army of Northern Virginia ceased to exist. Alex and Gardie were now civilians. Shortly afterward, they said good-bye to each other and left camp in different directions, one headed east and the other west.

Indisputable news of Lee's impending surrender came to Davis on the afternoon of April 10. During the day, stragglers had continued to drift into Danville. All claimed they had become separated from their units in the woods and marshes either at Sayler's Creek or in subsequent actions. None of them questioned had participated in the surrender or knew anything about one. Around 4:00 p.m., the president was in his office with his cabinet, except for Trenholm, when Capt. W. P. Graves and other scouts Davis had sent out returned in a heavy rain. Graves had come across Maj. Gen.

Thomas Rosser at Pamplin Station on the afternoon of April 9. Rosser, of Pickett's "shad bake" fame, had refused to surrender his cavalry division and had cut his way through Grant's lines that morning. He was able to provide Graves with a written message for Davis, confirming the surrender.

As the cabinet members sat around a table at the Benedict house, Rosser's message was solemnly passed from one to another. Stephen Mallory, paraphrasing Thomas Jefferson, recalled that the news "fell upon the ears of all like a 'fire bell in the night.'" The gloom that ensued was "more eloquent of great disaster than words could have been."[13] With the realization there was no army between Grant and Danville, and with rumors now flying that Stoneman's cavalry was headed for Davis, the time had come for the government to move farther south. Danville's tenure as capital of the Confederacy had passed. Departure time was set at 8:00 p.m., which did not give them much time to pull together the government records and their personal belongings. Fortunately, there was no need to worry about the treasury.

But there was the matter of foreign exchange, that is, Liverpool Acceptances in the amount of sixteen thousand to eighteen thousand British pounds sterling. For some reason, the promissory notes had been separated from the rest of the treasury and were now in the possession of navy assistant paymaster C. Lucius Jones, who was in Danville. On finding this out, Mallory apparently decided not to bother Trenholm, who was still ill. Instead, Mallory penned a formal order to Jones, directing him to surrender the acceptances to "Paymaster James A. Semple CSA, taking his receipt for the same." The secretary of the navy knew he could depend on Semple and that the acceptances would be in safe hands. Jones received the order, but he never connected with Semple; the foreign exchange ultimately ended up in the hands of Postmaster John H. Reagan.[14]

While the cabinet hurried to their rooms and offices to pack, Burton Harrison took responsibility for ensuring a train and cars were made up and ready at the station for loading and on-time departure. Placing a guard around the train, he gave specific instructions as to who and what could go on board. Back at the Benedict house, Harrison directed the repacking and removal of luggage and boxes to the train. In this, he was assisted by the president's chief clerk, Capt. Micajah H. Clark, who oversaw the sorting and packing of Davis's papers.

While the train was being loaded with records, luggage, and the horses of Davis and his staff, the president sent a telegram to Joseph E. Johnston:

"A scout reports that General Lee surrendered the remnant of his Army near to Appomattox C.H. yesterday. No official intelligence of the event, but there is little room for doubt, as to result. General H. H. Walker is ordered with forces here to join you at Greensboro. Let me hear from you there. I will have to see you to confer as to future action."[15]

Davis also wrote a note to Mayor James Walker, offering his "sincere thanks for your kindness shown to me. . . . I had hoped to have been able to maintain the Confederate Government on the soil of Virginia, though compelled to retire from the capital."[16] He also indicated that he had hoped he could protect Danville. Now, he was unable to do either. In fact, as he indicated in his earlier telegram to Johnston, Davis was reassigning H. H. Walker's small defensive force from Danville to Greensboro. They would not have been helpful to Danville anyway, for the town would soon be taken over by the Union Fifth Corps. Any defenders in the way would have been overrun or simply swept aside.

Reflecting on the events of the past week, Davis concluded, "The shadows of misfortune which were on us when I came have become darker." He asked for the mayor's "good wishes" as Davis "sought to discharge the high trust which the people of the Confederate States conferred on me."[17] Johnston was still in the field in North Carolina, and the Confederacy had other armies on both sides of the Mississippi. Reason enough existed not to give up.

Davis then made his way through the rain to the Sutherlin mansion, where he informed Mrs. Sutherlin that Lee had surrendered and that Davis and the government would be leaving that evening for Greensboro. Despite the glimmer of hope that remained and the president's determination to go on, the news brought by the couriers had been devastating. Only through sheer will was Davis able to concentrate on what needed to be done in the few hours before he had to leave. After packing papers and some belongings—cigars, toiletries, and a few changes of clothing—in a valise, he had a light meal and took time to thank his hosts for their hospitality. As he entered his carriage for the ride to the station, the Sutherlins tried to hand him a bag with a thousand dollars in gold coins they had managed to save during the war. "A mere trifle of gold—take it, and ask no further questions," said the major. With tears in his eyes, Davis declined. "I cannot," he replied and suggested that they would probably need it more than he.[18]

By 8:00 p.m. the streets of Danville and the platform at the railroad station were a mass of confusion as people sloshed through mud over their ankles and in some cases up to their knees. Horse- and mule-drawn wagons struggled through the morass, with whips cracking and drivers cursing, animals snorting and protesting, and train whistles piercing the air as more and more cars were coupled to the original four (boxcar, stock car, flat car, and passenger coach) authorized by the president.

Burton Harrison had his hands full. Panic took over, with rumors of Union cavalry approaching Danville, and soldiers and civilians pressing closer to the cars, attempting to push past the guards. No one was allowed on board without authorization, and because of this, Harrison was deluged with people begging, arguing, and even threatening, most to no avail. The engine—old, tired, and poorly maintained through four years of war—could pull only a limited number of cars. Twelve had already been hooked together, each of the department heads insisting on a boxcar to carry his department's records. Trainmaster Col. John H. Averill, who compiled the train for Harrison, had no idea if the locomotive was capable of leaving the station.

One of the cars was allocated for Mallory and the Navy Department, and Semple had no difficulty loading the records brought out of Richmond. He also included some of the supplies from the naval store he felt might be useful to Davis and his cabinet during the next leg of the journey. He had to have known that what he left behind would soon be gone. Only a couple of companies of Home Guard remained in Danville to keep order, not enough to contain an unruly crowd determined to get at the supplies. Within hours of the train's leaving, Semple's warehouse would be plundered, along with the warehouses of provisions for the army. With Lee's surrender and the government in flight, the war was over in the minds of those living in Danville and in the surrounding countryside. Why should the enemy be allowed to confiscate the supplies when Southerners who provided the food were hungry and in rags?

In the midst of the turmoil, Brig. Gen. Gabriel Rains, head of the Confederate Torpedo Bureau, showed up at the depot with his daughters, a staff officer, and a quantity of fuses and explosive devices, which he promptly pointed out were harmless. Rains asked to be allowed to join the president's car, but Harrison turned him down, no doubt because of what Rains had with him, despite the general's assertions that they were safe. Harrison explained to Rains there was no room in the car. Ultimately, Rains pleaded his case with Davis, an old friend from the Mexican War. The president overruled Harrison, and the Rains family was allowed to board, but the devices had to be loaded in one of the boxcars. Before the train left the station, Davis would regret his decision.

Around 10:00 p.m., well after the scheduled 8:00 p.m. departure time, the cabinet secretaries began to show up. There they huddled on their luggage, the rain subsiding somewhat as they waited for Davis, Judah P. Benjamin's cigar tracing a red glow in the night. The last of the cabinet officers to arrive was George A. Trenholm and his wife, Anna. Still plagued with nausea, Trenholm had been unable to negotiate the deep mud and was transported part of the way by ambulance.

When Davis reached the station with his aides, not long afterward, those assigned to the president's car boarded, including Rains and his daughters. The doors were then locked behind them to prevent others from intruding. Sharing the president's seat, as there was no other place to put her, was one of the Rains daughters, and Davis paid a price for his generosity to Rains. In the words of Harrison, "The lady was of a loquacity irrepressible; she discoursed her neighbor—about the weather, and upon every other topic of common interest—asking him, too, a thousand trivial questions." As the occupants waited to be off, a gloom settled over the car, the passengers "as silent as mourners at a funeral; all except for the General's daughter, who prattled on in a voice everybody heard."[19]

Perhaps the explosion was a relief. One of Rains's staff officers was seen to "bounce in the air, clapping both hands to the seat of his trousers." He had one of the general's "safe" fuses in his pocket, and when he sat down abruptly on the flat surface of an unlit woodstove, the fuse detonated.[20] The reprieve was probably only temporary for Davis, the young girl no doubt again demanding his attention.

Finally, the train began its Herculean struggle out of the depot, but within a few miles, the load proved to be too much for the dilapidated engine, which blew a cylinder head. After a delay in offloading a horse and sending a rider back to Danville, another engine was ordered up to take its place, and the train eventually resumed its trek toward Greensboro. Progress was excruciatingly slow, for the narrow-gauge track was in extremely poor condition. Until dawn, the engineer had to stop frequently to shine lights ahead in the night to watch for possible breaks by Yankee raiders and for rails that had come loose and shifted out of position. A little slower or one more delay would have spelled disaster for the president and his "government on wheels," for only five minutes after the train crossed over the Haw River, Union cavalry destroyed the bridge.[21]

For those inside the president's car, the trip could hardly have been more tedious and uncomfortable. The incessant chatter strained already strained nerves, and not long into the train ride, the car suddenly began to fill with smoke, the flue from the now-lit stove having become blocked. The occupants were unaware that soldiers had pushed past the guard at Danville and climbed onto the roof of the car. Once the train was underway, as the soldiers became colder and wetter from the night air and drizzle, they crouched around the stovepipe protruding through the roof. Still cold, they covered the flue with their blankets to capture the heat, causing billowing clouds of acrid smoke to envelop the passengers below. Since the blankets stayed in place, despite the outcry, the windows were opened, and the cold air was endured as a substitute for the smoke.

The distance from Danville to Greensboro was less than fifty miles, but with the train averaging only four miles an hour, the trip took about twelve hours. As the train approached the outskirts of Greensboro, the passengers were obviously relieved that the journey was nearly over. For the president, it was unclear whether his relief was due more to the fact that the train had passed safely over the Haw, and hence eluded capture, or because he was about to be free of the person who sat next to him. In any case, his spirits lifted; aide Col. William Preston Johnston described him "as collected as ever."[22]

During the morning of the next day, April 11, John C. Breckinridge rode into Danville with his son and others who had accompanied him since Richmond. Expecting to find the president still in town, he learned that the government had relocated to Greensboro. He was pleasantly surprised to find his younger son, Clifton, had resigned as a midshipmen when the treasury train moved south on April 6 and had remained behind to wait for his father . By the time Breckinridge arrived, the Home Guard had been brushed aside and most of the provisions had been taken from Semple's store and the warehouses, the plundering apparently ending when the arsenal, situated near two of the largest warehouses, had accidentally blown up after a match had been dropped by a soldier stealing powder. The explosion and subsequent bombardment of heated shells killed fifty people and maimed many others. Alarmed by the possibility that Union troops were firing into the town, the crowd quickly disappeared, much of their plunder being left behind in the hurried flight.

Late that morning, Thomas Rosser and his staff also rode into Danville, and since Davis was no longer around, he met with Breckinridge and gave him a full report of Lee's surrender at Appomattox Court House. After a day of collecting what remained of the Confederate supplies and distributing them to soldiers drifting into town from Lee's army, Breckinridge rode out of Danville for Greensboro with his two sons and the remainder of his party.

* * *

At Castleton Hill on Staten Island, Julia Gardiner Tyler was beside herself, not knowing where Alex and Gardie were and how they were doing. Had either one of them been injured? Or worse? Were they scared? Were they able to get food? Were they still together? Was Lee ahead of Grant, or was he under attack? Were they being fired on? Were they captured? The not knowing was wearing on her nerves, and for the first time since she had left Sherwood Forest, Semple was unable to help them—and her. Ever since her mother passed away the previous October, Julia missed the closeness of a confidante. Semple was beginning to fill that role as a relative and friend and as a man whose confidence and assurances put her at ease.

Until the fall of Richmond, he had taken care of whatever needed to be done for her while she was in the North, away from her home; if he had a concern or an opinion on any matter that could help her, he expressed it. To the best of his abilities, he had kept an eye on Sherwood Forest, writing to her former neighbors about its condition and who was living in it and querying those who had ventured into the Charles City area. Since Julia left the plantation, Yankees had been swarming over the area, looting and destroying property and threatening those who had chosen not to leave their homes. He had her silverware and family heirlooms crated and stored for safekeeping in a warehouse (which went up in flames during the evacuation from Richmond). He had acted on her behalf to get payment from the War Department for a horse that had been stolen by Confederate soldiers. He had worked tirelessly (and hopelessly) to obtain a midshipman's warrant for Alex. And when she had needed a brother figure to counsel her sons, give them a place to stay, and watch over them in Richmond, he had done so agreeably and well. The boys loved and respected him.

Decisions about their future had been theirs to make, but he had counseled them in such a way that their youthful ardor for the South and fighting for the Confederacy was ultimately met by joining the First Rockbridge.

Though the artillery unit had been actively engaged in numerous battles earlier in the war, Semple knew that it had seen very little action in months, having been camped, for the most part, safely behind Lee's outer lines. Plus, being in artillery meant they were not likely to be involved in hand-to-hand combat, or even fired at by enemy infantry, unless their position was being overrun.

For decisions like these, Julia was extremely grateful. Moreover, she had developed a sense of comfort and security, almost an expectation that nothing could really go wrong as long as Semple—Brother James, as he liked to call himself—was there to support her when she needed him. Was she using him? Certainly, but a familiarity was developing between them that made her feel that it was natural and right for her to depend on him, to discuss the children and finances, and to ask his advice on almost any subject. He brought a male perspective to their discussions. He was also close to Robert Tyler and John Tyler Jr., sons of her deceased husband, both of whom she liked, and he knew the Tyler family members as well as she did.

The fact that he was married to Letitia, who despised Julia, was a complication. She put that aside in her mind. Letitia was James's problem, one that he had chosen to resolve through separation. Their marriage had never been a happy one, and their relationship had continued to be contentious, even as they lived apart. When forced to communicate with one another, they were barely civil. At some point, Julia, who herself had stopped speaking with Letitia after being ignored and slighted by her "stepdaughter" over the years, realized that her opinion of Semple had been colored by her opinion of Letitia. She began to see him in a different light and took him for whom she had come to understand he was, not as the husband of Letitia, but rather as a resourceful, dependable friend who genuinely cared for her and her children.

Unfortunately, in the time it took for Grant to drive Lee from the trenches around Richmond, Julia's world changed. Her sons were in danger, and probably Semple was as well.[23] Then, after several days of rumor and speculation, the April 10 edition of the *New York Times* heralded the final defeat of the Army of Northern Virginia: "Union Victory! Peace! Surrender of General Lee and His Whole Army."

Yet the news brought no relief to Julia. She needed to hear from the boys, or about the boys, as to how they were and where they were. If paroled and unharmed, Alex and Gardie may possibly be headed back to

Sherwood Forest, but she had no way of knowing that. She was certain they had no money to go by train or boat to New York. James was probably still with the president, whom the paper reported as fleeing south. He could be returning to Richmond, but there was nothing to draw him back there, and if caught, he would almost certainly be arrested as a bureau chief in the Confederate government.

She would not hear from either of her sons for more than two weeks, and it would be months before Semple suddenly appeared.

6

ON TO WASHINGTON

President Lincoln was assassinated in the theatre in Washington. . . .
Seward's house was entered on the same night and he was repeatedly
stabbed and is probably mortally wounded.

—Secretary of War John C. Breckinridge to
Jefferson Davis, April 19, 1865

*C*ROSSING THE HAW RIVER before the bridge was destroyed lifted the spirits of the passengers, but the effect was short-lived, as the reception in Greensboro was less than enthusiastic. Davis's aide Col. John Taylor Wood wrote in his diary: "Houses all closed. The people are afraid to take anyone in."[1] Many of the residents believed that harboring Davis might bring retribution from the Union army, in particular, Stoneman's cavalry, which continued to roam south of Greensboro after burning Salisbury.[2] Then there was Sherman, whose army was near Raleigh and moving west and whose reputation preceded him.[3]

Burton Harrison saw the reaction of the people as indicative of feelings other than the Stoneman threat. In his mind, the people in "that part of North Carolina" were never committed supporters of the Confederacy. He noted, "As long as we remained in the state, we observed their indifference

111

to what should become of us. It was rarely that anybody asked one of us to his house."[4] While fear of having their homes burned by Yankees was certainly an understandable concern, the lack of enthusiasm for the Confederate cause, a history of dissatisfaction with the Davis administration in Richmond, and movements in North Carolina—as early as 1863—to end the war were undoubtedly underlying factors.

Greensboro's unhappiness with the Confederate government also surfaced in the form of bitter resentment against Brig. Gen. John H. Winder, who, in addition to being in charge of the prison system east of the Mississippi, was provost marshal. Thus he had been responsible for returning deserters and soldiers absent without leave from their units. Winder's detectives had been overzealous in Greensboro, as they undoubtedly were elsewhere. According to a formal complaint submitted to then Secretary of War James A. Seddon, the city was reportedly "haunted" by spies." Citizens were reluctant to walk the streets on legitimate business, for they were often accosted, arrested, and brought before Winder.[5]

Whether the accusations were valid or not, the combination of events explained the cool reception given the Davis government by the Greensboro residents. Perhaps unaware of the circumstances, and expecting the "generous hospitality . . . characteristic of the South," Stephen R. Mallory summed up his disappointment by commenting, "This pitiable phase of human nature was a marked exception to the conduct of the people upon this eventful journey."[6]

One bright spot in the otherwise gloomy conditions at Greensboro, at least for Col. John Taylor Wood, was the presence of his family. Before Richmond was evacuated, Wood had sent his wife and children south, to where he believed they would be safe. Even though the owner protested, Wood provided the president with a small, modestly furnished second-floor room in the house in which the Wood family had been boarding.

With the exception of Trenholm, the cabinet and staff were billeted in an old railroad passenger car. Trenholm was offered a room in the home of John Motley Morehead, former governor of North Carolina. According to Postmaster General John Reagan, Trenholm received special treatment, not because of his illness, but because Morehead had an ulterior motive. The owner of a large number of Confederate bonds, he hoped to persuade Trenholm to exchange some of the securities for gold from the treasury. The secretary, however, could not have helped him even if he wanted to, for the treasury was many miles away and under the protection of William H. Parker and his midshipmen. And Trenholm was still quite ill and incapacitated.

The "cabinet car," as Mallory referred to it, became a social center, the department heads and staff attempting to make the best of a spartan situation. They were not without provisions, however. Semple provided bread and bacon from his hoard, and by foraging, with help from others in the party, he was able to produce biscuits, eggs, coffee, and various other supplies. The less-than-luxurious accommodations were endured for almost a week. Nighttime was a particular challenge, as the "residents" were forced to contend with trying to sleep on a seat in the passenger car that was only four feet long. Reagan, who was more than six feet tall and weighed more than 250 pounds, probably got little rest.

Mallory found humor in their situation:

Here was the astute "Minister of Justice," a grave and most exemplary gentleman, with a piece of half-boiled "middling" in one hand and a hoe-cake in the other, his face beaming unmistakable evidence of the condition of the bacon. There was the clever Secretary of State busily dividing his attention between a bucket of stewed dried apples and a haversack of hard-boiled eggs. Here was the Postmaster-General sternly and energetically running his bowie knife through a ham as if it were the chief business of life; and there was the Secretary of the Navy courteously swallowing his coffee scalding hot that he might not keep the venerable Adjutant-General waiting too long for the coveted tin cup! . . . State sovereignty, secession, foreign intervention and recognition, finance and independence, the ever recurring and fruitful themes of discussion, gave place to the more pressing and practical questions of dinner or no dinner, and how, when, and where it was to be had.[7]

Not long after the Davis party reached Greensboro, P. G. T. Beauregard appeared at the railway car and was greeted hospitably by the cabinet members in their "new office." In private with Davis, Beauregard delivered a bleak assessment of the military situation. Their conversation was no doubt hampered by the fact that they had disliked each other since the early days of the war, when Davis rebuked Beauregard for taking too much credit for the Confederate victory at the battle of Manassas (Bull Run). Beauregard also had little respect for Davis's judgment in military affairs, and he was critical of the president's interfering with his generals. Nevertheless, Davis and Beauregard were stiffly courteous to one another. Further discussions were postponed until the next day, when both Breckinridge and Johnston would be in attendance.

Later, Davis telegraphed Johnston to inform him that Breckinridge would be joining him that afternoon and to ask if Johnston preferred to meet at his headquarters or at Greensboro. In the message, Davis still hoped that the information about Lee had been premature, noting, "I have no official report from Lee." It was clear that Davis expected Johnston to continue in the field: "The important question first to be solved is at what point shall concentration be made, in view of the two columns of the enemy, and the route they may adopt to engage your forces."[8]

In the initial meeting the next morning in the president's second-floor room, Davis faced the formidable task of gaining the support of Johnston and Beauregard for continuing the war. As reduced in numbers and as makeshift as their army might be, in the mind of the president, it still represented hope, and its existence bought time until stragglers, escaped soldiers, and others temporarily absent from their units could be rallied to it.

Joseph E. Johnston harbored an even stronger aversion to Davis than Beauregard. He was, and would remain, a vehement and persistent critic of the president. While their mutual rancor could be traced back to their days at West Point, Johnston was most offended by being placed behind Robert E. Lee and two others in the commissioning of full generals at the beginning of the war. This slight was especially hard to take since Johnston had been the highest-ranking U.S. officer to resign his commission and offer his services to the Confederacy.

Then there was Davis's decision to replace Johnston in front of Atlanta with John Bell Hood, who then lost the fight for the city and ultimately most of the Army of Tennessee. For Johnston, the insult added fodder to his growing hatred of the president. Yet there they were, Johnston and Davis, stiffly facing each other once again, each making an effort to be civil.

Personal feelings aside, Johnston and Beauregard probably assumed they could convince the president as to the hopelessness of the situation. Sherman's armies were at least four times the size of Johnston's, and Grant, with more than one hundred thousand veterans, was only a train ride away. They had figured wrong. Davis surprised them by expressing the belief that between Lee's veterans who had not surrendered and stragglers from other commands, an adequate force could be created to augment Johnston's troops. He further proposed that the war could even be conducted west of the Mississippi by uniting with Lt. Gen. Edmund Kirby Smith's Trans-Mississippi Department. Fully aware that neither of his generals agreed with him, Davis continued the meeting the next day, April 13, when Breckinridge would be there.

During the day, Capt. Robert E. Lee Jr. appeared in Greensboro and met with Davis. He had escaped through Grant's lines before his father surrendered. The president also finally heard from the senior Lee: "It is with pain that I announce to Your Excellency the surrender of the Army of Northern Virginia." Lee reviewed the military situation leading to the surrender and provided details of the meeting with Grant, including the parole terms. In his view, Lee had no other choice: "The enemy was more than five times our numbers. If we could have forced our way one day longer it would have been at a great sacrifice of life; at its end, I did not see how a surrender could have been avoided."[9]

Passing the telegram to John Taylor Wood and the general's son without comment, Davis was visibly shaken. He now had to face the fact that the largest, most powerful Confederate army was no more and that the valiant Lee was heading back to Richmond, not in victory, but as a civilian. Even Davis's optimism for forming scattered troops into a new army must have suffered as well. Were there actually remnants of Lee's army still willing to fight for the Confederacy? Wood later commented in his diary, "I can hardly realize this overwhelming disaster," adding, "it crushes the hopes of nearly all."[10]

Breckinridge arrived that evening and met with Davis, providing whatever details he could on the events leading up to Lee's surrender. Quite likely, he also mentioned commands such as the cavalry of Thomas Rosser and Lunsford Lomax that he knew had escaped. Breckinridge did this in his role as secretary of war and sense of duty, not because he agreed with Davis's proposal to form the scattered troops into a composite force.

The next day, April 13, Johnston and Beauregard joined Breckinridge in meeting with the president at Wood's quarters. Also jammed into the room were the cabinet members, as usual, sans the ailing Trenholm. Davis had miraculously recovered from Lee's grave news and delivered another soliloquy on the necessity of continuing the struggle, stating his belief that if Confederate forces remained in the field, Lincoln would ultimately be forced to accede to Southern demands for independence. As Mallory later recalled, the president acknowledged "[while] our late disasters are terrible;

we should not regard them as fatal. I think we can whip the enemy yet if our people will turn out. We must look at matters calmly, however, and see what is left for us to do. Whatever can be done must be done at once. We have not a day to lose."[11]

Johnston was anything but calm. After pausing, perhaps to compose himself, Johnston responded to Davis's request for his views in a biting, "almost spiteful" manner, according to Reagan. The general asserted, "My views are, Sir, that our people are tired of the war, feel themselves whipped, & will not fight. Our country is overrun, its military resources greatly diminished, while the enemy's military power & resources were never greater, and may be increased to any extent desired. My small force is melting away like snow before the sun & I am hopeless of recruiting it." Johnston concluded by suggesting that negotiations be opened with Sherman, seeking terms for peace.[12]

After Johnston finished, an uncomfortable silence fell over the room before a subdued Davis asked Beauregard what his opinion was, to which he replied that he concurred with Johnston. Cabinet members Mallory, George Davis, and Reagan also agreed. Only Judah P. Benjamin supported the position of the president and made a plea for Johnston to remain in the field. Of his cabinet members, Breckinridge's opinion probably weighed most heavily on Davis. The president may have been surprised to discover that his secretary of war, whose military abilities he respected, also backed the peace initiative.

In any case, Davis reluctantly authorized a meeting with Sherman to inquire about terms. In response, Davis was asked by Johnston to state his conditions for surrendering Johnston's amalgamation of troops. He had three: state governments must be preserved, personal and property rights must be retained, and amnesty must be granted against arrest and prosecution for participating in the war. Davis knew that while Sherman might accept the terms, Abraham Lincoln and Secretary of War Edwin M. Stanton would not. Johnston's men, however, would have a few days of relief from being attacked and perhaps a chance to regroup.

In the meantime, the treasury train, again under Parker's command, was headed even farther south. With the specie locked up in the mint at Charlotte and watched over by a local Home Guard, Parker had thought his responsibilities were ended with regard to the treasury and the bank funds. News of Stoneman's raid on Salisbury, however, changed his plans.[13]

After remaining in Charlotte for a few days, Parker attempted to tele-graph Mallory in Greensboro and found that the lines had been cut by Stoneman. Fearing that Yankee raiders might have heard about the treasury train and the fact that it had traveled through Salisbury, Parker was con-cerned that Stoneman might already be headed for Charlotte. Though lack-ing orders from Mallory, he decided that the specie would not be safe in the mint. As the senior naval officer on the scene, Parker had no choice but to assemble his midshipmen, load the treasury and the bank funds back into the boxcars (one for the government funds and one for the banks' funds), and head south to Abbeville, South Carolina, and ultimately, perhaps, to Macon, Georgia. At that point, he was unsure of the final destination. In fact, he had no word as to what was happening with the government in Greensboro; he was totally on his own in deciding the fate of the specie.

Accompanying him would be Varina Davis, who, through the efforts of Burton Harrison, had been renting a house in Charlotte. Concerned that, as the wife of the president of the Confederate States, she might not be safe once Stoneman—or any Yankee cavalry force—reached Charlotte, Parker persuaded her to accompany him to avoid possible capture.

On April 11, the packing of the cars was completed, and the train chugged out of Charlotte for Chester, South Carolina. Before leaving, Parker removed large quantities of food supplies from Semple's amply filled store-house. He also expanded the escort force to include a company of volun-teers from the Charlotte Navy Yard who agreed to accompany the train along with the midshipmen. He now had a small force of about 150 men to guard the treasury.

In Chester, baggage, specie, and passengers were offloaded from the train and transferred to wagons for the next leg of the journey to Abbeville. (At Chester, the train tracks only went southeast to Columbia, which had al-ready been captured and burned by Sherman's army.) In a way, the delay was welcome, for Varina had the opportunity to visit with a number of friends, including Clement Clay, John Bell Hood—who had ended up in Chester after the near destruction of the Army of Tennessee—and Brig. Gen. James Chesnut Jr. and his wife, diarist Mary Boykin Chesnut. Chesnut had been an aide to the president. Dining with Varina that evening, the Chesnuts found Varina "calm and smiling," though obviously changed by recent events.[14]

Before leaving Chester in the Parker caravan and heading for Abbeville, South Carolina, Varina sent a telegram to the president, informing him as to her plans, such as they were. She was also anxious to hear from him: "Would to God I could know the truth of the horrible rumors I hear of you. One is that you have started for Genl Lee but have not been heard of. Mr. Clay is here and very kind, will catch up with my train and join me tomorrow."[15]

Leaving Chester in the late afternoon, the party camped near a country church, where Parker organized his group and saw that each man carried a rifle. That night, he slept in the pulpit of the church, while Varina and others spent the night on the pews and on the floor. The party began its march from there the next morning.

This part of the trip was perhaps the most difficult for Varina. Between bouncing around on rough roads and struggling through muddy stretches, she and the children and two servants were tired and uncomfortable. At one point, the mud became too deep for the overloaded wagons, and she had to walk about five miles, carrying her youngest child in her arms.

That night, around sunset, arrangements were made for Varina and the children and other women in the party, including Parker's wife, to spend the night at a home along the route, while Parker and the men camped nearby. To Parker's surprise, the owner of the home was Edward Means, who had been a midshipman with Parker years before in the U.S. Navy. A lieutenant in the Confederate navy, Means most recently had commanded a gunboat on the James River before it had to be destroyed the night of the exodus from Richmond.

Very early the next morning, the group resumed its "line of march," reaching Newberry, South Carolina, two days later, during the afternoon of April 16. Supposing that Stoneman could be in pursuit, Parker left guards at every bridge crossed by the party, ready to burn it if necessary.

All along the way, from Chester south, Varina was greeted warmly, perhaps because of what was with her. "During the march," Parker recalled, "I never allowed any one to pass us on the road, and yet the coming of the treasure was known at every village we passed through. How this should be was beyond my comprehension."[16] At the same time, the popularity of the president and his wife in South Carolina, combined with the anger and contempt felt for Yankee soldiers, were enough to draw crowds anyway.

In Newbury, the baggage and specie were transferred back into railcars for the forty-five-mile trip to Abbeville. Despite the train's late-evening arrival, Varina was invited to the home of Armistead and Martha Burt. Colonel Burt had been a member of the U.S. Congress and a friend of Davis when he was in the U.S. Senate before the war. The next day, at the Burts' urging, Varina decided to remain in town while Parker repacked the treasury and bank funds in wagons to cut across country to Washington, Georgia, some forty miles away. All along the route, Parker "lightened ship," discarding books, stationery, and even now-worthless Confederate money to make better time.[17] Stoneman's raiders were much on his mind.

When the caravan arrived in the small town of Washington on the morning of April 19, the news greeting Parker was not good. Yankee cavalry under Maj. Gen. James H. Wilson was headed north through Macon, about a hundred miles to the southwest. Not knowing if Washington would be in Wilson's path, Parker transferred the specie to a house in town, placed a strong guard around it, and took the day to rest, recover, and ponder what to do next. The women were provided with rooms at a local tavern. Though no meals were served there, food was plentiful for the entire party, thanks to the provisions removed from Semple's Charlotte storehouse and what could be bartered in town. As ragged as the midshipmen and the company of Charlotte volunteers may have appeared, their stomachs were at least full on eggs, bacon, and poultry, as well as milk and butter and even coffee and sugar.

During the afternoon, Parker decided to confer with Judge Garnett Andrews about the specie. Andrews was a prominent figure in Georgia. He had been a successful lawyer for thirty years and judge of the northern circuit of Georgia before retiring. According to his daughter, Eliza Frances Andrews, a young girl of twenty-five who documented her perspective of the last days of the Confederacy: "He was stoutly opposed to secession, but made no objection to his sons' going into the Confederate army, and I am sure would not have wished to see them fighting against the South."[18]

Despite his views, Andrews was respected, liked, and widely known for his "Southern hospitality." Georgians recognized that his opposition was based on fear of what would happen to the people in his state *when* the war was lost. "I shall never forget that night when the news came that Georgia had seceded," Eliza recalled in her book. "While the people of the village were celebrating the event with bonfires and bell ringing and speech making, he shut himself up in his house, darkened the windows, and paced up and down the room in the greatest agitation. Every now and then, when the noise of the shouting and the ringing of bells would penetrate to our ears through the closed doors and windows, he would pause and exclaim: 'Poor fools! They may ring their bells now, but they will wring their hands—yes, and their hearts, too—before they are done with it.'"[19]

Parker and Andrews decided that the treasury and bank funds would be safer in Augusta, since troops were there that could at least protect the specie from rabble and paroled soldiers bent on paying themselves out of the treasury. In the morning, the gold and silver were reloaded into railcars and sent off to their destination almost sixty miles to the southeast. The women and some of the baggage remained in Washington.

Back in Greensboro, with the news of Lee's surrender, Johnston's already small army was shrinking steadily as entire companies were deserting together. Raphael Semmes, who had been attached to the army on arrival from Danville, lost most of his men in a matter of days. "I was ashamed of my countrymen," he later commented.[20] Talks with Sherman could not happen fast enough. Soon Johnston might not have an army to surrender, and the president's "conditions" would not matter.

As the ragged, undisciplined soldiers drifted into the city, disorder reigned, with bands of deserters roaming the streets and cavalry racing about. While the original intent was to find food and perhaps shoes and clothing, the bedlam escalated, with looters carrying off whatever they could take, and civilians eventually joining in with the soldiers. At this point, the president and the cabinet were unsafe in Greensboro, due as much to the rioting as to the proximity of Union forces. Eventually, a semblance of order was restored by the Forty-fifth North Carolina and others assigned to guard duty, but it would take the entry of Sherman's army into Greensboro to finally calm the city.

On April 15, Davis and the cabinet departed from Greensboro for Charlotte. Before leaving, the president gave a written order to Treasurer John C. Hendren, specifying that the kegs of silver coins in his possession, amounting to around thirty-nine thousand dollars, be delivered to Johnston so that "he may give to it due protection as a military chest to be moved with his army train."[21] While the purpose of the coins would be to pay those who remained of Johnston's troops, the general would be able to control when and where the disbursement was made. The day before, Davis had revealed his growing hopelessness in a short note to Varina: "Everything is dark—you should prepare for the worst. . . . I have lingered on the road and labored to little purpose."[22]

Unfortunately for Davis and his party—with Stoneman's cavalry cutting the rail line and burning bridges below Greensboro, at Salisbury—the archives and the baggage brought from Danville had to be packed into wagons. Capt. Micajah H. Clark, this time, was in charge of organizing the wagons and directing the process. Included in the contents being loaded were the thirty-five thousand dollars in gold sovereigns that had been set aside by Parker for the president's use, should he need the funds.

A welcome addition to the caravan was a brigade of some thirteen hundred mounted Tennesseans under Brig. Gen. George G. Dibrell and the Ninth Kentucky cavalry commanded by Col. William C. P. Breckinridge, cousin of the secretary of war. The combined force had been ordered by Johnston to escort the government procession to Charlotte.

As the line of wagons moved out of Greensboro, travel was slow and difficult due to recent rains and the heavy flow of people, animals, and vehicles along the route. The Davis party encountered paroled soldiers from Lee's army who were headed home as well as others who had been returning to the Army of Northern Virginia and traveling in the opposite direction when they heard of Lee's surrender. Bridges burned along the way by Yankee cavalry also added to the difficulty.

Because of the rains, the roads were generally bad, but in places, they were quagmires of mud with deep ruts in the sticky red clay caused by artillery and heavy wagons. Those on horseback—the president and his three aides, along with Reagan, Mallory, and Breckinridge—had little difficulty. The ambulances, on the other hand, carrying Benjamin, whose "figure was not well adapted for protracted use of the saddle," Trenholm, George Davis, Adj. Gen. Samuel Cooper, and Jules St. Martin, Benjamin's brother-in-law, struggled through the mud and were often forced to turn off the road and into adjacent fields in order to get around areas where they could easily get stuck.[23] Occasionally, St. Martin and George Davis had to get out of the wagon and put a fence rail under the wheels in order to gain traction. At one point, near nightfall, Harrison found Benjamin's wagon stuck in the mud with the wheels in a hole in the road and the hind legs of the horses stuck in the same hole. Fortunately, an artillery unit was camped nearby, where Harrison was able to get help to pull out the ambulance.

After covering only ten miles the first day, a hot meal and comfortable rooms were provided by a local resident just north of Jamestown, who was able to accommodate the president and those in his immediate party. The best room, with a "soft bed and snowy white linen," went to sixty-seven-year-old, white-haired Cooper, who was assumed by a servant to be the president.[24] When the mistake became known, Cooper was already in his room and Davis declined to make a change. The next morning, Harrison was able to replace the "old and broken down" team of horses that had been pulling Benjamin's ambulance, and the generous host, John Hiatt, presented Davis with a beautiful filly, "broken to saddle." He had kept the horse locked in his cellar to prevent her from being stolen.

Semple, riding with what remained of his records as paymaster and bureau chief, had no more idea as to where the government would end up any more than anyone else in the administration. He would follow the president wherever that might lead and do what he was asked to do for the South. He was, first and foremost, a naval officer, and as such, he followed orders. He did so while serving in the U.S. Navy for seventeen years, and he had continued to do so for the past four years as paymaster in the Confederate navy. His was not a blind allegiance to an individual but rather a respect for the chain of command. Without it, anarchy ruled, and he was beginning to see its effects as the Confederacy disintegrated around him,

Semple was also a Southerner in heart and soul. Despite the years spent at sea, he had been born and raised in Virginia and was committed to serving both his state and the Confederacy. His dedication was thus similar to that of Robert E. Lee, who, at the beginning of the war, had been offered overall command of the Union armies. Lee had declined, as he could not bring himself to be responsible for enemy soldiers crossing onto the soil of his native Virginia. No doubt, Semple had to wonder where his loyalty was taking him and what destiny was in store for Davis and his cabinet. He knew only that Charlotte lay ahead of them and perhaps that would become the new capital; he could not know that the role he would soon play in "helping" the South would consume the next two years of his life.

The planned route of the Davis party was through the small villages of Jamestown, High Point, and Lexington. By the night of April 16, the group was nineteen miles south of High Point, and the caravan camped the second night in a pine grove near Lexington, the president and some of the cabinet members finding beds in homes nearby. At the encampment, North Carolina Gov. Zebulon Vance caught up with Davis to discuss the military situation. Though the state had contributed about 125,000 troops to the war effort, Vance had been critical of the president, opposed secession, and never really felt that the heart of his people was in the war. Whatever had been in the past, he needed an honest assessment from Davis as to what he should do.

He did not get it. With his cabinet in attendance, the president proceeded to launch into his plan for rallying forces still in the field and raising a
new army to continue the war west of the Mississippi, where he could link
up with Edmund Kirby Smith. A "sad silence" followed Davis's discourse,
after which a few of the members offered support for the president's position,
probably none wholeheartedly. It took Breckinridge to bring the discussion
back to reality. He indicated that he felt the president was not being candid
with the governor, that the chances of what he was suggesting were "so remote and uncertain, that I, for my part, could not advise him to follow our
fortunes further." Instead, he suggested that Vance remain in North Carolina,
do what he could for his people, and "share their fate, whatever it may be."[25]

Davis, uncharacteristically, acknowledged that an opinion that disagreed
with his could be right and responded with resignation. "Well, perhaps,
General," he said, "you are right." He then stood up, shook the governor's
hand, and bade him farewell, saying, "God bless you and the noble old state
of North Carolina."[26]

After the meeting with Vance, a brief dispatch from Johnston reached
Breckinridge: "Your immediate presence is necessary, in order that I should
be able to confer with you."[27] Breckinridge was a skilled, charismatic nego-
tiator and was respected as a political and military leader by peers and
friends in the North as well as the South. Johnston knew that he and the
secretary of war agreed that the war needed to be over so the country could
begin to heal, and he evidently believed that Breckinridge could contribute
to Johnston's discussion with Sherman in gaining favorable terms.

Davis agreed to send Breckinridge, but he also wanted Reagan to go as
well. The postmaster general had originally proposed the terms of the discussion with Sherman, and the president believed that Reagan would be
useful in seeing that these were presented as approved by Davis. After getting instructions from the president, the men left that night for Johnston's
headquarters. Arriving in Greensboro the next morning, they discovered
that Johnston had relocated to Hillsborough, about forty miles to the east.
While these cabinet members waited in Greensboro to hear from Johnston
about the arrangements with Sherman, Breckinridge received the request
from Johnston to hurry to the general's headquarters so they could confer
before Johnston's meeting with Sherman the next morning.

Johnston had good reason for wanting to talk with Breckinridge. He had
spoken with Sherman at a preliminary meeting to discuss terms for surrender.

At that meeting, Sherman shared some information that stunned Johnston: three nights earlier, on April 14, Abraham Lincoln had been assassinated and Secretary of State William H. Seward had been severely wounded.

Around the time that Breckinridge and Reagan had arrived in Greensboro, the rest of the Davis party was breaking camp and continuing south toward Charlotte. Once on the road, Davis's spirits lifted, despite the fact the residents of Salisbury and Concord and places in between greeted the president and cabinet with the same cold indifference encountered at Greensboro. For Salisbury, the animosity toward the government was understandable, given the destruction wrought by Stoneman's cavalry, the ruins of the prison and railroad station still smoldering as the president entered the city. Davis was fortunate in that he was invited by the Reverend Thomas G. Haughton—an old friend—to stay in the rectory of St. Luke's Episcopal Church. Harrison and others slept on the rectory porch as guards.

A major manufacturing facility for the Confederate navy was situated at Charlotte. Established here because it was inland—and thus safe from invasion—and at a junction of several railroads, the Charlotte Navy Yard produced round shot, gun carriages, propeller shafts, and repair parts, employing some fifteen hundred people in the smithy, foundry, and machine shops.[28] Here also, as William H. Parker had discovered, were warehouses stocked with food and clothing by agents reporting to James Semple.

A few miles outside of town, Harrison sent a courier to the quartermaster in Charlotte, Maj. Gen. John Echols, to notify Varina Davis of her husband's imminent arrival and request her help in finding places for the group to stay. When Echols greeted the party outside of Charlotte, he had word that the president's family had already departed for South Carolina, but he did not know where she was going. Taking Harrison aside, Echols informed him that while he was able to arrange accommodations for those who were accompanying Davis, he was having difficulty finding suitable quarters for the president, because residents were fearful that the home of whoever gave shelter to Davis would be torched by the Yankees. Stoneman's cavalry had been extremely effective at intimidating the population.

Only one homeowner, Lewis F. Bates, offered Davis a place to stay. Bates was an agent of the Southern Express Company and rumored to be a Yankee sympathizer. In Harrison's opinion, the residence was "not at all a seemly place for Mr. Davis," but the president had little choice, unless he wished to sleep in an ambulance or outdoors with his escort.[29] The others were housed in residences around town, Harrison himself staying at the home that he had previously rented for Varina.

Davis went to the Bates house with his staff, and in the midst of a short speech he was asked to give to a small gathering outside the house, Davis received a dispatch from Breckinridge that momentarily stunned him: "President Lincoln was assassinated in the theatre in Washington on the night of the 11th inst. Seward's house was entered on the same night and he was repeatedly stabbed and is probably mortally wounded."[30]

Wondering if the news was true, and perhaps thinking that it was simply another unfounded rumor, Davis handed the telegram to a person standing nearby, who read the contents out loud. The news was as shocking to Davis and the cabinet members as it had been to Breckinridge and Reagan. The secretary of war and Lincoln had been friends before the war; First Lady Mary Todd Lincoln considered Breckinridge a distant relative.

Without question, Davis saw the death of Lincoln as bad news for the South, especially if the Confederacy could not win the war and the states needed a means by which to return to the fold. Stephen R. Mallory was not with the president when the message was delivered, but he spoke with him a few minutes later. According to the navy secretary, Davis said, "I certainly have no special regard for Mr. Lincoln; but there are a great many men of whose end I would much rather have heard than his. I fear it will be disastrous to our people, and I regret it deeply."[31] Mallory feared that the South would be accused of Lincoln's death and suffer for it, which was an opinion probably shared by most of the cabinet and staff. Even more ominous was the possibility that Davis would be accused of authorizing and masterminding the assassination; there would be a universal call for vengeance by the North.

Later that day, Davis signaled his distress over the death of Lincoln by confiding to Burton Harrison, "We have lost our best friend in the court of the enemy."[32] Shortly afterward, he sent Harrison to Abbeville, believing Varina would most likely be there. Harrison was to deliver a note to her and guide her and the children farther south, where they would be safer.

In Charlotte, the focus of Davis and the cabinet turned to the results of the Johnston-Sherman conference near Durham, North Carolina. Breckinridge and Reagan returned with a copy of the surrender document negotiated with Sherman. The agreement required Confederate disarmament, but state governments would remain in place and could return to the Union.

Southern property and citizens would be free from harassment by Federal officials. Reagan had not attended the meeting, but Davis's conditions had been met. The president and the cabinet agreed that the terms were quite favorable, but Davis doubted they would be approved by the newly sworn in U.S. president, Andrew Johnson. Though born in North Carolina, Johnson would be accountable to the Radical Republicans in Congress, and the prospects of any degree of leniency in accepting the South back into the Union were very slim now.

On April 24, in the Bank of North Carolina Building, Davis met with his cabinet for the last time. There he again presented his view that surrender was not their only option, but he asked for written opinions from each in attendance. Even the still-ailing Trenholm, staying at the home of William F. Phifer, was asked for a statement.

In the meantime, Davis wrote a lengthy letter to Varina. He remarked, "The dispersion of Lee's army and the surrender of the remnant which remained with him, destroyed the hopes I entertained when we parted. . . . Panic has seized the country. J. E. Johnston and Beauregard were hopeless as to recruiting their forces from the dispersed men of Lee's army, and equally so as to their ability to check Sherman with the forces they had. Their only idea is to retreat."[33]

Struggling with regard to the decision to surrender or not surrender, Davis weighed the suffering the people of the South would endure in returning to the Union versus the carnage that would come with a continuation of the war. Any decision, of course, also affected his family. "I have sacrificed so much for the cause of the Confederacy that I can measure my ability to make any further sacrifice required, and am assured there is but one to which I am not equal—my wife and my children—how are they to be saved from degradation or want is now my care."[34]

In terms of specific advice, he indicated that "during the suspension of hostilities, you may have the best opportunity to go to Mississippi, and there to sail for a foreign port or to cross the river and proceed to Texas, as the one or the other may be more practical." For himself, "It may be that, a devoted band of cavalry will cling to me, and that I can force my way across the Mississippi, and if nothing can be done there which it will be proper to do, then I can go to Mexico, and have the world from which to choose a location."[35]

Clearly, Davis anticipated the opinions of his cabinet. As he probably expected, they all agreed, even Benjamin, who believed that the terms presented could not be more favorable for the South. Moreover, they urged the president to leave the country as soon as possible.

Looking out at the streets, which were now filled with various commands of cavalry that had left the armies of Lee and Johnston before they could be surrendered, the president was bolstered and cheered by their enthusiasm and talk of continuing the war. He was also aware there were leaders, like Maj. Gen. Wade Hampton, who were vehement in their protests against surrender. In a letter to the president on April 19, Hampton said, "I shall fight as long as my government remains in existence," adding, "I beg to express my heartfelt sympathy with you, & to give you the assurance that my confidence in your patriotism has never been shaken."[36] These were comforting words. In the final analysis, though, should Washington approve the terms, Davis could do no better for the besieged soldiers in Johnston's army and for the people in western North Carolina, where the war would continue if Johnston were to remain in the field.

Reading through the opinions of his department heads, Davis finally capitulated, signed the surrender document, and sent it back by courier to Johnston. Furthermore, the president agreed to move farther south while he pondered where he would go next. If he could, he wanted to avoid capture, not for himself personally, but for Varina and his children. He also believed there was much he could still do for the South if he could make it across the Mississippi.

All this, however, was all for naught. The debating of ideas, the written opinions, the agony over the decision. Three days later, as he expected, Davis received a message from Johnston that Sherman's terms had been rejected in Washington. The United States was willing to offer Johnston the same terms as those provided to Lee at Appomattox. In fact, Secretary of War Stanton publicly criticized Sherman and accused him of disloyalty for offering such generous terms to Johnston.

On April 26, without Davis's approval, Johnston accepted the new terms dictated from Washington and surrendered his army, which included remnants of the Army of Tennessee in the Carolinas, Georgia, and Florida. That same day, after meeting in Trenholm's room to discuss the continued retreat of the government, Davis's party left Charlotte. The escort, now numbering more than two thousand, was reinforced by skeleton brigades under the commands of Brig. Gens. S. W. Ferguson, Basil Duke, and John C. Vaughan, all of whom now reported to Breckinridge, who had retained his military rank of major general. Capt. Given Campbell of the Second Kentucky Cavalry joined the escort as well, Company B being assigned scouting and courier duties.

Staying behind with his children was Attorney General George Davis, who was the first cabinet member to resign. Adj. Gen. Samuel Cooper also chose to remain in Charlotte. At age sixty-seven, the jolting of an ambulance over the poor roads had been too hard on him.

Before the group departed, Col. Robert G. H. Kean, head of the Bureau of War, was ordered by Breckinridge to leave the archives in Charlotte at a secure place and see that they were delivered into the hands of the commanding Union officer as soon as the city was occupied. Since Cooper was now planning to remain also, Breckinridge asked him to assist Kean in assuming responsibility for the archives. What Cooper actually did is unclear, for Kean turned the papers over to C. T. Bruen, the journal clerk for the Confederate Senate, who was planning to stay in Charlotte for a time. Bruen was holding on to issues of the senate journal as a future business venture and agreed to store the archives until they could be delivered to Union authorities. Kean was anxious to return to Virginia; he must have believed he had complied with Breckinridge's order, and he left shortly afterward with others who were heading home.[37]

Johnston, despite the details of disbanding his army, also took note of the archives. On May 8, he sent a letter to Union Maj. Gen. John M. Schofield, advising him that the archives were in Charlotte, "as they will furnish valuable materials for history, I am anxious for their preservation."[38] Schofield replied that he would send someone to retrieve them. "I fully share your desire for their preservation," he said, "as they will be invaluable for history and will take care that they be properly preserved for that purpose."

The archives—some eighty-three boxes—were actually in Union hands by the time Johnston wrote his letter to Schofield. Capt. M. C. Runyan of the Ninth New Jersey Volunteers reported that he was holding "boxes said to contain the records of the rebel war department and all the archives of the so-called Southern Confederacy."[39]

* * *

As Semple made his way south with the Davis administration, from Danville to Greensboro to Charlotte, the lifeblood of the Confederacy ebbed. What had begun three weeks earlier with a degree of hope and confidence, despite the loss of Richmond, was now ending in despair. But the war was not yet over. There were still Confederate armies in the field, in particular, Lt. Gen. Richard Taylor's command in Alabama, Mississippi, and Louisiana and the Trans-Mississippi Department in Texas under Lt. Gen. Edmund Kirby Smith.[40] Their surrender might be a matter of days or maybe months.

Then there was the matter of the specie. Though he was ill, George A. Trenholm must have agonized over what could be done with the treasury when the Confederacy finally collapsed. Should the coins and bullion be surrendered to the U.S. government? Should the funds be paid out to Confederate soldiers before the gold and silver ended up in the pockets and saddlebags of the Union army? Or should the specie be secreted someplace, perhaps offshore, to somehow benefit the South in the days ahead? With the Davis caravan headed out of Charlotte, the treasury train was not likely on the minds of those in the administration, except for Trenholm, and one other: Mallory. Instead, the focus was on escape, on how to stay ahead of the pursuing Yankee cavalry driven by a fixation on apprehending Jefferson Davis. Most Northerners, soldiers and civilians alike, were convinced that he had something to do with the murder of Abraham Lincoln. Within a week, a reward of one hundred thousand dollars was offered for his capture.

As to Mallory, he still had de facto responsibility for the treasury and, by association, the bank funds (they were still being transported together, although not commingled). William H. Parker remained in charge of protecting the specie, and for this reason, Mallory was involved in its destiny. Ultimately, it would be his decision and influence that decided the fate of the funds.

At Castleton Hill, to the great relief of Julia Tyler, a letter arrived from Alex. On April 16, he had written from Richmond, now occupied and under military rule, but the letter was apparently never received. A second letter, written on April 29, did reach Julia and brought her welcome news of her sons' safety.

Perhaps choosing not to mention in this letter what had happened to him and Gardie since the fall of Richmond, Alex began by addressing his foremost concerns: his appearance and money. He reported that he was "almost entirely ragged" when he reached Richmond, and he asked his mother to reimburse R. H. Maury of Richmond; Maury had loaned Alex thirty dollars, with which he bought underwear. Alex also needed his mother to immediately deposit funds in his account to cover a one-hundred-dollar check he had written on the Manhattan Banking Company to Lancaster and Co. Anticipating her objection to such an expenditure for clothing, he added, "Now I know that you will think it very extravagant in me my Dear Mother, but you will change your mind when I tell you that the whole $130 hardly supplied my wants."[41]

Still the defiant Rebel, Alex urged Julia to sell her property and move to Europe to avoid the insults she had been enduring in the North, the most recent being an invasion of Castleton Hill by three thugs looking for a Confederate flag she reportedly had in her parlor. (There was no flag, only a wall hanging, a tricolored, hand-sewn handkerchief display that was seized by the intruders.) "If the South is conquered," Alex railed, "which with the help of God, it will never be, neither G[ardie] or A[lex] ever will live here under Northern rule." He also informed her about Gardie's decision to return to Washington College in Lexington, at least until they heard from her, and that they had agreed that Alex—for whom resuming studies was less of a priority at the moment—should go to Sherwood Forest to see what could be done to salvage the plantation. Richmond was directly on his way home, and it was a stopping-off point in an effort to obtain money and clothing.

Ultimately, Julia heard from Gardie, who had returned to Lexington but was unable to attend the college, because classes had been dismissed for the summer. The brothers had fought for their country and were adamant supporters of the Confederate cause, but in the end, they were boys, and thus able to recover quickly from devastation, death, and poverty (though the latter would take awhile to overcome).

So while Johnston was surrendering his army and Davis was fleeing south, Gardie was planning to go fishing.

7

DISPERSAL
OF THE
TREASURY

It is with profound regret that I find myself under the necessity of withdrawing from the service of the country, at a time of so much difficulty and gloom.

—Secretary of the Treasury George A. Trenholm
to Jefferson Davis, April 27, 1865

S THE CARAVAN WENDED its way out of North Carolina and into South Carolina, members of the Davis party were greeted warmly by people along the way, a marked contrast with the cold reception in Greensboro and the reluctance to provide rooms to the president and his cabinet in Charlotte. Feelings toward the Confederate government were different here, as was the outlook on the war. The South's fight for independence had begun in South Carolina, with the state being the first to secede from the Union, and it was in Charleston where the war officially began with the firing on Fort Sumter. Of those lining the route traveled by the president, some undoubtedly believed they were watching the remnant of the Confederate nation passing by, but many others remained convinced that the South would prevail and Davis would somehow lead them out of their present difficulties.[1]

Noting the president's popularity, aide William Preston Johnston remarked, "It must be gratifying to find people with so much confidence in you, even now."[2] Davis was perhaps more embarrassed by the enthusiasm of the crowds than by the vitriolic treatment he often received from his critics.

Though now unburdened of the archives and the treasury, the long column of wagons, brigades of cavalry, and government officials on horseback advanced slowly through the countryside, reaching Fort Mill, twenty miles from Charlotte, late in the day. There Davis spent the night at the home of planter A. B. Springs, sharing accommodations with some of his cabinet, while Trenholm and others went to the nearby home of William White.

For the secretary of the treasury, bouncing around in an ambulance between Charlotte and Fort Mill had become unbearable, and he decided to resign his post. Trenholm needed a chance to recover from his illness, and the physical abuse caused by the rutted roads, combined with the stress of avoiding capture, only added to his misery. He and Anna wanted to be with their family, and he would wait for whatever the U.S. authorities had in mind for him, the likelihood being arrest and prison. Staying with the president as he moved farther south would be of no benefit to Davis, as Trenholm could contribute very little, if anything, to the functioning of the government. He would only slow the group down, and at some point, he would probably need to be left behind.

Davis had deep respect for Trenholm's intelligence, dedication, and accomplishments and expressed sincere appreciation for his service: "I . . . accept your resignation and in the name of our suffering country and sacred cause, I thank you, for the zeal and ability with which you have sustained its finances, reviving its sinking credit by the confidence you inspired at home & abroad and increasing its resources by new arrangements."[3]

While there was no denying Trenholm's abilities and the impact he might have had on the financial stability of the government, Davis's characterization of the treasury secretary's contributions was overstated. Trenholm had only been in office for nine months, a number of his proposals had been ignored by the Congress, military reverses had cut off any possibility of foreign loans, and inflation was so rampant that the economy could not have possibly recovered. The failure of the Confederacy to finance the war was ably symbolized by the boxcar sitting on a siding in Washington, Georgia, the day Trenholm resigned. Inside the car, the meager amount of coin and bullion represented the sum total of the entire Confederate treasury.

With Trenholm's resignation, Davis turned to his postmaster general, John Reagan, and appointed him secretary of the treasury. Reagan at first objected, indicating that he already held one post. Davis could have pointed out, however, that there was little Reagan could do with the mail, since he no longer had control over any deliveries. In a reply to Judah P. Benjamin, who jokingly suggested that it might be "unconstitutional for him to hold both places at once," Davis responded in kind by suggesting that the treasury probably would not be too onerous and time-consuming, also referring to the fact "there's but little money for him to steal."[4]

The following day, Davis assembled his cabinet on the lawn of the Springs home to plan the next leg of the journey. While all agreed that the most expeditious route possible would be necessary to avoid capture, none were aware of developments in Washington in the aftermath of Lincoln's assassination. Secretary of War Stanton had taken personal charge of the hunt for Davis. With allegations of official Confederate involvement in the death of Lincoln in the Northern press, coupled with rumors that Davis had left Richmond with a large trove of gold, public pressure was heightened to capture the president. Stanton repeated the rumors to his military commanders as he exhorted them to find Davis. The secretary of war saw to the deployment of Union forces in a wide area in the Carolinas and Georgia, while naval patrols scoured both the east and west coasts of Florida.

While Davis had little information about the disposition of Union forces, beyond rumors, the president was intent on continuing southwest and then, at some point, turning west and linking up with Richard Taylor, whose headquarters was reportedly near Meridian, Mississippi. With the fall of Mobile and the news of the meeting between Johnston and Sherman, however, Taylor was ready to surrender himself, and he had agreed to meet with Union Maj. Gen. Edward R. S. Canby. Included in the negotiations was the army of Maj. Gen. Dabney H. Maury, who had commanded the District of the Gulf, and Confederate cavalry genius Lt. Gen. Nathan Bedford Forrest. Maury had intended to join Johnston, but with Johnston's surrender, Maury became a divisional commander under Taylor. Events were spiraling down for Confederate forces in Mississippi and Alabama, and soon Davis would have no refuge with an organized command east of the Mississippi River.

Not knowing what was happening with Taylor, Davis followed the route he had planned to take with his cabinet. Ahead of him, in the same direction, were his wife and children and the treasury train. The caravan continued south from Fort Mill on April 27, crossing the Catawba River on a pontoon ferry, since the bridge had been burned. All along the route, scouts were sent out to check for signs and news of Yankee cavalry in the area.

The party stopped for the night at the small town of Yorkville, South Carolina. The next morning it set out again with Davis and Reagan in advance of the caravan. Stopping at a house to ask for water, Davis was recognized, the lady of the house asking him if he were the president. When he said he was, the woman nodded toward her small child and indicated, "He is named for you." At that Davis reached into his coat pocket and produced a gold coin, which he gave to her, telling her to keep it for the child. Later, as he rode away, he mentioned to Reagan that he had just given away his last coin.[5]

To help with morale, Davis and Breckinridge, as well as the other cabinet members on horseback, mingled with the escort, at times ahead, at times in the middle, and sometimes near the end of the column. Even Benjamin from a wagon managed to converse with the soldiers, his humor and easy manner winning over the hardened cavalrymen.

After crossing the Broad River, the party reached Unionville, where Davis rested at William H. Wallace's home for an hour or two. Wallace had not yet returned from surrendering with Lee at Appomattox, but after Davis woke, he and the cabinet were served an ample luncheon by neighbors before they moved on to Rose Hill, where Breckinridge arranged accommodations for Davis at the home of a Confederate captain who had died during the war.

On May 1, the party crossed the Saluda River and reached Cokesbury, where Davis was joined by Gen. Braxton Bragg. The general was a favorite of the president, a sycophant who said what he believed Davis wanted to hear, even to the point of distorting or creating "facts." As a field commander, Bragg had been incompetent, so much so, that Davis finally had to remove him when the Army of Tennessee essentially ceased to exist after it was routed at Chattanooga. To soften the blow, however, the president made his friend from the Mexican War a personal adviser on military matters. Disrespected by the officers under him to the point of mutiny, Bragg was also unpopular with the cabinet, especially with Breckinridge, whom Bragg had falsely accused of being drunk at the battle of Missionary Ridge, blaming his subordinate for the loss that was his responsibility. Even Varina recognized Bragg's failings. Early in her flight south, she begged the president not to place Bragg in command: "I am satisfied that the country will be ruined by his intestine feuds if you do so."[6]

As Bragg stood in front of Davis, hat in hand, the president probably expected the general to support his position on continuing the war west of the Mississippi. But even Bragg saw the hopelessness of the situation, and in a rare instance of honest appraisal, he sided with Breckinridge and what remained of the cabinet. Bragg then walked over and stood next to Breckinridge to emphasize his agreement with the secretary of war.

While Bragg's "rebellion" surprised and depressed the president, his mood must have improved with receipt of a letter from Varina, a response to the letter he wrote to her in Charlotte: "Your very sweet letter reached me safely by Mr. Harrison and was a great relief." She indicated that she was leaving for Washington, Georgia, and would probably then go on to Atlanta. As might be expected, Varina's plans were vague and perhaps fanciful. She mentioned, "subject to your approval," going to Bermuda or Nassau and from there to England, in order to put her two oldest children in "the best school I can find." Then, with the two youngest, she would join him in Texas, "and that is the prospect which bears me up, to be with you once more."[7]

On his arrival in Abbeville, Harrison had tried to convince Varina to remain in town until it was quietly occupied by Union troops, assuring her that "some officer would take care that no harm should befall her," adding that "she would then be able to rejoin her friends."[8] The Burts also tried to persuade her that it would be best to stay with them rather than endure the hardships of the journey and risk capture on the road. Their arguments had been to no avail, and the decision was made to travel to Madison, Florida, where they would then figure out how to get to the coast.

Harrison was able to find an ambulance and horses to convey Varina and the children through the generosity of Brig. Gen. John S. Williams, who had commanded some Kentucky regiments in the cavalry corps of Lt. Gen. Joseph Wheeler and was recovering from an illness a few miles from town. With the ambulance and horses, Williams also provided a driver, who would take them to Washington and then return the horses and rig to Abbeville. Three young Kentuckians, well mounted on fresh horses, volunteered to be an escort.

For some reason, Parker sent Lt. George Peck ahead of them to Washington.[9] Peck was given the task of transporting seven large boxes of papers and some instruments belonging to the Navy Department. Parker instructed him to see if Judge Garnett Andrews, a resident of Washington, would be willing to store the items. Most likely, the primary purpose of Peck's mission was to determine if Yankee cavalry was operating in the area and if it would pose a significant risk in Varina's traveling there.

Approaching the Savannah River, Varina became concerned on hearing about an epidemic of smallpox in the area they were passing through. Her youngest had not yet been vaccinated. While the risk of infection was small, since they had little direct contact with people along the way, Varina found a planter willing to vaccinate Winnie, using the scab of an infected child. Needless to say, unless the infected child had cowpox, and not smallpox, the danger to the baby was probably higher than not being vaccinated at all.

As Varina's small party entered Washington, Georgia, she must have been struck by the beauty of what had been, until recently, a sleepy, picture-book village, the center of a wealthy plantation district. Untouched by war and teeming with yellow jessamine, forget-me-nots, fragrant myrtles, and a variety of other flowers populating gardens, lining pathways, and hanging from verandas, Washington had grown around an open square. Aged live oaks acted as sentinels along the common, while the yards of most houses boasted white and pink magnolias.

No longer "sleepy," the town bustled with paroled soldiers and refugees, "unemployed" Confederate generals who had migrated there, and somewhat more than two thousand townspeople. On the north side of the square was a building that had formerly housed the Bank of the State of Georgia. Now closed as a bank, the building was simply referred to as the old bank building. On the first floor were rooms for various businesses, and on the second floor was the residence of Dr. J. J. Robertson, a former cashier of the bank, who lived there to protect the interests of the stockholders, who still owned the building.

While Varina was taking in the town and, with the help of Harrison, looking for a place to stay, the townspeople were eying her as well. Eliza Frances Andrews noted, "The poor woman is in a deplorable condition— no home, no money, and her husband a fugitive. I am very sorry for her, and wish I could do something to help her, but we are all reduced to poverty, and the most we can do is for those of us who have homes to open our doors to the rest."[10] Varina found lodging at the home of Dr. Fielding Ficklen, a town physician.

Varina and the children stayed in Washington for two nights. Here she learned of Johnston's surrender, which gave Union Gen. James H. Wilson command over a region that included Washington and at least as far north as Abbeville. With the surrender of the scattered elements of the Army of Tennessee in addition to Johnston's main body of troops, Varina realized that any attempt by the president to reach Texas by crossing the Mississippi River would be made considerably more difficult by Wilson, and she was anxious to see her husband by waiting for him to arrive in Washington. Unsure of the president's plans, however, and when, or if he would be arriving in Washington, Harrison apparently convinced Varina that she should move on for the safety of her children and the rest of her party.

Before leaving town, however, they needed money. Fortunately, also in Washington was Judge William W. Crump, the assistant secretary of the treasury for the Confederacy. A few days before the evacuation of Richmond, Trenholm had sent Crump to Augusta on a mission for the Treasury Department. With Augusta no longer safe after the surrenders of Lee and Johnston, Crump had traveled by wagon to Washington, where he was a guest of a fellow judge. Crump was now in charge of the specie belonging to the Richmond banks, which he had brought back from Augusta, having taken over the responsibility from the clerks traveling with the deposits. Harrison heard that Crump carried a small amount of gold, independent of the bank funds, which he had placed in the vault of the old bank. "We were to start in the morning," he recalled, "and as nobody in our party had a penny of the money needed to prosecute the intended exit from the country, I was determined to get some of the gold."[11]

Harrison enlisted the support of a treasury clerk and awakened Crump. After considerable persuasion, the assistant secretary gave Harrison an order for "a few hundred dollars in gold and one hundred and ten dollars for myself."[12] The withdrawal was to be charged to the presidential account. With Crump's order, the treasury clerk was able to withdraw the gold that night.

Earlier in the evening, Harrison requisitioned supplies at a quartermaster's camp near town, along with three or four army wagons, drivers, mules, and several men to help with the baggage, promising that the wagons would be given to them at the end of the journey. He had then moved the wagons to a separate bivouac in the woods, which turned out to be a wise decision, since the quartermaster's camp was raided that night, and a number of mules were stolen.

The next morning, May 2, the wagons were loaded with luggage, rifles and ammunition, tents, cooking utensils, and food for the travelers and their animals. In a message to Davis by courier, Harrison informed the president that, because of Johnston's surrender, the safest route seemed to lie between Macon and Augusta, running through Sandersville, and from there, south and southwest into Central Florida, "whence we can strike for the coast as we may find it practical, with a view to procuring shipping."[13] Part of the planned route would be through an area devastated by Sherman's army, and the other would be through mostly uninhabited piney woods. The supplies would be essential.

Varina also sent a message to "Banny," her term of endearment for the president: "Now in the danger of being caught here by the enemy and of being deprived of our transportation if we stay is hurrying me out of Washington. I shall wait here this evening until I hear from the courier we have sent to Abbeville." She may have waited a few hours, but she never heard back from the courier, so before leaving, she sent another note to her husband by way of two acquaintances. In it, she informed him that they had to leave and thought "it best to cross the railroad before nightfall. . . . We will make a march tomorrow of 25 miles to pass beyond the point of positive danger between Mayfield & Macon by day after tomorrow."[14]

The party traveling with Varina and her four children had expanded by the time the group left town that day. Originally, the first lady of the Confederacy had been accompanied by her sister, Margaret; her servant, Ellen Barnes; and Jim Limber, an orphaned black boy of around five or six who had become a member of the Davis household. To the three Kentuckians who were serving as escorts, Harrison had added drivers for the wagons plus two artillery officers who had been returning from furloughs through Augusta only to find out there was no army for them to rejoin. The officers volunteered to set out with Varina to provide added protection for the caravan. Ultimately, they would head west to their homes in Mississippi and Louisiana.

On the way out of town, the procession passed by Brig. Gen. Robert Toombs. An ardent secessionist and former secretary of state under Davis, Toombs had stepped down to command a Georgia brigade and later retired to Washington, when he was denied promotion. Despite being an outspoken critic and archenemy of the president, Toombs greeted Varina warmly when she first arrived in Washington. As he stood there, dressed in an "ill-cut black Websterian coat the worse for wear" and wearing a "broad brimmed shabby hat," Harrison called out a good-bye and may have reflected on how far even the most affluent and elite had fallen during the four years of war.[15]

Toombs was subject to arrest, as was every official of the Davis government. Fortunately for him, he would escape capture and flee to Cuba and then Paris before returning to the United States two years later. Because he refused to request a pardon from the U.S. Congress, however, he never regained his citizenship.

Meanwhile, at Cokesbury, some sixty-five miles north of Washington, Davis had hardly arrived before a scout reported that Union horsemen had been seen about ten miles away, but not necessarily headed for town. Davis decided to spend only a few hours to rest before moving on. About two o'clock in the morning, news of a more imminent threat was received, a scout predicting that Stoneman's cavalry could reach town in three or four hours. According to Mallory, Davis's escort was assembled into a single command under Breckinridge, but nothing came of the presumed attack. Around six thirty the next morning, the president departed Cokesbury.

Davis's presence and direction of travel, however, had not gone unnoticed. Following in his path was the First Brigade of Stoneman's corps, which was commanded by Col. William Palmer, who was a couple of days behind the caravan. Capturing stragglers from Davis's escort, Palmer learned that the president was headed for Abbeville. For some reason, instead of chasing down the Davis caravan, Palmer chose a parallel route and targeted a location west of Abbeville. There he waited, expecting Davis to ride into his web.

On May 2, Davis rode into Abbeville to an enthusiastic reception. He had missed Varina by only a few days. He immediately went to the home of his friend, Armistead Burt, while the cabinet members and staff were hospitably received in other homes nearby, one of the homes being that of Col. Henry Leovy.

Waiting for the president in Abbeville were William H. Parker and the treasury. Since departing from Abbeville on April 17, the government specie and the accompanying bank funds had traveled a circuitous route of more than two hundred miles only to end up in a warehouse back in Abbeville, reunited with the president.

For Parker, the journey from Washington, Georgia, to Augusta and back through Washington to Abbeville had been an exercise in frustration.

On reaching Augusta, Parker learned of Lee's surrender and became con-cerned about the safety of the specie. Both soldiers and citizens were grow-ing unruly. Food was scarce, Confederate money no longer had any value, and the expectation was that Yankee cavalry would soon overrun the town. In such circumstances, people were ready to take what they could, when they could, and the treasury train was a tempting target. Parker, accordingly, threw a heavy guard of midshipmen around it.

Word of the armistice between Johnston and Sherman brought a few days' reprieve, and although Parker was frequently "advised by officious persons to divide the money among the Confederates, as the war was over and it would otherwise fall into the hands of the federal troops," he refused to make any disbursements. He later wrote, "The treasure had been put in my safekeeping, and I would hold it until I met President Davis; and that, if necessary, the command would be killed in defense of it."[16]

Ultimately, Parker decided to retrace his steps and attempt to meet Presi-dent Davis in his retreat. He had been advised by Brig. Gen. Birkett D. Fry, the local commander at Augusta, to move the specie out of town, as disci-pline among the Confederate troops there was evaporating and he could pro-vide no protection. Navy Paymaster John Wheless, also in Augusta, had a similar bleak assessment about the safety of the treasury. Dining with Parker and William Wood Crump at the Planters Hotel, Wheless warned that sol-diers at the local arsenal and workers at the government shops "with no means to buy food now, would almost certainly try to take the money." He suggested moving the specie back to the vicinity of the army.[17] Though there was no army, Davis had a few cavalry brigades with him that could at least fend off attacks from unruly soldiers and mobs of civilians.

While at Augusta, Parker received a confusing telegram from Mallory directing him to disband the midshipmen, an order he decided he could not immediately obey. Otherwise, the treasury would be unguarded as it was transported north. On returning to Washington, the specie was loaded again into wagons, and the women who had been left behind in Washing-ton, including Parker's wife, rejoined the procession for the trip back to Abbeville. Parker was guessing that this would be where he might meet up with Davis and the cabinet.

At Abbeville, Parker made sure the treasury and the bank funds stored in a warehouse on the public square were heavily guarded. The town was now filled with soldiers from Lee's and Johnston's armies. Some were passing through on their way home while others were milling about, causing turmoil in the streets and posing a risk for the gold and silver. News of Union cavalry in the area also kept Parker on edge. Around sunrise on May 2, a cavalry company could be seen winding down the hills in the distance, and Parker hurriedly had the specie loaded onto a train, ready to leave for Newbury. On sending out scouts, however, Parker was relieved to learn that the horsemen were the advance guard of the president's caravan. He had guessed correctly.

With Davis's entry into Abbeville, Parker's responsibility for the treasury came to an end. He transferred the coin and bullion to the acting secretary of the treasury, John Reagan, who instructed Parker to deliver the specie to Gen. Basil Duke. Parker did so at the railroad station and then disbanded his command, granting official "leave" from the naval school to each of his charges, along with ten days' rations. Also discharged was the company of volunteers from the Charlotte Navy Yard.

At some point afterward, Parker called on Davis at the Burt house to report his disbanding of the midshipmen in accordance with Mallory's orders. He also took the opportunity to urge the president to leave the country as soon as possible, as he was in definite danger of capture. Brigades of Union cavalry were scouring the countryside and would surely soon close in on the Davis party. Parker's efforts were in vain, as Davis refused to take any action that could be portrayed as fleeing.

During the day, reports were received of Union cavalry raiding to the northwest of town, about thirty miles away. Concerned that the enemy was moving toward Abbeville, Davis called for a "council of war" during the late afternoon in a parlor of the Burt mansion. Attendees included Breckinridge, Gens. Braxton Bragg, S. W. Ferguson, George G. Dibrell, John C. Vaughn, and Basil Duke, and Breckinridge's son, Col. William C. P. Breckinridge. Cabinet members Benjamin, Reagan, and Mallory were not invited. Davis already knew their opinions.

The president's position was similar to what it had been with his cabinet: collect as many soldiers as could be rounded up east of the Mississippi River and continue the war in the West. "It is time that we adopt some definite plan upon which the further prosecution of our struggle shall be conducted," he said, adding, "I feel that I ought to do nothing now without the advice of my military chiefs."[18] The last remark was probably taken by some in the room as glib. Almost certainly, not lost on them was the fact that the

Confederacy of Robert E. Lee, Thomas J. "Stonewall" Jackson, and Joseph E. Johnston had been reduced in "military chiefs" to Breckinridge, Bragg, four brigadiers, and a colonel.

As in Charlotte with his cabinet, an embarrassed silence enveloped the room, the president's plan falling on deaf ears. There was simply no way to present the military situation in a favorable light, and the president's statement that "three thousand brave men are enough for a nucleus around which the whole people will rally" bordered on foolishness.[19] One by one, the generals stated their belief that there was no hope for victory, Southern resources were exhausted, and the people were "broken down and worn out."

In terms of continuing the war west of the Mississippi River, Ferguson reduced the question to two considerations: were they strong enough to cut their way to the Mississippi through the enemy forces blocking their way, and would they have any men left as they passed by the homes of the men in their brigades? His answer to both questions was no.

Visibly stiffened by the response, Davis managed to ask, "Then why are you still in the field?"

"We are here to help you escape," Duke replied. "Our men will risk battle for that, but they won't fire another shot to continue the war."[20]

Pausing for a moment to collect himself, Davis indicated that he would not accept any proposal that "looks merely to my personal safety," and he made a final appeal to them as Southerners and soldiers. The "sorrowful silence" that followed was a clear answer to his plea. "All is lost indeed," he said, as he slowly rose and walked unsteadily from the room, supported by Breckinridge. When the opportunity presented itself, Breckinridge also urged the president to leave the country as soon as possible.

With that meeting, the character of Davis's southward journey changed considerably. No longer was this an effort by the Confederate government to reestablish its capital in a location where war could best be conducted. Instead, it became what it appeared to be: an effort to protect the president from being captured, whether he was willing to see it that way or not.

Soon after the meeting, Breckinridge took command of all the cavalry—which until then had technically been under Bragg's authority—and directed the repacking of baggage and the specie in wagons for the next leg of the journey to Washington, Georgia. A few boxes of papers that had not been included in what was left behind in Charlotte with Kean and Cooper were entrusted to Mrs. Henry Leovy. She and her husband had been staying in Abbeville as refugees from New Orleans, the city having fallen in 1862. Evidently, New Orleans was a stronger draw for Henry Leovy than for his wife, for he joined the Davis caravan with the intent of eventually making his way back home. His wife chose to remain in Abbeville.

Other government papers were burned, in particular, some of Benjamin's State Department records, which he may have felt could prove to be incriminating, given the fact that Benjamin ran the Confederate Secret Service. At the very least, they might have "added fuel to the fire" were he and Davis caught and imprisoned.

Breckinridge had also been giving thought to the reliability of the escort. Without question, morale was low, especially among some of the brigades, and in particular, Vaughn's Tennesseans. Accustomed to moving with speed, the cavalry commands found the casual pace set by the president and the need to protect the "dressing cases on wheels" hard on the nerves, along with the constant threat of being attacked by a superior force of enemy horsemen. The time had come to pare the escort down to a core of dependable riders and release all those who wished to return home. The brigade commanders were also told to inform those staying that, at some point, payment in silver would be made from the treasury funds. Ferguson, returning to his camp from meeting with Breckinridge, found that a portion of the Second Alabama Cavalry had already deserted.

When the Davis party left Abbeville around 11:00 p.m. on May 3, the escort numbered about half of what it was before. Included with the baggage of the president were the boxes containing the thirty-five thousand dollars in gold sovereigns that had been separated out, dropped off in Greensboro by John C. Hendren for Davis's use and later picked up and added in with the president's trunks. For the remainder of his trek south, Davis had little to do with his baggage, except for a change of clothing and an occasional cigar, and nothing at all to do with the gold. He probably knew of the gold being transported in his wagon, however, since Breckinridge had assigned Capt. Watson Van Benthuysen, a nephew of Davis, to command a small guard that included two of his brothers and five young soldiers from prominent Maryland families to watch over the president's wagons. Ferguson's cavalry formed the rear guard for the procession.

Somewhere in the column were the remaining cabinet ministers—Benjamin, Breckinridge, Mallory, and Reagan—the president's staff . . . and Semple.

Early on the morning of May 4, Davis crossed over the Savannah River on a pontoon bridge below Vienna, South Carolina, and rode a few miles to a farmhouse to get breakfast and to have the horses fed. Now that the pace had picked up, Benjamin was uncomfortable jouncing around on horseback. He decided that he would part from Davis for a time and catch up with him in the Trans-Mississippi Department. In discussing with Davis his plan to make his way to Florida, where he would find a way over to Nassau or Bermuda, Benjamin was entrusted to perform certain "public duties" by the president, which neither he nor Davis ever revealed. Traveling in a buggy and disguised as a Frenchman who spoke only a few words of English, Benjamin probably never intended to rendezvous with Davis in Texas. In leaving, accompanied by Henry Leovy, who would travel with him to Florida before returning to his home in New Orleans, Benjamin indicated to Reagan, "I am going to the farthest place from the United States if it takes me to the middle of China."[21]

Breckinridge rode for a while alongside Davis, near the head of the column, as the president continued to express his frustration at the lack of will by his generals to save the South from tyranny. The secretary of war used the opportunity to reiterate his belief that Davis had to leave the country by boat, that it was too dangerous to try to reach the West by trekking across Alabama and Mississippi.

After a while, Breckinridge drifted back behind the wagons containing the specie and fell in with Ferguson's rear guard. With each mile, grumbling among the men increased, as they saw little reason to continue to risk their lives. Some had thrown away their arms. Talk of surrender was increasing.

The rear guard had left Abbeville two or three hours after the head of the column started out, and as a result, the caravan was spread over many miles. Ferguson's cavalry thus reached the Savannah hours after Davis had crossed over, though it was still only daybreak. Here, discipline broke down among Ferguson's men, a number of them threatening to seize the treasury rather than have it taken from them by the enemy. They wanted to be paid and began to move forward and around the wagons. The guards assigned to protect the wagons were outnumbered and would be powerless to fend off the mutinous cavalrymen. Breckinridge, who was popular and widely respected by the rank and file, appealed to their patriotism as Confederate soldiers. "You're Southern gentlemen," he said, "not highway robbers. . . . As soon as we reach Washington, you will be paid from the treasure train— just as I told you yesterday."[22]

The primary Confederate leaders involved in the tale of the missing Confederate treasury are President Jefferson Davis (upper left), Secretary of War John C. Breckinridge (upper right), Secretary of the Treasury George A. Trenholm (center), Secretary of the Navy Stephen R. Mallory (lower left), and Postmaster General (later acting Secretary of the Treasury) John H. Reagan (lower right). Of this group, only Breckinridge managed to escape capture. The others all served prison terms. In March 1866, Mallory was the last to be released.

VALENTINE RICHMOND HISTORY CENTER

Julia Gardiner Tyler (above) was known for her beauty, independence, and energy. Her poise and charm captivated suitors prior to her marriage to President John Tyler (below left).

LIBRARY OF CONGRESS

MRS. MARY MORRIS BOOTH, LYNCHBURG, VIRGINIA

David Gardiner "Gardie" Tyler (right) joined the First Rockbridge Artillery late in the war. He was photographed in uniform at age eighteen in 1864. His letters to his mother were opinionated, entertaining, and written with the skill of a wordsmith.

In 1842, when John Tyler purchased the estate, Sherwood Forest (left) consisted of some sixteen hundred acres. The house was built around 1730 and is the longest frame dwelling in the country. Although damaged and stripped of furniture by Union soldiers in 1864, Sherwood Forrest survived the war and has been continuously owned by Tyler descendants.

At age nineteen, Julia Gardiner allowed her image to be used in an advertisement by Bogert and Mecamly, a New York City clothing and dry goods store. Her humiliated parents soon left for Europe with Julia in tow. But from the advertisement, Julia received the nickname "the Rose of Long Island."

On April 2, 1865, the Confederate government (personified by President Jefferson Davis's first cabinet, above, during a briefing with Robert E. Lee) fled Richmond. Destruction of war materiel and tobacco warehouses in the capital led to a conflagration in the city that consumed more than seven hundred buildings and all or part of fifty-four city blocks.

Capt. William H. Parker (above) was superintendent of the Confederate Naval Academy on the school ship *Patrick Henry*. Parker commanded the midshipmen who guarded the Confederate treasury during the flight south from Richmond.

Adm. Raphael Semmes (above) spent twenty-two months at sea capturing or sinking more than sixty Union vessels. After his ship was sunk off the coast of France, he escaped to England and found his way to Richmond to command the James River Squadron.

A thirteen-hundred-ton side-wheel gunboat, CSS *Patrick Henry* (below) was attached to the James River Squadron, and the vessel was modified as a school ship for the Confederate Naval Academy. It was burned at the time of the evacuation of Richmond.

In the former Georgia Branch Bank, known then as the "old bank building" (above), Davis held his last cabinet meeting on May 4, 1865. The pencil sketch was done at the time.

After the surrender of Robert E. Lee's Army of Northern Virginia, only small remnants of the former Army of Tennessee under Gens. Joseph E. Johnston (right) and P. G. T. Beauregard (left), Johnston's second in command, were left to stem the relentless onslaught of the Union juggernaut under William T. Sherman. With an army four times the size of Johnston's, however, the match was decidedly uneven. Johnston surrendered his army on April 26, 1865, to avoid the useless loss of his men.

Jefferson Davis's exodus (pictured above) wound from Virginia, through the Carolinas, and into Georgia before he was captured by Union cavalry. He was imprisoned at Fort Monroe (pictured below) for two years before bail was allowed to be posted. The U.S. government never prosecuted the case against Davis.

U.S. Senator, railroad magnate, lawyer, and statesman David L. Yulee built the first cross-state railroad in Florida. His five-thousand-acre sugar plantation, Cotton-wood (a.k.a. Cotton Wood) was where the personal baggage of Jefferson Davis ended up before it was found and seized by Union soldiers. Because of his support for the Confederacy, although he played no active role in the administration, Yulee spent ten months in prison.

Augusta, Georgia (below), became a mecca for families uprooted by the burning of Atlanta and William T. Sherman's March to the Sea. In April 1865, the city's waterfront was busier than ever with those who wanted to leave the state for safer homes.

Situated on a bluff along the Savannah River several miles inland from the Atlantic Ocean, Savannah was Georgia's largest city as well as a busy commerce and ship-building port for the Confederacy (as portrayed below, although it appears deceptively peaceful in the above photo). In fact, the port was a primary destination for blockade-runners and a key player in the South's naval program. Three ironclads were built here, and two more were under construction when the war ended. Protected by obstructions and a line of river batteries, the city was safe from attack for much of the war. The fall of Fort McAllister, however, during Sherman's March to the Sea, opened the back door to the city, which surrendered on December 21, 1864.

Situated at 221 Broadway in New York City, the Astor Hotel was only a few blocks south of Fenian headquarters and close to Sweeney's Hotel, where Fenians tended to congregate. James A. Semple usually stayed at the Astor when he had to be in the city.

FACING PAGE: The Ottawa Hotel in Montreal was an unofficial gathering place for Union soldiers, officials, and sympathizers during the war. For some reason, Confederate agent James A. Semple generally stayed here during his business dealings in Canada after the war.

Edward M. Tidball was chief clerk of the Confederate Navy Department. He accompanied James A. Semple and the gold from the Confederate treasury from Washington, Georgia, to Augusta. When the two men divided the gold between them and separated, Tidball returned to his home in Winchester, Virginia.

Two years in a damp prison took a toll on Jefferson Davis's health. Here he poses with his wife, Varina, after his release from Fort Monroe in May 1867.

The house (above) Tidball built after the war still stands today in Winchester, Virginia. Known as Linden Farm, the property is presently undergoing restoration. During the renovation, papers were found in a wall in a bedroom (below) that listed Tidball's assets in February 1866, including twenty-seven thousand dollars in gold coins from the Confederate treasury.

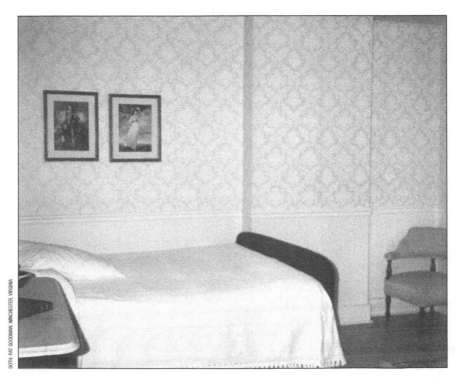

This Mexican silver dollar, also known as an 8 reale coin, is similar to the coins left behind by the Confederate government and possibly still buried in Danville.

The Confederate naval warehouse in Danville, Virginia, was situated on this hilltop, now part of the Greenhill Cemetery.

Letitia Tyler Semple is buried in an un-marked grave in the Cedar Grove Ceme-tery (above) in Williamsburg, Virginia.

Letitia Tyler Semple (right) would have been buried at Williamsburg's Bruton Parish Church, but at the time she died (1907), the cemetery was closed to new interments. Today, the marker at Bruton Parish (above) noting the death of James A. Semple (as well as his mother and fa-ther and a family servant) carries an in-scription to the "memory" of Letitia.

James A. Semple died in 1883 (as opposed to the date on the marker above and to the right) and is buried in the small cemetery behind Bruton Parish Church in Williamsburg, Virginia.

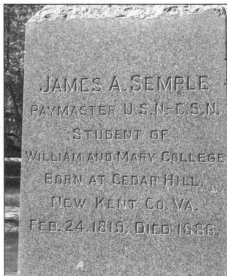

Sitting calmly on his large charger, he was successful at getting them to listen to him, but not at changing their minds. With the enemy raiding around them, they were not about to take a chance of being attacked before they could get the wagons to Washington, and they wanted to be paid immediately. Finally, Breckinridge agreed and ordered the wagons to be drawn up and the boxes of silver coin belonging to the treasury to be broken open. Quartermasters were ordered to fill out payrolls, and payment was made to each man. After the disbursement, the wagons were loaded again.

The specific pay actually received by each soldier has never been satisfactorily accounted for, though numerous claims have been made, mostly that the amount was around $25 or $26. What is known is that a total of $108,322.90 was later recorded as being "paid out."[23]

In a note delivered to Davis, Breckinridge reported, "Nothing can be done with the bulk of this command." He indicated that he had to open only a few boxes to pay out the silver and that he would move the wagons forward again into Washington, where he could, hopefully, turn the remainder of the treasury over to Reagan. For the record, he requested Davis's written approval of the distribution. This was really a formality, because the distribution had been made by the time Breckinridge received Davis's authorization.

Breckinridge also noted that some of the men—mainly the brigades of Vaughn and Dibrell—were going to stay where they were and surrender to the enemy. Others went looking for Yankees so they could be paroled. Only a few hundred men from Basil Duke's and Col. William C. P. Breckinridge's commands and forty or fifty from S. W. Ferguson's cavalry could be considered reliable. In the final analysis, however, the secretary of war was not really sure how dependable any of the men would continue to be. For that reason and concerned about the safety of the chest of jewelry and silver, he apparently found a way to leave it secretly with Mrs. J. D. Moss, who lived nearby.

As Davis neared Washington, Georgia, or on reaching it, Secretary of the Navy Mallory spoke with the president, and their discussion very likely included the treasury. If Davis was still determined to reach the Mississippi, and even if he was not, the specie would eventually be seized, probably sooner rather than later. Every mile traveled and every road traveled presented an extreme risk. Eventually, the wagons would be stopped, if not by Union cavalry, then by Confederates seeking food, clothing, money . . .

whatever could be taken. Even the wagons themselves and the horses and mules pulling them would be an enticement to soldiers walking back to their homes, in some instances, hundreds of miles away.

Between William H. Parker, Raphael Semmes's sailors, and the midshipmen guards, the Navy Department had borne much of the responsibility for the protection and safety of the specie, including the funds belonging to the Richmond banks. Quite possibly, Mallory offered his opinion as to what to do with the gold and silver. Given the respect that the president had for the intelligence and accomplishments of his naval secretary, Mallory would have had the president's attention. As events proved out, Mallory almost certainly made a recommendation to Davis concerning his bureau chief and paymaster, James A. Semple, and Davis almost certainly listened.

By the time the Davis party reached Washington, Mallory had also decided that he could no longer be of any particular use to the president, and during their conversation, the secretary handed the president a brief note of resignation. Mallory recalled, "In taking leave of Mr. Davis, I told him that I would accompany him if he would determine to go to South Florida and thence leave the country, for I believed I could aid him materially; but up to 4:00 p.m. in the afternoon of the day he reached Washington he was still unable to determine his future course." Mallory, accordingly, took his leave that evening and stayed the night with Confederate Congressman Louis T. Wigfall and his wife. The next day, he and the Wigfalls left by train for Atlanta. Mallory's wife and children were in LaGrange at the time, about seventy miles southwest of Atlanta. He would wait with his family for whatever fate was in store for him.[24]

On entering Washington, Davis was greeted warmly by the townspeople, as he had been in Abbeville, and he went to the home of Dr. J. J. Robertson in the old bank building. There, he was able to get a few hours of sleep, and the wife of Maj. Gen. Arnold Elsey saw to it that he was not disturbed. When he rose later in the afternoon (which explains, perhaps, why Mallory had no further word from the president and assumed no plans had been made), he spoke with many of the people who flocked to see him—in particular, the Confederate officers in town.

Around 6:00 p.m., Paymaster John Wheless arrived at the bank building. He had been sent by Parker, who realized soon after Davis left Abbeville that his navy escort had not been paid for their services in protecting the treasury. While Parker delayed his departure for home, Wheless asked Reagan to authorize payment while he waited; he intended to return to Abbeville as soon as he could obtain the funds. Reagan, accordingly, gave Wheless authorization for payment of $1,500 in gold for the escort. He was to be provided also with $300 in gold for Lt. David Bradford of the Confederate marines, who was under orders for the Trans-Mississippi Department. Disbursement was to be made the next day, when the wagons containing the treasury were expected to arrive in town.

During the evening, John Reagan, William Wood Crump, and staff officers John Taylor Wood and William Preston Johnston joined the president in his room. Though he had resigned, Mallory was also present. James Semple was requested to attend as well.

At the meeting, Reagan suggested that Capt. Micajah Clark be made acting treasurer, and Davis agreed. The appointment was the last official act of the president. Clark's qualifications were well known to Davis. Not only was he the president's chief clerk, his overseeing of the archives as they were transported south had much to do with the fact that there were records to be left when Breckinridge ordered them to be turned over to the Union army. Reagan and Davis also both knew they could rely on Clark's integrity and dedication to duty. The captain was to be given the responsibility of disbursing the specie in the treasury and for taking charge of the president's baggage, including the thirty-five thousand dollars in gold sovereigns. Over the coming days, Clark's new responsibilities would make full use of his organizational and record-keeping skills.

Semple was also given an assignment, one considerably more difficult and dangerous. If caught by the enemy, he would face a lengthy prison term. His mission would be to secretly transport the gold coins and bullion of the treasury out of the country and then see that the funds were deposited in a secure account. While Clark would be making a few additional disbursements the next morning, the bulk of the specie entrusted to Semple, a bonded paymaster, would be what was contained in the wagons soon to arrive in Washington. Semple's objective was to get the gold to Charleston or Savannah and then to Bermuda, Nassau, or ideally, Liverpool, England, where the specie could be placed with Fraser, Trenholm, and Company, the Confederacy's commercial agent in Great Britain. All three ports were familiar to Semple. Though Davis later claimed the gold was intended for settling "incurred liabilities," the president—at the time, still holding on to the possibility of continuing the war in the West—probably wanted to have access to funds to help finance the effort. The amount, of course, would have been much too small for even minimal expenditures in maintaining an army, but he may have hoped to use the specie for short-term needs or as a nucleus for raising additional financing.

Mallory no doubt played a part in the choice of Semple, but Davis knew him also and was well aware of his resourcefulness. The well-stocked warehouses encountered along the route to Washington were simply a reminder of Semple's abilities. Then, too, Col. John Taylor Wood, a nephew of Davis, was a friend of Semple and would have wholeheartedly seconded his selection for the mission.

When told about it that evening, Semple probably had no idea how he was going to get the specie past the Union troops filling the streets of Southern cities and swarming over the countryside. He had until the morning to figure it out, because at that time, the president was planning to ride out of Washington with whatever remained of his escort. Semple would be on his own, without any sort of a guard to protect the gold from being seized at gunpoint or by a mob. He would also need to leave the next day, probably under the cover of darkness, as Yankee cavalry was known to be closing in on the town.

The next morning, William Preston Johnston notified Micajah Clark of his appointment and the role to be played by Semple. While the president readied himself to leave town, the acting treasurer waited for Breckinridge and the wagons to appear. The first order of business would then be to record the funds paid out by the secretary of war. He would determine specifically the exact amount of specie left in the treasury and make the final distributions.

Semple, in the meantime, had a plan for transporting the gold—and soon he would have a partner, Edward M. Tidball.

8

FINAL DAYS OF FREEDOM

Do not try to meet me. . . . Why not cut loose from your escort? go swiftly and alone with the exception of two or three.

—Varina Davis to Jefferson Davis, May 1865

AVIS AWOKE THE NEXT morning, May 4, having come to some conclusions. In a sense, his "plan" was consistent with what he had been wanting to do all along, which was to reach Edmund Kirby Smith in Texas. With reports of Union cavalry moving toward Washington and Augusta, he knew he had to move quickly farther south, far enough to get past Union-occupied areas. He would then turn west, cross the Chattahoochee River, and seek out the forces supposed to be in the field in Alabama. The plan was similar to what he had proposed in Charlotte, the difference being that he would no longer be accompanied by brigades of horsemen, which would be too conspicuous to escape detection and too few in number to cut through the opposition. Instead, with the two remaining cabinet members, his staff, and a much smaller escort, he would attempt to blend in with soldiers returning home and slip through the web of Union forces ahead of him.[1]

In a sense, he would be following Varina's suggestion in a letter that found him shortly after he had arrived in Washington. She had urged him to "cut loose from your escort" and not to try to meet up with her; she cautioned him against making a "stand this side of the river."[2]

Davis had no knowledge as to what was happening "this side of the river." He had received no recent word from his generals east of the Mississippi, though he realized they had no idea where he was and were dealing with increased pressures from the enemy on all fronts. Not hearing otherwise, he continued to believe the illusion that Richard Taylor, Dabney H. Maury, and Nathan Bedford Forrest still led effective forces in the field. That very day, however, Taylor had begun the process of surrendering the Department of Alabama, Mississippi, and East Louisiana—which included Forrest—to Union Maj. Gen. Edward R. S. Canby. The next day, May 5, Maury would surrender his troops, and by May 12, the last Confederate forces east of the Mississippi would lower the battle flag and pass into oblivion.

Ultimately, Davis's hope rested with Smith and Maj. Gen. John B. Magruder, who, under Smith, commanded the District of Arizona, New Mexico, and Texas. The Trans-Mississippi Department was a vast area consisting of Arkansas, Louisiana, Missouri, Texas, Indian Territory (present-day Oklahoma), and the territories of Arizona and New Mexico. Few Union troops were stationed there—though that would change—and many of the engagements in those regions had been more like skirmishes (unlike the large pitched battles in the eastern theater). Davis knew the Southwest well, having served in the area early in his career, and he knew how difficult it would be to defeat highly mobile armies and guerrilla forces that took advantage of the varied terrain of that region of the country. He reasoned that the Union would eventually tire of chasing Confederate forces that could operate effectively in such a large area.

As commander of all Confederate forces in the Trans-Mississippi Department, Gen. Edmund Kirby Smith exercised almost total control over military affairs. Essentially cut off from the rest of the Confederacy after the loss of Vicksburg, "Kirby Smithdom" had received minimal direction from the War Department in Richmond. By 1864, Smith had been promoted from lieutenant general to a full general.

The interdiction of communications that resulted after the fall of Vicksburg forced Smith to obtain supplies and finances on his own. He built and contracted with factories and foundries for weapons, textiles, tools, and other essential items, while he fed his troops by producing grain and cattle. One of the most successful ventures, and one that enabled Smith to finance his operations, was the continuing cotton trade through Mexico. The general's agents were able to purchase Texas cotton for "three or four cents a pound and sell it for fifty cents in gold."[3] The cotton was shipped to Matamoras and thence abroad or via Galveston, Texas, en route to Havana, Nassau, and Europe. Some of the cotton was exported by blockade-runners under Smith's control. By using Union ships captured in Texas ports, Smith had the vessels reconfigured to run the blockade with exports and return with supplies for his command.

By 1865, Union forces were making gradual incursions into the Trans-Mississippi Department by occupying parts of Arkansas and attempting to invade Texas. In Indian Territory, Confederates turned back enemy forces in western Arkansas, primarily with cavalry units consisting of white volunteers and Indians from the Cherokee, Chickasaw, Choctaw, Creek, Osage, and Seminole nations. Commanded by Maj. Gen. Sam Bell Maxey, the Indian units were particularly adept at harassing Union troops and cutting supply lines, as opposed to large-scale frontal engagements. The largest Indian force was commanded by Stand Watie, chief of the Cherokees, who in 1864 was recognized by the Confederacy for bravery and loyalty with promotion to brigadier general.

Considering the nature of the region and Smith's success in financing and commanding a self-sufficient army, Davis likely reasoned that the war could be prolonged, if not sustained, in the West. Smith's empire, in the president's mind, was the only hope for the Confederacy and the only part of the country that could provide safe refuge for Davis, his cabinet and staff, and his family. And if Semple were to somehow get the treasury gold to one of the intended destinations, there would be additional funds to combine with those of Smith. Between the two, sufficient financing might be possible, especially if a viable cotton trade could be maintained through Mexico.

In the meantime, Union cavalry commander James H. Wilson had cast a wide net to capture Davis and the Confederate leadership. In March, Wilson and his troopers had pushed south from Tennessee into the heart of Alabama. Selma and the naval works there were destroyed, Forrest was defeated, and the capital of Montgomery was captured. Wilson then turned east and captured Columbus and Macon, Georgia. With fifteen thousand troopers in Georgia, Wilson was now ready to sweep southward to find Davis.

With a reward of one hundred thousand dollars for capture of the president and twenty-five thousand dollars each for the cabinet members and other Confederate leaders, Union soldiers and civilians alike had a substantial incentive to pursue Davis's party. And there was an additional inducement: a reward for locating the Confederate treasury, which was now falsely bloated in estimation to several million dollars.

While Wilson's cavalry was crisscrossing parts of Alabama and Georgia, the Union navy was on alert to the possibility that Davis might try to escape by sea. By the time the president reached Washington, Georgia, the U.S. secretary of the navy, Gideon Welles, had notified the commanders of his blockading squadrons that Davis and the cabinet intended to escape the country either via Cuba or across the Mississippi. Welles noted, "All the vigilance and available means at your command should be brought to bear to prevent the escape of the leaders of the rebellion."[4]

Early in the morning of May 4, Davis met with his remaining advisers: John Reagan, Braxton Bragg, Francis R. Lubbock, John Taylor Wood, William Preston Johnston, and Charles E. Thorburn. (Breckinridge had not yet arrived with the wagons containing the treasury.) Davis spoke with "surprising calmness" about his plans.[5] Noting that he intended to reduce his escort considerably, he asked Capt. Given Campbell, either during or after the meeting, to see if ten men of his company would be willing to accompany him as he continued south. Campbell reported back that all of his men volunteered, and Davis asked him to choose ten.

James Semple may have been in the meeting as well. Either he alone, or in collusion with someone else, perhaps Wood, had devised a means of secreting the gold while it was transported to the coast, and Semple would have felt obliged to report this to Reagan and probably the president. His plan entailed building a false bottom in a carriage, with the gold being loaded into the hidden compartment. Modifications to the carriage would take time, but they must be completed so that Semple would be able to depart the next night and put quite a few miles behind him before daybreak. He could begin to modify the carriage, but he needed for the treasury to arrive and for some funds to be disbursed so he could determine the volume and weight of the gold to be transported.

Reagan, Davis, and the others must have recognized the odds against Semple's reaching the coast. Too much could go wrong. The bottom of the carriage might not be strong enough to hold the gold, especially with regard to the rutted and bumpy roads that lay ahead. Union soldiers might detain Semple, search the carriage, and discover the false bottom. Semple might even be arrested. Of the possibilities, the greatest concern was that Confederate soldiers returning home might seize the carriage and horse. With thousands of soldiers traveling the roads and most seeking transportation, Semple would be at risk every mile of the way.

Given the odds and the difficulties ahead, either Semple or Reagan—or most likely Mallory the night before—must have suggested that Semple be accompanied on the journey. The person they recommended was Edward M. Tidball, chief clerk of the Navy Department. A precise, dapper, and orderly accountant-type, Tidball may not have appeared to be well prepared for the rigors of what faced the two men en route to the coast, but during the first two years of the war, he had traveled extensively throughout the South, negotiating contracts for warship construction. At the very least, he could help figure out what they should do in the situations that might arise, and he could assist in unloading the gold when they reach their destination.[6]

By 10:00 a.m., Davis was ready to go himself. He visited briefly with Garnett Andrews and others who had called on him to wish him well. Before leaving, Davis gave Mrs. J. J. Robertson some of his personal belongings, including books and an inkstand, and he spoke for a few minutes with Micajah H. Clark, who had received his commission from Reagan. The presidential caravan was now reduced to a single wagon, two ambulances, and extra horses. Clark, who was asked by Davis to take charge of the president's baggage and the thirty-five thousand dollars in gold, planned to catch up to Davis after the authorized disbursements were made. With Capt. Watson Van Benthuysen and his small guard riding alongside, the wagon and ambulances moved out behind the president's staff.

Reagan decided to stay behind until the treasury gold was loaded into the carriage and Semple was on his way out of town. Breckinridge still had not yet arrived with the treasury, and with things to do when he arrived, he would be delayed as well. The funds of the Richmond banks were to remain in the vault of the old bank building under the nervous eye of William Wood Crump.

As part of his duties in watching over government property and the personal effects of the president, Clark had documents belonging to Davis and his letter books sewn up in blankets, which were hidden in town, perhaps with Mrs. Robertson. His intent was to return when he could safely retrieve the contents, after the turmoil of surrender and occupation had abated.

Shortly after the president rode out of Washington to catch up with his staff, the treasury wagons appeared, followed a couple of hours later by Breckinridge and S. W. Ferguson's cavalry brigade. The wagons pulled up about a mile outside of town, where Basil Duke was camped on both sides of the road. As soon as he learned about the wagons, Clark rode out to the camp and presented his commission to Duke, who was relieved to be rid of the responsibility. Clark set up shop beneath a large elm tree and performed his first official responsibility as acting treasurer by carefully counting the remaining assets of the treasury: $179,700 (after Breckinridge's disbursement of $108,322.90 to the mutinous troops the night before).

After recording the $108,322.90 payout and noting that the receipt was signed by A. R. Lawton, Clark executed payment of the silver and gold coin to the troops at hand, recording the amounts and taking receipts in return. Most of the payments were in silver and were for services rendered. Five thousand dollars went to the Quartermaster's Department in Washington to supply the troops; $1,472 went to the president's escort that was now being disbanded; and $4,000 in gold went to Maj. J. Foster for payment of troops whom Breckinridge intended to keep in his command. John Wheless received $1,500 in silver for William H. Parker's midshipmen and $300 for Lt. David Bradford's mission to the Trans-Mississippi Department. Braxton Bragg was provided with $2,000 to "transmit" to the Trans-Mississippi Department for Davis's eventual use. Capt. Joseph M. Brown had requested $3,000 for the Quartermaster's Department but received approval for $520 in gold instead. Five commissioned officers and twenty-six men belonging to a Louisiana Brigade received $806; three auditors in the First Auditor's office received $50 each; and Breckinridge received $1,000 to be transmitted to the Trans-Mississippi Department.[7]

Around sunset, Clark left Duke's camp with two wagons containing silver bullion and the remaining specie for Semple. He was also bringing back an ambulance he had borrowed from Breckinridge, empty now, except for a small iron safe. Though the distance to town was short, Duke provided an escort of twenty to thirty men.

Before reaching town, Clark was halted by Maj. Raphael J. Moses, who had been authorized by Davis to receive an amount of silver for feeding Confederate soldiers passing through Washington. Clark moved all of the gold to the ambulance and turned over the wagons to Moses, with twenty boxes of silver bullion totaling about forty thousand dollars.

Clark was down to the one wagon with the gold. Finding Semple, he delivered some eighty-six thousand dollars in gold coin and bullion. Now that they could determine the size and weight of what they would be transporting, Semple and Tidball finished construction of the hidden compartment, after which the gold was placed inside and covered with the false floor. The horse they hitched up to the carriage may have belonged to Tidball; he had brought extra horses with him. One he gave that day to Wood before he left town.[8] He may have had one other that he would ride, while Semple drove the carriage. Given the load—no more than two men and a little over three hundred pounds of gold—one horse was all that was needed for the carriage.

Finally ready to go, Semple and Tidball stowed their baggage and headed out of town. The gold coins and bullion they secretly carried would be valued at more than two million dollars today.

The Confederate treasury was now mostly disbursed. All that was left was the Liverpool Acceptances held by Reagan, an amount of gold still in Clark's possession, a keg of pennies, thirty-five thousand dollars in gold sovereigns with the president's baggage, and a mass of Confederate currency and bonds, which Breckinridge and Reagan authorized Clark to destroy. Not long afterward, the nighttime sky was lit by the burning of millions of dollars (face value) in Confederate money.

By 11:00 p.m. all the financial transactions had been completed, Semple and Tidball were on their way, and the paper money had been destroyed. Reagan and Clark left Washington, escorted by a few of Duke's men, who also acted as guides. After several miles, the guides were dismissed so they could go home, and riding through the night, the two men came upon Davis's camp at sunrise. The president was probably mildly surprised to see them so soon. He had chosen a secluded, "miserable, out of the way place" near the hamlet of Sandersville, Georgia, according to Tench Tilghman, one of the Marylanders guarding the wagons.[9]

While Reagan and Clark wended their way in the dark along the route taken by Davis, Breckinridge was finishing up affairs in Washington so he could get out of town before Yankee cavalry rode in. He had moved into the room in the Robertson home previously occupied by the president, though he would need it only for a matter of a few hours. In those hours, he disbanded the War Department, ordering the bureau heads to rejoin him in the West, if and when he called on them.

Breckinridge also ordered that any public property be disposed of either by directly providing it to Confederate soldiers or by turning it over to Union authorities to aid the men who had formerly served in the Confederate ranks. Covered by the order were the funds given to Moses. The major left ten thousand dollars with the Quartermaster Department in Washington and took the remaining thirty thousand dollars to Gen. Edward L. Molineaux, commanding the Union garrison in Augusta. With the Yankees entering Washington on May 5, the next day, and confiscating all public property, almost certainly none of the bullion was used to assist Confederate soldiers. And though Molineaux promised to use the funds to feed them as they returned or passed through—as well as the sick and injured in the local hospitals—probably very little of the specie was used for that purpose either.

With the president headed south, Breckinridge's intention had been to have the remaining troops in Ferguson's and Duke's brigades ride westward to decoy Yankee scouts seeking the presidential party. Now, late at night, discipline broke down completely with Ferguson's men, and the secretary of war had to put his plan into action with around 350 volunteers from Duke's brigade and some 50 men from William C. P. Breckinridge's brigade.

The two groups were large enough, however, to attract attention as they traveled slowly along two separate roads toward Woodstock, Georgia. Eventually, they would be confronted by a superior Union force that would block them from continuing. When that happened, the men were to surrender and ask for their paroles. Hopefully, by then, Davis would have had enough time to slip farther south. The plan was for Breckinridge and his sons to melt into the woods and attempt to catch up with the president. The secretary of war did not intend to be arrested. Instead, after seeing the president to the relative safety of a boat and sending his sons back home, Breckinridge would leave the country himself. As events turned out, Breckinridge would not return to the United States for almost four years.

What Breckinridge could not know is that, at Sandersville, Davis revised his plans somewhat. Perhaps he was finally ready to move as quickly as he could to escape the net closing around him, or he could have been nervous about Varina, now that the roads were filled with riffraff—Union and Confederate—in addition to the men who had honorably served the cause and were now anxious to get home to their families. In any case, he decided to pare his party down again by sending the slow-moving wagons off under Clark on a more westerly route to Madison, Florida, while he continued his path southward, toward the Florida border. The wagons would still be guarded by the small group of men under Van Benthuysen.

Before departing from Davis, Clark made a few disbursements from the gold he still had in his possession. He provided $1,500 in expense funds and $10 in pocket money to each of the president's aides—William Preston Johnston, Francis R. Lubbock, Charles E. Thorburn, and John Taylor Wood—stipulating that whatever was not used for boats and supplies should remain Confederate property for a later accounting. Reagan, already weighed down with a money belt containing some of his own funds, was persuaded to carry $3,500 in his saddle bags; Given Campbell received $300 in gold for services he and his men were rendering as guides and couriers. These payments reduced the amount of gold carried with the president's baggage to $25,720. Davis refused to take any coin for his own use.[10]

While neither knew where the other was, Varina was, in fact, not that far ahead of the president and was following roughly the same route toward Florida. After leaving Washington, her caravan traveled for about ten miles that day, camping at night in a remote location. The ground seemed exceptionally hard to Varina for sleeping and the night exceptionally dark. The second night out, the party camped in a pine grove, where they were warned that an attempt would be made during the night to steal their horses and wagons. The situation was defused, however, when Capt. George Vernon Moody in Varina's party learned that the leader of the potential attackers was a fellow Freemason.

Two or three nights later, another attack was anticipated. During the day, one of the party on horseback lagged behind the wagon train by a couple of miles. His horse was stolen at gunpoint, and he had to run ahead to warn Burton Harrison that the horses and mules were at risk. Pulling off on a side road and reaching higher and open ground, Harrison chained the wagons in a circle, with the animals enclosed inside. There they waited, as prepared as they could be. Soon they heard the soft tread of horses slowly approaching. Varina crouched quietly, gripping the pistol her husband had given her the night she left Richmond.

AS THE Davis party rode deeper into Georgia, his aides finally persuaded him to agree to change his identity, though he declined to wear a disguise.

To those who asked, he was now a Confederate congressman from Texas, while Reagan was a Texas judge (not much of a stretch for him since he had been such ten years prior).

While camping alongside the Oconee River, William Preston Johnston overheard a conversation about a wagon train that passed through the area hours earlier, trailed at a distance by former Confederate soldiers who intended to rob it at night. Alarmed that it might be Varina's caravan, Davis immediately saddled up without any thought as to his own safety or what he might do when he reached her, if he reached her and if it were she. "I'll probably be captured or killed for this," he remarked in his haste to leave. "I don't feel that you're bound to go with me, but I must protect my family."[11]

Without hesitation, the others, including the escort, quickly mounted and joined the president. After riding hard for several hours, Given Campbell reported that his men's horses were too tired to continue. While he and the ten Kentuckians stopped to rest them until morning, Reagan, Davis's four aides, and the president's servant Robert Brown pushed on, with Davis trying one road and another as he raced through the night at a pace that belied his age. Shortly before sunrise, several men were encountered walking along the road and carrying bridles. They said they were from the Thirty-sixth Alabama and admitted they knew of wagons nearby with women and children. Johnston was convinced these were the men he had heard about back at the Oconee.

Near dawn, dim figures emerged from a grove, and Burton Harrison stepped into the middle of the road. He called out, "Halt," from the gloom that still enveloped the wagons and demanded to know who was there. The horsemen reined in, and the man in front replied, "Friends," in a familiar voice. The exhausted president had found his family.

There was no attack; the Alabamians had been possibly discouraged by the reinforcement that appeared in the form of Davis and his men. After the president rested for a while, the caravan resumed its journey, with Davis and his men riding alongside the wagons and camping with Varina's party that night. Staying together, though, was much too dangerous, and after breakfast the next morning, Davis moved on with his men, leaving Varina and Harrison with their "wagons and encumbrances."

That night, riding through a pouring rain, the president found a deserted house on the outskirts south of Abbeville, Georgia, where he spent the night. The people in the village were not aware of his presence. Varina, in the meantime, arrived at the Ocmulgee River a few miles behind Davis. Crossing on a ferry, her group set up camp on the western bank as night fell.

In the middle of the night, Burton Harrison was awakened by a courier sent by Davis, who somehow learned that the enemy was reported to be near Hawkinsville, about twenty-five miles to the north. Though the Yankees there were apparently interested in confiscating supplies, Harrison decided that Varina's party should move on, despite thunder and lightning and a driving rain. Passing through Abbeville, Harrison caught up to Davis at the abandoned house, finding the president resting on the floor and wrapped in a blanket.

Davis urged Harrison to continue on and indicated that he would meet up with them as soon as his horses had rested. With the rain still coming down in torrents, Varina's party wound through a forest of tall pine trees, the night so pitch black, the drivers found their way along the road and around fallen trees by waiting for lightning flashes.

In the midst of the storm, Davis and his men appeared, and the combined parties rode together all day, stopping in the late afternoon in a grove of pine trees with a creek for water about a mile north of Irwinville. The grove was off the road somewhat, and behind the wooded patch was a marsh. There would be no fear of the enemy coming upon them from that direction. The mules pulling the wagons were worn out, but as the parties were now roughly fifty miles south of Hawksinville, Davis believed they were probably safe for the night. While the camp was being set up, William Preston Johnston rode into the village to buy eggs.

As Davis and his staff advanced closer to the Florida border, John Taylor Wood and Charles E. Thorburn thought the time was right to share with Davis a plan they had conceived as far back as Greensboro. For a period during the war, Thorburn had captained a blockade-runner, bringing goods and war supplies into the Confederacy via such ports as St. George, Nassau, and Havana, his holds filled with cotton. Since officers on blockade-runners were considered pirates by the Union navy, Thorburn was not sure if or when he might need to flee the country. For that reason, he kept a "small, but seaworthy vessel" hidden on the Indian River on the east coast of Florida. Their plan, which must have been discussed with Johnston and Breckinridge as well, was to use the boat to convey the president around the peninsula and across the Gulf of Mexico to Matamoras. From there, Davis could then make

his way to Texas. Now that the group had reached Irwinville, Davis authorized Thorburn to ride ahead to make arrangements and then meet him at
Madison, Florida. Since the president had sent his baggage and the gold to
Madison in the care of Micajah Clark, he likely had known about Thorburn's
boat before he left Washington.

But the plan was doomed to failure for at least two reasons. First, almost 250 miles separated Madison from the Indian River at Titusville.
While much of the state they would be crossing was lowland and sparsely
populated, there would be a constant danger of encountering Union cavalry
intent on tracking down the president and his "plunder," now claimed by
Secretary of War Stanton to be "between $6,000,000 and $13,000,000 in
specie."[12] The closer Davis was to the Indian River, the greater the danger,
and with Union vessels patrolling the coastline, the chance of sailing around
the peninsula and across the Gulf to Matamoras was, at best, slight.

The second problem was that, unbeknownst to Davis, Varina's wagons
had been noticed passing through Abbeville. With Union troops in Georgia
on full alert, Lt. Col. Benjamin D. Pritchard, commander of the Fourth
Michigan Cavalry, an element of Wilson's cavalry corps, was in full pursuit
along the road from Hawkinsville to Irwinville that paralleled the route
taken by the Davis parties.

Meanwhile, Harrison and the staff were pressing Davis to ride on immediately. The wagons were slowing him down, and he still had sixty-five
miles to go to get to the Florida border. Though the site chosen by Harrison
was somewhat hidden from the road by thickets, the campfire was easily
seen as soon as darkness fell. Davis gave his word that he would leave after
supper. Harrison, suffering for days from dysentery, fell into a sound sleep
after eating and forgot to post any guards. With Campbell and his scouts
riding ahead to check for a river crossing, the Confederate president's camp
was completely unprotected.

When William Preston Johnston returned from Irwinville with the
eggs, he reported that the camp had been seen and there were rumors of an
attack on the caravan during the night. It was familiar threat, but one that
could not be ignored, and Davis decided to delay his departure a while.
There was no way he could leave Varina and the children susceptible to assault. He would wait to see if the marauders showed up, hoping, if they
were Confederate soldiers, he might be able to convince them not to molest
the camp. With his horse saddled and tethered to a tree and his pistols

nearby, Davis decided to rest for a bit. He lay down fully clothed on a cot in his wife's tent and was soon asleep. John Reagan and the presidential aides sat around a campfire for a time, waiting for Davis, ready to leave. Soon, they succumbed as well, and by midnight the camp was quiet and a light drizzle reduced the fire to embers. And Given Campbell and his men had not yet returned.

Around 1:00 a.m. on May 10, Pritchard arrived in Irwinville with 136 troopers.

Before dawn, Charles E. Thorburn woke, dressed, and rode out of camp with a servant. He soon blundered into Pritchard's men but managed to escape after shooting the lead pursuer. On fresh horses, the Confederate fugitives easily outdistanced the Yankees in the early morning darkness.[13] Learning from a villager where the Davis party was camped, Pritchard moved slowly and silently into position, within a hundred yards of the wagons, and waited for sufficient light to attack.

Around the same time, the First Wisconsin Cavalry under Col. Henry Harden, which had been following the road south from Abbeville, deployed around the camp and also waited for morning. Apparently, neither Union group knew the other was there, so as each advanced toward the camp in the low light of an overcast dawn, the two commands fired on each other.

The gunfire just outside the camp immediately alerted Davis's servant James Jones, who was rebuilding the fire to boil water for washing the baby's diapers. Jones rushed to wake Harrison, Moody, James Taylor Wood, and William Preston Johnston before moving on Davis's tent.

As Harrison sprang to his feet and grabbed his revolver, he saw Pritchard and his horsemen charging up the road from Irwinville. There was not much he could do. The camp would be overrun, and killing or wounding any Yankee soldiers would only add to the Confederate party's problems. The "din of battle" was thus restricted to the clash between the two Union cavalry regiments.

Despite the confusion caused by the rifle fire (which ended only after one of the regiments captured a trooper from the other), yelling soldiers, and horses racing through the camp, Davis had no chance to escape, although Wood urged him to try. While Varina attempted to distract one of the guards placed by her tent, the president threw a waterproof cloth over his shoulders—which by mistake was Varina's—and began to walk into the woods. He was quickly followed by Varina's maid Helen, who was carrying a bucket to give the appearance they were going for water. The subterfuge failed, and Davis was soon ordered back by a Union soldier, who leveled his carbine and threatened to shoot him if he did not immediately obey. As he turned, Varina became hysterical and ran to her husband to keep him from charging at the trooper and possibly being shot. According to Wood, by throwing her arms around him, Varina also ended any possibility of escape. "Mrs. Davis by her appeals—the children by their crying, the servants by fear and howling destroyed all," he said.[14] Within minutes, Davis was recognized. The chase was over.

After the "battle" with the First Wisconsin ended, in which two men from the Fourth Michigan were killed, Pritchard's soldiers returned to the camp and began to search the prisoners and the wagons, no doubt motivated by the possibility of finding the much-sought-after treasury. Taken from Reagan was the fifty-five hundred dollars in gold he was carrying plus the Liverpool Acceptances. While Johnston lost his fifteen hundred dollars in gold, he was robbed of something much more valuable to him: the pistols his father—Gen. Albert Sidney Johnston—was wearing when he was killed in April 1862 at Shiloh. Harrison had an amount of gold taken as well, but he managed to dump some official papers unnoticed into the campfire. Francis R. Lubbock, somehow, because of his stubborn resistance, was able to hold on to his saddlebags containing his fifteen hundred dollars in gold but lost a gold watch, fifty dollars in gold he had in his pocket, and his horse.

John Taylor Wood was the most fortunate. As the plundering reached its peak, with Union cavalrymen swarming over the wagons and the baggage, throwing clothing around and stripping the gold and jewelry from the prisoners, Wood picked out a trooper he thought he could bribe, a German who spoke little English. Pointing to the creek, Wood held out a twenty-dollar gold coin. Grasping the meaning, the soldier escorted his prisoner to the edge of the swamp, supposedly so Wood could relieve himself. Once there, Wood motioned for the guard to go back, but he refused to do it until Wood had given him another twenty-dollar gold piece and turned his pockets inside out to show him that was all he had. Now alone, Wood moved deeper into the swamp. Though he had lost his horse and personal belongings and had to crouch in a cramped position in the swamp for three hours, the resourceful and quick-thinking colonel regained his freedom.

After a time, bugles sounded and the Union cavalrymen fell into formation. Slowly, the wagons with Varina and her children and the rest of her party moved off. Following behind on horseback and closely escorted by guards were Davis and his staff (minus Wood) and the last remaining member of his cabinet, Postmaster General and Secretary of the Treasury John Reagan.

As Wood was about to leave his hiding spot, he noticed Capt. Stephen Barnwell leading a couple of horses out of the camp. Barnwell, an artillery officer, had been traveling in Varina's party, and he had managed to escape into the brush with the horses when Pritchard's troops appeared. Picking through the debris left behind, Wood found a small derringer that belonged to Johnston, which he pocketed. They were also able to fashion two saddles and bridles out of remnants of both, though the horses were too decrepit to be ridden much. In fact, Wood and Barnwell found themselves mostly on foot, driving the horses ahead of them.

Bedraggled and with animals nobody would steal, the two men made themselves out to be paroled soldiers on their way home and had little fear of being accosted, though Wood kept a wary eye out for Pritchard. Most probably, the Union commander was well on his way to Macon to deliver Davis to Wilson and was giving little thought to the whereabouts of lesser "Rebels"—at least for now. But that would soon change.

About twenty miles south of Irwinville, Judah P. Benjamin hailed Wood and Barnwell. Wearing goggles with a hat pulled down over his face and allowing his beard to grow for about a week, the former secretary of state was difficult to recognize—even for Wood. With a much better horse to pull his carriage than the unfit animals of the two "paroled" soldiers, Benjamin was intent on getting to Madison, where Yankees had not yet appeared and he had friends who could help him escape. Wood and Benjamin decided to go by separate ways but to meet up in Madison. There they would decide what to do next.

By May 13, Wood and Barnwell had reached the town of Valdosta, some seventy miles from Irwinville. Osborne Barnwell, the captain's uncle, lived in a large log cabin outside of town, and Wood was happy to have the opportunity to rest for a couple of days without concern for being seen and captured. He even had enough confidence in his safety to venture into town to purchase much-needed "hickory shirts" and socks. Remembering that Benjamin could be waiting for him, Wood left the Barnwells on May 15, fortunately riding a better mount.

On May 25, Pritchard filed his report on Davis's capture at Irwinville. In addition to Davis and his wife and four children, the other captives were

John Reagan, William Preston Johnston, Burton Harrison, a major named Maurin, Capt. George Vernon Moody, a lieutenant named Hathaway, Jefferson Howell, Maggie Howell, and several servants. Among the materiel seized were five wagons and three ambulances, along with fifteen horses and twenty-five to thirty mules.

WITH THE capture of Jefferson Davis, his family, and most of his advisers, and with a number of the former cabinet members—namely George Davis, Stephen R. Mallory, and George A. Trenholm—about to be rounded up, only four men who had played essential roles in extending the life of the Confederacy eluded capture: Judah P. Benjamin, John C. Breckinridge, John Taylor Wood, and James A. Semple. All four would be arrested if they were caught. Benjamin and Breckinridge were cabinet officers, and in the case of Benjamin, there was his added role as head of the Confederate Secret Service. Wood was wanted for his exploits in seizing and destroying Union shipping on the high seas. Semple, if he were captured, would probably not receive an extensive prison sentence for being a bureau head. His shepherding of the gold from the treasury, on the other hand, and his attempts to transport it out of the country made him very much a wanted man. Quite possibly, Union authorities had already been told who last had possession of the coins and bullion. In any case, his concerns about being captured were real and were justified by known attempts to find him.

After leaving the president south of the Savannah River on May 4, Benjamin had used his nom de plume as a French journalist, Monsieur Bonfals (which translates as "Mr. Good Disguise"), to reach Florida. He passed through Madison but was too nervous to wait for Wood because of reports of Union soldiers in the area. Though he originally planned to try for the east coast, he decided to head for the Gulf coast.

On entering Florida, Benjamin also changed his disguise and presented himself as a farmer named Howard, looking for some land on which to settle. To authenticate his disguise, he had a farmer's wife make him some homespun clothes "just like her husband's." With the help of a Confederate underground, Benjamin arrived at the prestigious former home of Maj. Robert Gamble in Ellenton, on the Manatee River. While staying there, he had to hide in a canebrake twice as Union troops searched the area and the mansion for him and other Confederate leaders. Eventually, he reached

Sarasota Bay and boarded a boat to Knight's Key, which was owned by former blockade-runner Frederick Tresca.

From the Keys, Benjamin sailed to Bimini and took passage on a small sloop to Nassau. His troubles, though, were not over. The next day, the boat sank thirty miles from land, leaving him and other passengers just enough time to jump into a leaky skiff with a single oar. Fortunately, they were seen and rescued late that afternoon by a lighthouse-inspection ship, and he returned to Bimini. A second try on another sloop was successful, and six days later, Benjamin arrived in Nassau, where he boarded a schooner to Havana. From there, he reached St. Thomas in the Virgin Islands and took passage on the steamer *Seine* to Southampton, England. While he was probably congratulating himself on his successful escape, a fire was discovered in the hold of the steamer some sixty miles offshore. With the crew managing to contain the flames long enough by pumping water into the hold, the boat returned to St. Thomas.

Benjamin finally arrived in Southampton on August 30, 1865, about four months from the time he parted ways with Jefferson Davis. After arranging for a portion of Davis's salary to be paid to Varina by a third party, Benjamin almost never talked or wrote about his years in the Confederate government and never returned to the United States. He became a distinguished member of the British bar in 1866, and he was elected in 1872 to the Queen's Counsel.

WITH THE surrender of the brigades deployed to Woodstock to decoy the Yankees away from Davis, John C. Breckinridge followed his plan of escape: melting into the woods with his small band of followers. To disguise himself, Breckinridge merely cut short his highly recognizable drooping mustache and assumed the alias of "Colonel Cabell," based on his middle name. Riding south, the secretary of war hoped to meet up with the president at Madison (which is where Davis was supposed to unite with Micajah Clark).

In the group initially were Breckinridge's sons, Cabell and Clifton, cousin William C. P. Breckinridge, Basil Duke, Lt. James B. Clay Jr. (Henry Clay's grandson), and a few others. The number was reduced by two when Duke and William C. P. Breckinridge decided they could do nothing more for Davis and left to seek paroles so they could return to Kentucky. Much to twelve-year-old Clifton's and James Clay's disappointment, Breckinridge sent them to a friend living at Fort Valley, Georgia, near Macon. The secretary of war hoped that the boys could stay there until the turmoil subsided and the roads were less crowded with soldiers. Then the boys could find their way back to Kentucky without risking as much to the dangers of the journey.[15]

Continuing south and around Hawkinsville after being warned of Yankee cavalry in the town, Breckinridge had no way of knowing how close he was to Davis and how close Davis was to being captured. At one point, with elements of Pritchard's cavalry pushing down the road toward Irwinville, Breckinridge apparently advanced toward Davis's camp with Yankees in front of him and behind him, but neither he nor the enemy were aware of the other's presence.

On May 14, Breckinridge learned of Davis's capture. He dismissed his small escort and rode on with just his son Cabell, Lt. Col. James Wilson, and Tom Ferguson. Finally reaching Madison, he was surprised to find John Taylor Wood at the home of Brig. Gen. Joseph J. Finegan. The general formerly commanded the Confederate troops in Florida and had been recently paroled. Wood provided Breckinridge with details concerning the president's capture and his own bold escape from Pritchard.

Both Breckinridge and Wood were wanted men and, if caught, would spend time in prison. As Breckinridge was the highest-ranking government official and military officer left in what remained of the Confederacy, the focus—and resources—of any Federal manhunt would now shift from the president to him. Wood, who had been branded a pirate for commanding the Confederate raider *Tallahassee,* also faced serious charges and could even be hanged. They now needed to think of themselves, and that meant finding a way to get out of the country. They would join forces, but first Breckinridge would send his son home, because he was allergic to mosquito bites, and they were certain to encounter the pests through the marshy Florida lowlands.

The initial decision had to be which Florida coast they believed they could find safe passage from: east or west. Wood favored sailing from the east coast to the Bahamas, and because he was an experienced seaman, Breckinridge deferred to his judgment. Reaching Gainesville on May 18, they met the next morning with Confederate Congressman James B. Dawkins, who introduced them to Capt. J. J. Dickison, known as the "Francis Marion of Florida" because of his intimate knowledge of the area. Dickison confirmed for them that they would be safer leaving from the east coast because of the greater difficulty the Union navy had in patrolling both the coastline and the inland waterway. Also, in the St. Johns River, Dickison had a seventeen-foot boat with a small sail hidden, though it needed to be raised and repaired. During the war, Dickison had captured the Union gunboat *Columbine* and had saved one of the lifeboats.

Wood took a side excursion to search for Benjamin, while Dickison saw to the repair of the boat. On his return, not having found Benjamin, Wood rode with Breckinridge and the rest of the party twenty-four miles south to Millwood Plantation, where they were guided to the boat at Fort Butler on the St. Johns River.

With the help of three former Confederates from Dickison's command to row and help with the sail, and after loading provisions, firearms, and camping equipment, the party made its way downriver to a point where it had to be hauled by wagon about 28 miles east to the Indian River. There, on the last day of May, they found themselves separated from the Atlantic Ocean by a narrow barrier of sand dunes, which protected the inland water-way from winds and waves and enabled them to travel some 250 miles down the peninsula with relative ease. On June 3, near Jupiter Inlet, they tugged the boat across 150 feet of sand, finally launching it in the ocean.

The day before, unknown to them and perhaps little noticed in sections of the South already overrun with Union soldiers, Lt. Gen. Edmund Kirby Smith formally surrendered the Trans-Mississippi Department. Davis's dream of continuing the war in the West was no longer possible.

Hugging the coastline, the party encountered a Union navy steamer, which lowered a boat to investigate. With Breckinridge hiding ashore, Wood and two of the crewmen rowed out to meet the boat. Wood played the role of a Florida fisherman who was salvaging items from wrecked ships, and the Yankees allowed him to go on. After overtaking a sloop believed by Wood to be transporting escaped convicts from the Dry Tortugas (Fort Jefferson), Breckinridge and his crew traded the lifeboat for the sloop at gunpoint and sailed through gale winds and rough seas to reach Havana on June 10. All three men—Benjamin, Breckinridge, and Wood—had reached safety over-seas. Of the four former members in the Davis administration being sought by Union authorities, only James A. Semple remained at large on U.S. soil.

9

INTO
THE
NIGHT

Billy slandered, and belied me—and strictly between us I am afraid took
public money, and went to Canada, giving Semple the slip.
—Varina Davis to William Preston Johnston,
October 3, 1865

AMES SEMPLE AND EDWARD TIDBALL rode past the lighted homes of Washington, Georgia, and into the black of night, with the gold coins and bullion secured in the hidden compartment of their carriage. Fortunately, there was enough moonlight to make out the road ahead: a ribbon of gray cutting through fields and the woods that loomed around them. Given only a matter of hours to figure out how to transport the gold and where to take it, Semple had settled on Augusta as their initial destination and Savannah as the port from which he would try to ship the gold out of the country.[1]

Neither John Reagan nor Jefferson Davis had issued specific instructions as to how Semple should transport all that remained of the Confederate treasury out of the country. Charleston, suggested as an alternative port, made less sense than Savannah. It would mean another day on the road, an added day of risking the loss of the horse and carriage—and the gold.

Nassau had been mentioned as a possible destination, but St. George, in Bermuda, was closer to Savannah and might be a better choice. The Confederacy still had agents in both places (as well as in Havana, Cuba). The problem was that any ship traveling between Savannah and Bermuda would be closely watched and probably carefully inspected in port. Yet the vessel had to be seaworthy and capable of handling the rough seas, strong currents, and high winds that frequented the coastal waters.

A commercial steamer with a cargo hold would be a better choice than a sailboat hidden in a marsh or a stream somewhere along the coastline. The ship would be safer, and the boxes of gold could perhaps be obscured among bales of cotton and other exports. Semple would need to see, if possible, what was in port and where it was going. The difficulty would be in transferring the boxes of specie—still with the markings of the Confederate government—from the carriage to the hold of a ship under the noses of Yankee guards ordered to be suspicious about everyone and everything leaving port. In all probability, he would need to repack the gold in innocent-looking trunks and then hope the trunks were not singled out for inspection.

On the road, Semple and Tidball had less to fear from the Union army than from paroled Confederate soldiers, deserters, and those who walked away rather than surrender at the end. The Yankees already had better horseflesh and little reason to confiscate a carriage. Thousands of the demoralized and ragged former soldiers of the Confederate armies, however, were on foot. Many were asking for help along the way, desperate for food and clothing, and needing a means to get home. Others were simply taking whatever they wanted, occasionally at the point of the sidearms they had been allowed to keep.

Semple took some comfort in the fact that Tidball was with him. They knew each other well. Both had reported to Mallory and worked in the same building. Traveling together would reduce the tension and physical strain of the almost sixty-mile ride. They realized they were headed directly into the lion's den, because Augusta would soon be under Union control, if it was not already, and they had no idea what to expect. Most likely, though, Semple was not overly concerned. Self-confident and coolheaded, he was counting on the fact that no Yankee would ever expect an official of the Confederate government to ride into the midst of a Union garrison with a cache of gold. The faith that he had in his own abilities would serve him well in the coming months.

The main road to Augusta ran through the towns of Aonia and Appling, but Semple likely chose back roads through the hamlets of Wrightsboro and White Oak Post Office. That way, he and Tidball would encounter few travelers—and almost certainly no Union cavalry—that night. The condition of the roads, though, was poor, and the subdued light of the half moon gave them little opportunity to avoid potholes and dried ruts. It would take them until well after sunrise to reach the outskirts of Augusta.

While Savannah was where Semple hoped to arrange shipment of the gold to an intermediate port, and from there to Liverpool, he had a particular reason for stopping first in Augusta. William F. Howell had been a civilian naval agent who had worked for Semple's predecessor, John DeBree. When the war began, Howell had served as a second lieutenant in a Louisiana infantry company before resigning to become a commissary agent. Somehow he managed to gain the title of captain, a rank that stuck with him after the war. In April 1864, when Semple took over DeBree's position at the Navy Department as chief of the Bureau of Provisions and Clothing, he inherited Howell and expanded his responsibilities. Semple was well aware of Howell's resourcefulness, because he had been assisting, advising, and bolstering DeBree for several months.

Howell had originally been stationed in New Orleans, and then the city fell into Union hands in April 1862, and Howell moved briefly to Montgomery, Alabama, before ending up in Augusta in the summer of 1863. There he developed a supply network for collecting fruits and vegetables from farmers in Alabama, Georgia, and the Carolinas and then having them dried and processed. Dried peas and beans were a common staple in the diet of Confederate seamen, while fresh fruits and vegetables were luxuries because of spoilage. Whatever was provided for fresh produce typically came from paymasters local to naval installations and ships in harbors.[2]

Howell collected wheat from the same states and shipped it by rail to private mills for grinding. Facilities in Augusta, Columbus, and Montgomery were employed for baking bread. Supplies of sugar, tea, and coffee were also warehoused, and Howell arranged for purchases of large quantities of beef and salt. To reduce costs, ensure availability, and optimize the preservation of the meat, he also purchased carloads of live hogs and saw to the butchering, curing, and packaging.

In meeting the provision needs of the Confederate navy, Howell's most effective negotiating tool was bartering. He traded molasses, flour, and textile goods—which he had little difficulty in obtaining until the last months of the war—for bacon, beef, and pork. His biggest problem was his competition—the Confederate army, which had priority over all sources of supply. In one instance, after Howell had contracted with a South Carolina mill for yarn and cloth, the materials were seized by the army's quartermaster general. Howell was told he could purchase shirts and pants at cost, but he wanted the fabric, not the finished goods, so he could use it to barter for food.

Most of the fabric obtained by the navy, other than what Howell bartered away, ended up at cutting operations in Mobile, Richmond, and Savannah. Ultimately, with the army appropriating whatever came out of Southern textile mills, the navy was forced to bid at auctions for fabric brought in by blockade-runners primarily from Havana.

Shoes in the Confederate navy lasted longer than they did on the feet of soldiers constantly on the march, but eventually they also wore out, even on ships, and supplies were extremely scarce. Howell's most notable accomplishment for improving the comfort of navy personnel may have been his procurement of a British cutting machine for mass producing leather uppers and soles of shoes, enabling him to keep up with the demand. The distillery he set up in Augusta for supplying the navy with whiskey was undoubtedly a close second. In short, Howell had proven himself to be creative and competent. But he was now needed for a different assignment.

Semple knew that the odds were against his being able to get the government gold to Savannah and past the Yankee guards on the wharves. For this reason, he had decided, probably before leaving Washington, that he was better off entrusting a portion of the specie to someone he could depend on to hide and protect it. That way, if the contents of the carriage were confiscated, at least some of the gold would hopefully be safe and available to the government wherever it might reestablish itself.

The obvious choice was Howell, not only because of his talents and accomplishments, but also because he was Varina Davis's brother. Semple was sure that Howell would do whatever he was asked to do to support the president and the Confederate cause. Though riding into the midst of the enemy at Augusta might seem foolhardy, Yankees would soon be encountered in towns and on roads throughout Georgia and the Carolinas. It hardly mattered where he went; meeting up with Howell and unloading some of the gold seemed to be worth the risk. From Augusta, Semple would then continue on to Savannah with the remainder of the specie and see about the possibility of shipping the gold to an offshore port.

As the sun rose on Augusta, Semple and Tidball approached the outskirts of the town. The blue uniforms of Union soldiers could be seen on the streets and onboard a steamer in the Savannah River edging toward the docks. Obstructions had been removed from the river below the town so that Yankee infantry could be transported by boat from Savannah. Augusta had been a busy industrial town when Semple last visited the navy commissary here. Barges filled the canal, trains chugged in and out of the three stations day and night, and the tall chimneys of the mills lining the river spewed black smoke into the sky. He could not have helped but notice the difference.

The town had changed considerably. The sprawling Confederate States Powder Works, which produced more than seven thousand pounds of gunpowder daily, was now closed. Only months ago, it was unsurpassed in output and quality by any other powder mill in the world. Factories that once had housed thousands of spindles for producing thread and hundreds of looms for weaving cotton from the thread were now empty. The Confederate pistol factory was gone, and the Confederate arsenal, as well as the government foundry, were in Union hands. Twelve-pound Napoleon cannons and other artillery pieces abandoned in the foundry yard were a stark reminder of what had been an immense production facility for the Confederacy. Something else was missing. The smell of baking bread no longer permeated the streets along the canal.

In recent days, the army quartermaster store on Broad Street had been looted by a mob bent on getting to the supplies before the Yankees took over. Howell's warehouse of provisions, however, had been saved by a citizen guard, which fired into the crowd. On the same day that Semple entered the town, Union Bvt. Maj. Gen. Edward L. Molineaux and additional troops appeared, restoring order and setting up a military government. Howell's provisions would be among those distributed to Augustans and Confederate soldiers passing through town.

Semple was undoubtedly anxious to move on, since the town was filling up with Yankee soldiers disembarking at Sand Bar Ferry. After he found Howell, he had little difficulty in convincing the unemployed agent to take responsibility for a portion of the gold. Twenty-five thousand dollars in gold bullion, valued at almost six hundred thousand dollars today, was placed in his care.

Then Semple modified his plans. The gold was divided again. For some reason, Semple decided to send Tidball back to his home in Winchester, Virginia, with a portion of the gold. Possibly, Tidball refused to go any farther and intended to return home anyway. In any case, Semple entrusted him with twenty-seven thousand dollars in gold coins, while he moved on to Savannah with the rest of the coins, amounting to about thirty-four thousand dollars. Perhaps Semple believed that the chances of holding on to the gold were so slim, it should be divided to ensure that at least some of it escaped seizure. In any case, he wanted the rest of the coins with him, as opposed to the bullion. Given the poverty in the South and the desperate straits that most banks were in, gold bullion would be less liquid than coins; whatever Semple would be able to accomplish in terms of transporting his portion to safety, he would still need access to the funds in order to take care of myriad expenses. Paying for anything—food, hotel rooms, fees for river crossings, passage on a steamer, etc.—with nuggets or ingots would be considerably more difficult than a twenty-dollar coin. Semple assumed that Howell had a secure hiding place, and the bullion could remain with him until Semple would return that way in a few months, after the turmoil had subsided and the city had returned to some degree of normalcy.

One thing was clear, the majority of the gold would never make it out of the country and probably would never be used for the purposes intended by the president. Perhaps it could be used to help the South in another way. Semple decided to continue to Savannah anyway to weigh his chances of shipping the gold in his care to St. George or Nassau. He still had in the bottom of the carriage a substantial portion of the treasury, which would be valued at almost eight hundred thousand dollars today.

How Tidball carried the gold back to Virginia is unknown. He could have obtained a carriage or a small wagon and somehow concealed the specie. He could have even carried the coins in saddlebags. What is known is that he arrived in Winchester with the gold.

In returning to Washington, Georgia, Tidball had to pass through a large contingent of Yankee cavalry on its way to Augusta, but he managed not to attract their attention. Back in Washington, he met with Judge William Wood Crump, who was also ready to return to the Old Dominion, since he no longer had any authority over the Virginia banks' funds. Though the bank funds had been confiscated by Union troops, they remained as yet untouched in the vault of the old bank building. Before leav-

ing town, Crump convinced Union Capt. Lot Abraham of the Fourth Illinois Cavalry, commander of the local garrison, to release the specie to the
bank tellers and allow it to be transported, under guard, back to the Richmond banks.[3]

Crump decided that his official papers might not be safe on the road,
and asked Judge Garnett Andrews to hold on to them until he could return
to pick them up. He then joined Tidball, and around noon on May 8, the
two men rode north, out of Washington, along with Capt. Henry Irwin,
who was returning to his wife and home in Norfolk. Since they had no
money, Irwin and Crump filled their saddlebags with food donated by Andrews plus letters of introduction from Andrews to friends along the way
who might be of help. Very likely, neither knew that Tidball carried a hundred pounds of gold.

In returning to Winchester and his wife, Helen, Tidball turned his interests to agriculture. On August 29, 1865, he sought and received a full
pardon from the Federal government. Two years later, he purchased a tract
of land on which he built Linden farm. The property was valued at thirty-
one thousand dollars in 1870, which meant it was an expensive piece of
property for the time. Though the town of Winchester had been overrun by
Confederate and Union armies, exchanging hands some seventy times, and
despite the hard times experienced by his neighbors, Tidball evidently survived the war without financial difficulty.[4]

For Semple, both the present and the future were much less certain. He
had no home to return to and no profession to resume in earning a living.
After he and Letitia were married, they had lived at Cedar Hill for four
years, but he had sold it after receiving his commission as a navy purser.[5] He
had been a career navy man; his home had mostly been a ship, and he had
very little experience in any particular business or trade. Farming was a possibility, but his short tenure as a planter and slaveholder during those four
years provided him with little actual experience in raising crops. The farm
had been run by a manager. Most people working the land in the South
were dirt poor, and that was not about to change with the end of the war.
Many would be forced to sell what they owned for a price considerably less
than their property was worth before the war.

Semple probably wondered about the condition of Sherwood Forest. He
knew that Julia Tyler would be weighing whether she should sell the plantation. For a long time, he had been able to check on it through neighbors,

even when the Union army had settled in the area. The last he knew, the field hands had scattered, and the fences and outbuildings had been pretty much destroyed. The main house, however, was intact, though it had been stripped of everything of value and squatters were living in it at the time. Unfortunately, there was little he could do to help her in his present situation, but if Alex and Gardie had made it safely through the last days of the war, they could at least visit the property and see what needed to be done.

As Semple made his way toward Savannah, a ride that would take him through the night, his thoughts no doubt turned to Julia and how much her family had come to mean to him. They represented warmth and contentment, a "happy home & cheerful fireside," as he would write to her in a future letter.[6] He knew he could not go back to Letitia. The bitterness between them would never subside. During John Tyler's presidency, Semple's father-in-law had realized that the union was in trouble, which had to be why he ensured that Semple spent most of his married years at sea or overseas. Unfortunately, the prestige of the Tyler family extended to name and reputation only. Letitia was without funds. Semple would continue to support her to the extent he could, and while he would encourage her to resume her own name (Tyler), he knew that, despite their acrimony, there would be no divorce. She had too much to lose. They would simply live separate lives.

For now, Semple had to stay focused on what he was doing and on keeping his wits about him when he ran into what for him was still the enemy. Following the main route through the villages of McBean and Springfield meant a ride of more than a hundred miles along a road at times clogged with refugees, Union and Confederate soldiers, and Northerners already attracted by the spoils of war and defeat. The confluence of people, animals, and vehicles was actually a benefit for Semple, as a carriage pulled by a horse was likely to be unnoticed in the midst of the distractions caused by cursing teamsters, baying mules, and jostling wagons in the road. Still, Semple had to be careful to avoid being stopped for he had no parole papers. He decided to assume the name Allen S. James, which he later claimed to Julia had been granted to him legally by the Alabama legislature.[7]

Semple had not seen Savannah for months. The city bore the rundown effects of war and the blockade, but it was intact. Unwilling to surrender his troops, Confederate Gen. William J. Hardee had left the city and fled north to join P. G. T. Beauregard on December 20, 1864, with about ten thousand men, allowing William T. Sherman's army to enter Savannah unmolested the next day. The result had been twofold. Ultimately of little consequence, Hardee had been able to add his troops to those of Johnston in opposing Sherman when the Union commander began his sweep through the Carolinas. A more notable and lasting benefit was the fact that the city had escaped being shelled by Union artillery or being burned to the ground.

By the time Semple reached the end of East or West Broad Street, either of which would take him down to the waterfront, he realized the impossibility of what he had hoped to accomplish. The city, especially the dock area, was heavily guarded by soldiers in blue. Bay and Canal streets were teeming with wagons and drays queuing up to the various wharves to unload bales of cotton and hogsheads of tobacco destined for points north and overseas, depending on the ship. Other wagons were hauling goods from the ships to the railroad stations, to warehouses, and to businesses. The noise and the chaotic atmosphere belied the close attention being given by clusters of guards watching both the gangplanks and the goods being lifted by stevedores into the holds of ships. Bills of lading were being checked carefully while boxes and trunks were occasionally opened for inspection.

There was no way Semple could arrange shipment of the gold. As a matter of fact, sitting on more than 123 pounds of gold (about 90 pounds had been left with Howell and 100 pounds with Tidball), and with Union guards scrutinizing everyone and everything, Semple must have felt at least a twinge of nervousness. In any case, he had to do something else with the gold; he could no longer continue to drive around the countryside with it in his carriage. He had to store most of it somewhere, and certainly a bank would not do. Deposits and withdrawals were surely being watched and monitored, and thirty-four thousand dollars in gold coins would attract the attention of any employee, even if smaller amounts were deposited in two or three financial institutions in the city. There could not be that many people in Savannah who were fortunate enough to survive the war with a substantial amount of gold in hand to deposit in the banks now that the conflict had concluded. Questioning by military authorities (if the depositor could be found) and frozen assets would be a strong possibility.

Fortunately, Semple had friends in Savannah, people he had known for years and could trust. While the names of these friends have not been revealed, except verbally to Julia, the gold was known to have been left with them and stored in places where he could access the funds when he needed money—which he would, from time to time. He undoubtedly traded the carriage for saddle and tack, purchased supplies, and rode out of Savannah with a quantity of gold coins on him and stored in his saddlebags.

The odyssey of James Semple becomes somewhat vague for a few months, since he essentially went underground as Allen S. James, convinced that he was being sought as a wanted fugitive. Unlike Tidball, he would not be allowed to take the oath of allegiance to the United States and be pardoned (not that he wanted to). As chief of the Bureau of Provisions and Clothing in the Confederate Navy Department, which meant that his rank was equivalent to a brigadier general, he was disqualified from seeking a parole.[8] Then, too, he had resigned his U.S. naval commission to join the Confederacy. That also disqualified him from receiving a pardon.

Most important, the Confederate treasury was being looked for in every possible direction from Washington, Georgia, and its worth was escalating daily. Rumors abounded. Private homes and public buildings were searched, and Union cavalry, former Confederate soldiers, and even treasure hunters from the North were combing the countryside. At some point, someone might mention that Semple had conveyed the gold toward the coast in a carriage. Perhaps the modification of his carriage had been observed. In any case, Semple believed, with reason, that the search would eventually center on him, and he needed to maintain a low profile for a while.

He did this very well, and though he apparently had contact by letter with his brothers-in-law—Robert Tyler in Richmond and Montgomery and John Tyler Jr. in Baltimore—the only person who eventually learned the full story of his travels, and the gold, was Julia Gardiner Tyler. What is known is that, from Savannah, he crossed Georgia into Alabama and likely stayed with relatives in Perry County. When questions arose about him in that part of the state, he reversed direction to the east and spent weeks hiding in Okefenokee Swamp in southern Georgia.[9] He must have suffered miserably from the heat, humidity, and insects.

In late July or early August, Semple made his way to the Florida coast and took passage on a boat to Nassau.[10] He was not there long. Apparently short on funds, he arrived back in Savannah to retrieve a supply of the gold coins. After signing in at the Pulaski Hotel under his alias of Allen S. James, he soon learned that Varina Davis had been under house arrest at the hotel since late May, after Jefferson Davis had been captured and transported to Fort Monroe, Virginia. Just recently, she had been allowed to leave Savannah for the home of a friend who was living in Mill View, a few miles outside of Augusta. George Schley and his family had offered to take Varina in for as long as she needed a home. The arrangement was a good one for her, allowing her some privacy, and she occupied comfortable quarters with her family in a small building behind the main house.[11] In the meantime, her three oldest children were en route to Canada in the care of her mother, Margaret Kemp Howell.

In disguise, as he often had been during the months he spent avoiding the Union authorities in the South, and still using the alias of Allen S. James, Semple decided to return to Augusta. There he could check on gold being held by William Howell, and afterward he could ride the few miles to Schley's farm and visit Varina. He had much to tell her.

In Augusta, Semple was in for a surprise: Howell and his wife had fled to Montreal with the gold. They supposedly escorted his mother and Varina's children on their journey.[12] But in Semple's view, Howell's motives had less to do with his family and more to do with the gold. The number of trunks belonging to the three children, the three adult Howells, and Robert Brown, a black servant employed by Varina, must have discouraged close inspection, especially with three young and energetic children accompanying the trunks on the steamer. Most likely, the coins were confined to the Howells' trunks, and no one else knew about them. The gold would tide them over nicely for a while and enable Howell to begin a new business in the Montreal area—which he did.

An emotional man, quick to become riled, Semple must have angrily shared his suspicions with Varina when he reached Schley's. Despite her shock, there was nothing she could do. She supposedly had no idea her brother was with her family, she had no address for her mother yet—they were still in transit to Montreal—and while she was allowed to write to her husband, she certainly could not mention anything about the missing treasury funds—"public money" as she called it. She could not mention Semple, though she knew the president would be wondering what had happened to him and the gold.

As much as she wanted to, Varina was not quite ready to write to William Preston Johnston, often a confidant in the past. She had grown fond of Johnston during the months he had lived in the Davis home, and he was held in high esteem by both the president and the first lady. To her regret, she had quarreled with him on the road, either shortly before or after they had been captured. There had been no opportunity to discuss what happened, as Johnston had been shipped off to prison at Fort Delaware, near Philadelphia. When he was released on July 19, he and his family had moved to Montreal, which seemed to be the destination of many self-exiled "Confeds."

It would be a couple of months more before Varina would have the courage to write to Johnston and apologize. In the meantime, she had to stew about the fact that she had not heard from her brother at all since her arrival in Savannah—no words of comfort, no offers of help. More important, she was furious over his quick departure with the gold and his using her children as an opportunity to do so. When she finally did write to Johnston, she was still angry: "Billy slandered, and belied me—and strictly between us I am afraid took public money, and went to Canada, giving Semple the slip."[13]

Semple was stirred enough by Howell's disappearance that he decided to chase him down. The family was only days ahead of him. At the same time, he could attend to business in both New York and Montreal. Wasting no time, he replenished his "expense money" from the supply of gold coins held by his friends and purchased a ticket on the steamship *Ariadne,* bound for New York City.[14] He was upset enough that he neglected to use his alias and bought the ticket under the name of J. A. Semple. Arriving in New York on August 22, he wasted little time in the city and left as soon as he could for Montreal.

* * *

WHILE SEMPLE was spending his days hiding in the Okefenokee Swamp, Gardie Tyler was wiling away the time in Lexington with very little to do until school opened in the fall. The time seemed to weigh heavily on him, so much so that his normal optimism had turned to gloom. "Here I am," he wrote in a June 26 letter to Julia:

> without home, without means and, I may almost say, without hope. Sometimes I begin to think that I will have to hire myself out as a day-laborer. My clothes are entirely played out and I have had them patched. So you see, I am a perfect "rag, tag, and bobtail." . . .
>
> How much happier I was in the army than I am now. I would rather have remained in it twenty years than be in the situation that we are in now. No country, no home, no freedom. What a deplorable case we present. I will not

be able to come to you as I (even if I could get the necessary funds) have only my uniform which I am not permitted to wear.[15]

Meanwhile, Alex, who had reached Sherwood Forest on May 1, had reason to be depressed: the plantation was in serious disrepair. Everything had been destroyed, except for the main house, and that could not be lived in. The squatters were gone, but the doors and windows had been smashed and all the furniture had been carried off. The soil was so hard, not having been worked for so long, two horses or mules would be required, instead of one, to plow the furrows. The burned-out buildings and fences needed to be replaced; the house itself had to be repaired and furnished with at least tables and beds; and money was necessary for purchasing tack, seed, farm equipment—and the mules—just to be able to plant a crop.

During the late spring and summer, Julia began to be concerned about the boys for a different reason than when they were in the army. She had no need to worry about their safety like she did when they were carrying a gun and walking a picket line. Her new concern was that both of them seemed to be wasting their time. Alex was clearly failing in his efforts to bring the plantation back. It was too big a job for him, even with the help of a farm manager who chose to hire Swedish immigrants instead of former slaves. Gardie in his boredom had flirted with the thought of going to Mexico with the stream of other Confederates leaving the South, but he dismissed the idea after a while. He then turned his hopes to a war between the United States and France in which he would fight for France, but he cooled on that also, especially when he could see there was not going to be a war.[16]

Julia began to think that they would be better off attending school in Germany, where they could focus on studying instead of being burdened with the trauma of reconstruction and the problems of Sherwood Forest. She had decided to keep the plantation and would find a way to do so. When nothing more exciting turned up for Gardie and as Alex could see that he was making little headway at Sherwood, the idea of study abroad became appealing to both brothers. In September 1865, along with their cousin Harry and accompanied by the Reverend John Fulton and his wife, who would be their guide and mentor there, Alex and Gardie sailed for Europe to attend college in Carlsruhe (Karlsruhe), Germany.[17]

Schooling for the boys, resurrecting Sherwood Forest, taxes and operating expenses on the two properties in her name, helping out her family and her destitute friends in the South, even maintaining her standard of living as a Gardiner and as the wife of a former president of the United States would all take money. For a time, Julia was not sure where she could find help. Then Semple appeared.

10

GOLD RUSH

Things are getting squally & the time is close at hand when we shall be free or prisoners.

—Diary entry for Tench Francisco Tilghman,
May 16, 1865

*A*s MICAJAH CLARK'S WAGON train moved south into Florida, it was escorted by ten handpicked Confederate cavalrymen, selected because of their loyalty to the president through either family relationships or personal friendships. The three Van Benthuysen brothers from New Orleans were related to Davis; their aunt was the wife of Davis's brother, Joseph. Capt. Watson Van Benthuysen was the quartermaster of Clark's baggage train. Alfred C. Van Benthuysen and Jefferson Davis Van Benthuysen accompanied him. Alfred had previous military experience, having served on the staff of Garibaldi in Italy and later in Confederate service. He was wounded and captured at Fort Fisher in January 1865 and later released. While serving in a Louisiana infantry regiment, Jefferson lost an eye and was captured at Gettysburg. He, too, was later released.[1]

The others included five troopers from Maryland, one of whom was Tench Francisco Tilghman from a distinguished Maryland family. His great-grandfather, of the same name, had been an aide-de-camp to George

Washington during the Revolutionary War, and he had carried the news to the Continental Congress of Cornwallis's surrender at Yorktown. Other Marylanders were William E. Dickinson, Fred Emory, J. W. Scott, and W. S. Winder. Rounding out the escort were five servants and two scouts who had formerly been with Capt. Given Campbell.

As Clark and his group moved south through the pine barrens of southern Georgia, they were acutely aware of the threat of Union patrols, and the scouts were vigilant in watching for signs of raiders. The group entered Florida on May 15 and left the barrens behind; the landscape changed to open country. Eventually, they began to see signs of civilization, and as they passed a plantation, they were offered a welcomed supper of fish, bread, and clabber. Weary from the trek, they decided to camp nearby for a couple of days. Here they learned that former Confederate soldiers were being required to apply for paroles in the next ten days or they would be considered outlaws. None in Clark's group were about to do that, but continuing on would be a risk because the countryside was teeming with Union troops on the prowl for Confederate leaders and whatever was left of the treasury. On May 16, Tilghman recorded in his diary: "Things are getting squally & the time is close at hand when we shall be free or prisoners."[2]

The following day, the wagons traveled twenty-three miles and camped at a farm owned by a man named Beason. The weather was hot on May 17 as they pushed farther, fording the Withlacoochee, a dirty, smelly tributary of the Suwannee River. After crossing over the Pensacola and Georgia Railroad, they set up camp nearby, awaiting news of Yankee activity from the scouts. Soon the scouts reported back that John C. Breckinridge's sons were in Madison, and "we fear the General has been captured." Breckinridge had, in fact, been at the home of Lewis Moseley on the Suwannee, but he was safely headed south.[3]

During the encampment, a deserter wandered into their midst who had "joined the Yanks and is now home." His appearance and sudden departure concerned them all; they thought he might be part of a band of marauders planning to attack the wagon train.[4] The threat never materialized, however, and the group moved on the next morning. Under a cooling spring shower, they covered twenty miles, arriving at the home of a man named Ivins.

The rain was actually a welcome relief from the heat. Also welcome was the blackberry wine provided by their host, accompanied by a butchered pig and "plenty of chickens." Ivins also offered them much-needed supplies for their journey. Heretofore the group had had little success in foraging for food because the area was sparsely populated.[5] Late that afternoon, they crossed the Suwannee River at Mosley's Ferry. This was the same ferry where Breckinridge and Benjamin had crossed only a few days earlier. While at the ferry, the officers heard that Jefferson Davis had been captured, but no one believed the news.

Under a sweltering Florida sun, the party moved deeper into the state, finding relief in the afternoon from a thunderstorm. After traveling twenty miles, Clark camped at a residence belonging to a man named Martin who had been an officer in the Florida militia. As Ivins had predicted, foraging continued to be difficult for the next couple of days. Their grueling ordeal finally ended when they were able to camp next to good water and a gristmill, where they were able to purchase some cornmeal. That night, Tilghman was on watch when a bugle call awakened the camp. Everyone expected an attack from bushwhackers, but it never came.

After traveling eighteen miles the next day, the group camped near "the only tolerable water." Eager to find out what was happening with the president, Watson Van Benthuysen and William E. Dickinson rode ahead to Gainesville but returned with little news, only a rumor that no Marylanders or Kentuckians would be allowed to return home. Though the rumor bordered on the ridiculous, it had a negative effect on morale. Tired and discouraged, many of the party had to be thinking of home.

On May 22, the wagon train left early in the morning and later passed to the west of Gainesville, being careful to avoid the town, which was now occupied by Union troops. At noon, they reached the home of plantation owner Edward Hailes, who fed them lunch and offered them "a very nice drink of brandy."[6] By the end of the day, they had reached Cottonwood, the plantation home of David Yulee, a U.S. senator before the war who was currently president of the Florida Railroad. Yulee had been a close friend of Jefferson Davis before the war when they both were in Washington, but they had a misunderstanding early in the war that had a lasting impact on their relationship.[7]

Yulee was on his way back from Jacksonville, where he had met with U.S. Chief Justice Salmon P. Chase. In January 1861, while still a U.S. senator, Yulee had written to a friend, Joseph Finegan, urging that Florida take over the forts and arsenals within its borders and that a confederation of states be formed. Chase told Yulee that the letter was probably enough to justify his arrest and trial for treason.

Clark's group camped near the railroad tracks of the Fernandina and Cedar Keys Railroad, which transected the sizable Yulee property. The news they received that evening from area newspapers devastated them. They learned of the surrender of both Johnston's and Taylor's armies and of the capture of Davis. Tilghman noted "a general gloom pervades our camp. Of course, the last hope is gone of the Confederacy and our only course as we are in the Department surrendered by General Johnston is to go somewhere [and] deliver ourselves up and be paroled. This I had hoped to have been spared but there is no alternative. Our little crowd of officers will still remain together."[8]

Realizing that it would be useless to continue the journey, Clark and the rest of the party had to decide where to go and what to do with the cargo of gold and baggage they had faithfully guarded. As leader of the group and acting treasurer of the Confederacy, Clark met with the escorts and told them that he would pay each man a fair salvage of the estimated twenty-five thousand dollars in gold that remained. He then intended to place the balance in an English bank to be used at the discretion of either Davis or Acting Treasury Secretary Reagan.

The plan did not sit well with Watson Van Benthuysen. He argued that since both Davis and Reagan were in prison, he, as quartermaster, had exclusive control of the funds. The others in the escort immediately supported him. Clark and Van Benthuysen apparently came to some agreement as to the division and ultimate disposition of the gold. Van Benthuysen said that he would set aside a quarter of the gold for Varina Davis and her family, and he would take control of her portion of the gold since he was related to the Davis family. The remainder of the gold would be divided equally among those who had guarded the contents of the train. Each of the guards was given $1,940 in gold coins as well as an additional $55 for traveling expenses. Clark retained $125 for one month's pay, and the two scouts were paid $250 each. The five servants each received $20. All agreed that Watson Van Benthuysen would keep the remaining $6,790 for the first lady.[9]

After deciding how to divide the money, there remained the issue of how to hide Jefferson Davis's personal baggage and papers. Clark and Watson Van Benthuysen asked Mrs. Yulee, whose husband had not yet returned, if they could hide the papers and baggage on the plantation. She agreed to hide the two chests and a trunk, as well as Davis's personal trunk, and entrusted the task to Lt. John Purviance, who was a friend of the family.

Purviance went to the stall of a Cuban pony that was kept separate from the other horses. After leading the pony out of his stall, Purviance dug a hole in the middle of the stable and buried the trunk. He hid the other chests and trunk elsewhere on the property.

Clark decided not to take his share of the gold with him. He hid the $1,940 that was given to him when the gold was divided and remained close to Yulee's plantation, waiting to see if any Union patrols had followed the wagon train. After about a week, Clark assured himself that he had not been followed, and he left for Washington, Georgia, to check on the security of some of the archives he had left there.

Owing to a large number of Union troops in the town, Clark thought it wise not to take any of the papers with him. In Abbeville, Clark went through the papers he had left with Mrs. Henry Leovy and destroyed "all applications for exemptions, detail appointments, and promotions." He preserved letters and telegrams from governors, general officers, cabinet members, and senators and congressmen, as well as records that pertained to the organization of the Confederate army. Finally, Clark selected those papers that he thought would be important to future chroniclers of the history of the Confederacy.

After packing the papers in a trunk, Clark told Mrs. Leovy that the papers should be moved out of town and into the country. While in Abbeville, he also arranged for the care of Braxton Bragg's papers and those of Attorney General George Davis, which had been hidden with "confidential friends." Satisfied that he had done his duty, Clark departed Abbeville for Baltimore, where he arrived safely, despite never taking the oath of allegiance. Clark later slipped back to Florida to recover his share of the British sovereigns.

While Clark lingered near the Yulee plantation, watching for signs of Union troops, the Maryland officers departed for Jacksonville to apply for their paroles and obtain passage on a ship northward. They arrived in Jacksonville on May 27 and attempted to apply for their paroles. There they were disarmed, but for some unknown reason, Gen. Israel Vodges would not permit them to take the oath of allegiance. They applied a second time the following day and were again refused. They were given, however, a pass and transportation to Hilton Head, along with orders to report to the provost officer there. On June 7, the group left Jacksonville and arrived at Hilton Head the next day. There, they were finally able to take the oath and receive their paroles. Afterward they boarded the SS *Haze* for New York and then went on to Baltimore.[10]

David Yulee returned home from Gainesville the day after Tilghman and his Maryland friends had left for Jacksonville. Shortly before sundown, Yulee was surprised to find "two strange gentlemen" at his plantation. The two were the Van Benthuysen brothers, who had remained at Yulee's home. They told him of their journey to Florida "with the purpose and expectation of reaching Texas from the coast."[11] Yulee advised them that they should "report at once to the proper officer in Florida, take their parole, return home to their families, and resume the duties of civil life."[12] The former senator indicated that he considered it futile to continue the military struggle and that Edmund Kirby Smith's forces had no hope of winning against the large Union armies that could be sent west of the Mississippi River, now that all the Confederates east of the river had surrendered. Yulee offered to accompany them to Gainesville the following day to receive their paroles and find transportation home. What Yulee said made sense to the brothers, and they decided to do as the senator suggested.

Watson Van Benthuysen told Yulee that he had two "blooded mares" purchased from soldiers in the Kentucky Brigade, and he wanted to keep the horses. He asked Yulee if he could find someone to care for the horses until he could transport them back to New Orleans, when the lines of communication were reopened. Yulee agreed to keep the horses himself until Van Benthuysen could retrieve them. Van Benthuysen also asked if Yulee could keep some baggage until he could arrange to have it shipped along with the horses, and Yulee agreed again. In a statement to Federal authorities on June 16, Yulee reported, "I afterward had reason to believe that this baggage comprised some of the personal private effects of Mr. Davis."[13]

With regard to Davis's papers, Yulee made the distinction, "Public archives I would have considered property which was subject to capture," but he did not agree that personal items should be retained by the enemy.[14] The senator reported that Watson Van Benthuysen had no duty to turn in the trunks to the Federal government, as they were the private property of an individual and did not belong to the Confederate government. For his part, Yulee believed that he was only being gentlemanly by keeping Davis's possessions, but he told Van Benthuysen that since he was preparing to take his family to Kentucky to visit relatives, he would place the trunks with a friend for safekeeping.

The next day, Yulee left Cotton Wood before breakfast and accompanied his visitors to Gainesville to receive their paroles. The Van Benthuysen brothers immediately reported to the appropriate authorities and were paroled. Yulee was not as fortunate; he was arrested on orders issued by Union Maj. Gen. Quincy A. Gillmore. Fearing for the safety of his family, Yulee sent them to Kentucky to stay with his wife's family. He had Davis's baggage moved to Waldo, Florida, to be kept by friends. Yulee was sent to Jacksonville to report to Gen. Israel Vodges. The general did not detain him and allowed him the freedom to move about the city. The lenient treatment did not last long, however, as orders from Washington sent Yulee under guard to Fort Pulaski, Georgia.

At Fort Pulaski, Yulee was treated well by the officers, and his family was able to visit him. In Washington, however, rumors circulated that an effort was underway to have Yulee tried, court-martialed, and executed. The alleged charge was that Yulee had tried to ascertain information on the quantity of armaments stored at the Federal forts at Pensacola and that he had urged that they be seized by the state of Florida. The judge advocate general of the army, Joseph Holt, was behind the charges against Yulee in what may have been a personal grudge. Kentucky governor Charles A. Wickliffe, Yulee's father-in-law, met with friends in Washington, including the attorney general, members of Congress, and even President Andrew Johnson to negotiate Yulee's fate. After a year in prison—only Jefferson Davis and Clement C. Clay had been held longer—Yulee was finally released. A note from Joseph E. Johnston to Ulysses Grant was probably instrumental in securing Yulee's release.

Eventually, Union troops in Jacksonville learned about the wagon train from one of the wagon masters who was with Clark, a former slave named James Jones. On being questioned by Union authorities, Jones related to them the details of Davis's baggage train and provided the names of the escort. Union officers checked their parole records and saw that two of the Van Benthuysen brothers had received paroles on May 26 and were intending to go to New Orleans. General Vodges dispatched the provost at Gainesville, Capt. Oliver E. Bryant of the Thirty-fourth U.S. Colored Troops, to Cottonwood to retrieve the trunk and chests that belonged to Davis. There, Bryant questioned Yulee's wife about the trunk, and she reluctantly told him that the baggage had been moved to Waldo, Florida, to the home of a man named Williams who was a railroad agent and a friend of the Yulees. The next day, Bryant arrived at Waldo, located Williams, and inquired about the trunk. Williams led the soldiers to an unlocked storeroom adjoining his house.

In addition to the information about the trunk, Yulee's wife gave the Union troops a French rifle that belonged to Davis, described as "a most murderous weapon" by Bryant. And en route to Waldo, Bryant's patrol stopped at the residence of Thomas Haile (Edward Haile's brother), with whom the Van Benthuysens had stayed. Bryant confiscated several horses that the brothers had asked Haile to sell for them.

Bryant reported the results of his mission and provided the details of finding the trunk and some significant papers contained therein. Those documents included the written opinions of the cabinet members on the surrender terms negotiated between Sherman and Johnston on April 18, a letter from Eugene Musson with an endorsement by Benjamin, and a March 14 letter from E. G. Booth of Wilmington, North Carolina. In addition to the letters, one of the documents was a key to the Confederate cipher, along with an explanatory letter on how to use the cipher.

The report included an inventory of the exact number of socks, underwear, ties, and scarves, and noted the inclusion of a nine-shot revolver and ammunition. The list also described the condition of the various items of clothes, noting that eight linen shirts were dirty. Vodges forwarded the report to Washington and offered to send Bryant along with the trunk and papers to the capital. The War Department responded that the trunk should be sent to Washington for examination. A portion of the contents were returned to Davis in 1874.

Overlooked for a time, except by William Wood Crump and the bank tellers, was the specie in the vault of the old bank building in Washington, Georgia. Having received permission from Union Capt. Lot Abraham to return the privately owned funds to the Richmond banks, the tellers decided not to waste any time. On May 24, the gold and silver were removed from the vault, loaded into five wagons, and covered with canvas to mask the contents. Accompanying the gold was a small cavalry escort. The plan was to take the specie by wagons to Abbeville, where it could then be taken by train to Richmond.

The caravan and its mounted guard naturally drew suspicious looks from the citizenry and the paroled soldiers who had flooded the town on their way home. Despite an attempt at secrecy, the plans for the movement of the funds had leaked out. Former Confederate soldiers, in particular, believed the money was part of the Confederate treasury and felt that they had as much right to the gold as the Union soldiers who were guarding it.

As the wagon train departed Washington, word quickly spread regarding the contents of the lightly guarded train, and apparently the wagons were shadowed by renegade cavalrymen almost from the time it left town. Late in the day, the wagons stopped for the night near the home of the Reverend Dionysius Chenault in Lincoln County, about fifteen miles north of Washington. There the wagons were circled inside a fenced-in area with a double gate, and the escort camped for the night. Even though the soldiers and the bankers kept a nervous eye on whatever they could see outside the fence, especially looking for movement of any kind, they eventually fell asleep.

In the middle of the night, shouting and cursing riders burst through the gate and into the camp, restrained the guards and tellers, and began to plunder the wagons. Smashing the kegs open, the raiders scooped up whatever they could carry. In their haste, they left more than forty thousand dollars scattered on the ground. Eliza Andrews wrote that the men "waded ankle deep in gold and silver. The raiders filled their haversacks and their pockets. They tied bags of gold to their saddles. They went away so heavily laden that they were compelled to throw away much of their booty by the wayside."[15] The next morning, the bank tellers salvaged the coins that the raiders could not carry away.

Lewis Shepherd, a former Confederate soldier from John C. Vaughn's brigade who witnessed the melee, said that the heads of the kegs were knocked off and many of the thieves filled their forage sacks with ten-dollar and twenty-dollar gold pieces. Some, Shepherd believed, were able to get away with as much as $60,000. He claimed that he knew two men who rode away with more than $120,000 and went to Kansas City, Missouri, "where they engaged in business, becoming great men of large wealth."[16] Shepherd also stated that "one of the wealthiest planters in Texas got his start with money secured from these kegs, and still another in the same state has made good as a stockman, being now a cattle king."

Some of the raiders hid their sacks of the specie in the woods, planning to retrieve them later. The bankers went to Danburg, a village nearby, and organized a posse to try to recover the money; although they overtook some of the raiders, they were unsuccessful in recovering any of the money carried off in the night. The next morning, the bankers approached Confederate Brig. Gen. Edward Porter Alexander for help in apprehending the raiders. Alexander, who had recently returned from Virginia and had been the chief of artillery for the Army of Northern Virginia, organized a posse from members of a local battery, "boys armed with pistols" as he described them. A judge named Reese, a former officer of the local bank, was approached to issue the appropriate warrants for the raiders, but he declined, claiming that he did not want to usurp the authority of the Union officials.

Porter Alexander encountered some of the raiders who had about eighty thousand dollars taken during the raid. They said they did not know that the funds were private and believed they were taking Confederate funds, which they felt were owed to them. Alexander's men returned the full amount to the bank vault in Washington, where it remained until two tellers could make arrangements to send the funds back to Richmond.

After this initial success, Alexander, along with Reese and several former Confederate soldiers from Washington, continued to search for other raiders who might have stolen funds. Needing a larger force to confront the bands of renegades still roaming the area, Alexander added "seven or eight citizens of the neighborhood" to his posse. But the strategy backfired. After recovering more of the specie, while heading back to Washington with his prisoners, the former artillery chief was confronted by sympathetic and armed townspeople. He recalled, "I was in about as close quarters as ever I was in my life. The friends of the guerillas had increased in number, while we had nothing but pistols. For a moment affairs looked dark. A dozen or two loaded guns and pistols were leveled at the heads of each other, and the first shot would have been the signal for a bloody affray." Alexander quickly calmed the group and promised that there would be no arrests if his prisoners would return the remainder of the money by the next day.[17]

Some of the money recovered by Alexander had been left temporarily at the Chenault home, and after the encounter with the armed townspeople, Alexander collected those funds and delivered them to Washington, where they were placed in the bank vault. He estimated that about $120,000 had been retrieved, leaving $250,000 to $300,000 at large.

In the view of Eliza Andrews, "All the money and plate that lives through these troublous times will have strange histories attached to it." She also related a likely apocryphal story about a citizen "who had $1,000 in specie which he went out to conceal as soon as he heard that the Yankees were in his neighborhood. Before he could get it buried, he heard a squad of horsemen coming down the road, so he threw his bag of money over a hedge to get it out of sight, and lo there it struck a skulking Yankee pat on the head!"[18]

Union Gen. Hiram A. Wilde, the new commander in Washington, upon hearing of Alexander's actions, seized the funds and arrested the bank officers. Wilde sent a detachment to the site of the attack to recover more of the money. He also ordered the arrest of anyone who might be suspected of involvement in the raid. Since the wagon train had camped near the Chenault house, the reverend and his family were arrested. This included his wife, his brother, his sixteen-year-old son, his seventeen-year-old daughter, and some servants. The soldiers shot the family's dog, Jeff Davis, and then took the three-hundred-pound Methodist minister, his brother, and his son into the woods. There they "put them to the most excruciating torture in order to force a confession from them." The men were strung up by their thumbs until their feet were lifted from the ground. But the soldiers' efforts to extract confessions were for naught. No one in the family knew anything about the raid or those who perpetrated it. Nevertheless, after torturing the men and strip-searching the women, the Chenaults were sent to Washington and "submitted to the most humiliating treatment during an investigation, which resulted in their complete vindication and release." Daughter Mary Anne later wrote about the missing money, asserting that the soldiers found most of the money, but there "were oceans more of it scattered all over Wilkes and Lincoln counties, besides what was carried off. Some of it was hid about in swamps and woods, some was buried in the ground, and there is no telling how much has been forgotten and not found again."[19]

While Union troops searched throughout Wilkes County for the remains of the bank funds, they discovered the chest of jewelry that John C. Breckinridge had left at the home of Mrs. J. D. Moss. The jewelry had been donated to the Confederate government by the women of the South. Mary Anne Chenault described the chest as being filled with "bracelets necklaces and rings . . . and silverware of all kinds."[20] The chest was taken to Washington along with jewelry confiscated from the Chenaults. Several weeks later, the family jewelry was returned, but the original contents remain unaccounted for to the present day.

11

THE
PRISONER

My dear, dear Husband, tell me precisely how you are. Do not let my
inevitable sorrow be swelled by uncertainties. You do not save me anything.
—Varina Davis to Jefferson Davis,
September 14, 1865

T. COL. BENJAMIN D. PRITCHARD was at the head of the grim procession making its way toward Macon. Though his primary concern was Jefferson Davis and his aides, he also treated the Davis family as prisoners of his
detachment. Each of the prisoners was allowed to ride his own horse except
for Davis and his family, who traveled in an ambulance. News of Davis's
capture had already spread throughout the country as soon as Secretary of
War Edwin M. Stanton received word by telegram from Gen. James H. Wilson. When the Pritchard party paused at a cavalry camp, the soldiers hurled
insults at the Davises.[1]

While they were at the camp, the former Confederates learned that a
proclamation had been issued in Washington offering a reward of one hundred thousand dollars for Davis's capture and asserting that the Confederate
president had participated in the assassination of Abraham Lincoln. Pritchard,

who saw the notice for the first time when he arrived at the camp, handed a copy to Davis, "who read it with a composure unruffled by any feeling other than scorn."[2] The charges had been made by Stanton and Judge Adv. Gen. Joseph Holt. According to Burton Harrison, "Stanton and Holt, lawyers both, very well knew that Mr. Davis could never be convicted upon an indictment for treason, but [they] were determined to hang him anyhow."[3] Despite a lack of evidence, newspapers picked up on the charges and created a frenzy and even called for Davis's execution.

After a four-day march, Pritchard and his prisoners arrived in Macon and were taken to Wilson's headquarters in the Lanier Hotel. Surprisingly, Davis was greeted by an honor guard that formed a cordon along the walk leading to the hotel entrance and presented arms as Davis passed through their lines. Davis graciously accepted their salutes. Inside the hotel, Davis and his family were given a large room, and dinner was delivered to them. On the dinner tray, a black waiter presented Varina with a rose, which brightened an otherwise gloomy day for her.

After dinner, Davis and Wilson talked of mutual acquaintances on both sides of the conflict and of their experiences at West Point, although their graduating classes were separated by a number of years (Davis was a member of the Class of 1828; Wilson graduated sixth in the Class of 1860). Wilson had experienced rapid promotion based on his successes in Tennessee, capped by an invasion of Alabama and a victorious campaign against Nathan Bedford Forrest. Turning east, Wilson captured Montgomery and then marched to Macon. As their conversation came to a close, Davis responded to Wilson's reference to the Stanton-Holt proclamation by saying, "There's one man who knows it is false: the man who signed it. Johnson knows that I preferred Lincoln to himself."[4]

Burton Harrison renewed his acquaintance with Gen. John T. Croxton of Kentucky, one of Wilson's subordinate commanders. Croxton was two classes ahead of Harrison at Yale. After exchanging pleasantries, Croxton assured Harrison he would have "a special outlook for my comfort while a prisoner."[5] Harrison also learned from Croxton the details of the movement of the Union pursuit of Davis. From this, he concluded that if Davis had not stopped after crossing the Ocmulgee River or had ridden on after having supper with Harrison and Varina, and "gone about five miles beyond Irwinville, passing through that village at night, and so avoiding observation, there is every reason to suppose that he and his party would have escaped either across the Mississippi or through Florida to the sea-coast."[6] Harrison attributed Davis's concern for the safety of his family above that of his capture.

Stanton ordered Wilson to send Davis north, although the exact location of his pending imprisonment had not been announced. Wilson asked Davis to select his mode of transportation: either land or sea. Davis chose to travel by boat, believing that such would be less stressful for his family. But in order to reach the coast, the Davises would have to travel to Atlanta and then to Augusta to take a steamer to Savannah. John Reagan became concerned about the travel arrangements; he had heard from some of the soldiers that only Davis was to be sent to Washington, and his aides were to remain in Macon. Reagan asked Wilson if he could accompany Davis, owing to his deteriorating physical condition. But his request was trumped by events; the War Department ordered Wilson to send the entire group to Washington.[7]

As the Davis party arrived at the train station in Macon, they were met by Clement Clay and his wife, Virginia. Clay had also been accused of conspiring in the Lincoln assassination and had the same bounty placed on his capture as did Davis. Clay had been in LaGrange, Georgia, visiting Senator B. H. Hill, when he met with Stephen R. Mallory. All were unaware of Davis's capture as well as the rewards offered for Clay's arrest; Virginia Clay heard the news on the way to LaGrange. Clay contemplated escaping to the West, but he decided to surrender himself to Wilson and sent a telegram to the Federal commander informing him that Clay would do so at Macon. Once in Macon, the Clays were told that they too would be traveling north with the other former Confederate leaders.

Departure from Macon was scheduled for late afternoon. Virginia Clay described Macon as a city in an uproar: "Cavalry clattered through the streets and gazing sightseers scarcely alight from our carriage when, looking back, up the street we saw a company of cavalry approaching. There was an increasing activity in the gathered crowds, which were composed of silent citizens of Macon, elbowed by Freedmen and Union soldiers, who lounged among them."[8]

As a cavalry detachment drew closer, the Clays realized that the passengers in the broken-down carriage were Jefferson and Varina Davis. The former president was dressed in a gray suit, and his face was "more ashen than his garb."[9] Another wagon followed with the Davis children and their baggage. When the procession passed, "The alien and motley crowd along the walks yelled and hooted in derision." Virginia Clay heard one "heartless Union soldier shout, 'Hey, Johnny Reb, we've got your President!' 'And the devil's got yours' was the swift reply."[10]

At the station, Jefferson and Varina Davis were escorted to their car by two soldiers, and the Clays were shown to the same car. The two couples sat together, and Varina and the senator chatted. When the doors to the car were slammed shut and the butts of the soldiers' rifles struck the floor in unison at the command of "Order arms!" Virginia Clay realized the gravity of the situation and their status as prisoners of the Federal government.

The trip to Augusta was tiring for all, except the Davis children, who had slept all night. Passing through Atlanta to Augusta, Virginia Clay found both towns to be in turmoil. When the train stopped at several stations along the way, meals were delivered to the passengers, but no one was allowed off the train until it arrived in Augusta. The prisoners were transferred to a steamboat amid a scene of emotional support for Davis and the others.

Virginia Clay described boarding the boat as "neither stately nor awe-inspiring" after she slipped and fell into the arms of "a soldierly little figure in undress uniform who stood close to the crude gang-plank." Her rescuer was "Little Joe" Wheeler, a Confederate cavalry commander. Wheeler had been captured a few days earlier and asked for a parole. Instead, he and his officers were made prisoners and were being sent to Athens and Augusta and ultimately to Washington.[11]

Virginia Clay described the steamboat to Savannah as a "wretched little craft." There were no chairs for the passengers. Davis suffered from a pain in one of his eyes, and the ladies "bathed his temples with cologne in vain attempts to lessen his tortures."[12] In Savannah, the prisoners embarked on a coastal steamer for the short trip to Hilton Head. This was a large boat with three decks similar to the excursion boats that were common at the time in New York Harbor. Before departure, Varina Davis sent her servants ashore with a letter to Brig. Gen. Rufus Sexton, inspector of plantations and settlements, asking him to ensure that they were treated kindly. Joseph Wheeler recalled that, later in the trip, when all the servants were gone, he spent "many an hour walking the deck with little baby Winnie in my arms."[13]

Lt. Col. Benjamin D. Pritchard and about sixty men of the Fourth Michigan Cavalry continued to escort the prisoners. The men were in "high spirits," according to Wheeler, because they believed they would receive the one-hundred-thousand-dollar reward for capturing Davis. The general euphoria over the expected bonus created a lackadaisical attitude among the guard and, in Wheeler's opinion, "rendered possible our escape in a way that would have been in the highest degree dramatic." He observed that the soldiers were stationed on the upper deck of the steamer with their guns, "but when breakfast-time came I saw that they would have to go below." Wheeler expected the guards would go below in shifts, but instead, almost the entire contingent left for breakfast with their guns still on the top deck. Only two guards remained at their posts.[14]

Wheeler talked to William Preston Johnston about overpowering the guards taking over the boat. The two men discussed where they might go and what the consequences would be if they were recaptured. Wheeler argued that they were all prisoners of war and, as such, could not be tried for piracy. One of the aides went to Davis with the plan, but he was not enthusiastic about it and did not endorse it. Meanwhile, the soldiers returned from breakfast and the opportunity passed.

Arrival in Hilton Head brought some relief, as the group boarded a large steamboat capable of ocean travel, the *William P. Clyde*. The vessel was escorted by the gunboat USS *Tuscarora*, "whose guns bear directly upon us, day and night," observed Virginia Clay, as "fears are entertained of the *Stonewall* or *Shenandoah*" coming to rescue Davis.[15] When the group departed Hilton Head on May 16, they still did not know their final destination. Anxiety arose over a possible engagement with the *Stonewall*, a Confederate gunboat.[16] All of the axes on the *Tuscarora* were removed for fear that the prisoners might use them should the vessel be attacked. "Cowards!" remarked Davis. "They're afraid of this handful of Confederate men."[17]

As the *William P. Clyde* steamed north on a course paralleling the eastern seaboard, Wheeler, ever the fighter, continued to look for avenues of escape. He proposed another plan to Davis that would require the president to jump overboard while Wheeler and Johnston overpowered two guards at the stern of the ship. Davis refused, arguing that an escape at that point would serve no useful purpose, and it was doubtful that he would have survived the ordeal. Wheeler believed that Davis "took a certain inward satisfaction in the knowledge that by refusing to escape, he would cause the Union government more embarrassment than if he did so." Davis had possibly recalled a remark, according to Wheeler, made by Lincoln that "if Mr. Davis could only escape unbeknown to us, it would be a very good thing."[18]

The *William P. Clyde* and the *Tuscarora* arrived off the Virginia coast at noon on May 19, entering Hampton Roads rather than turning into the Chesapeake Bay. Shortly the two ships arrived at a point just off of Fort Monroe. Virginia Clay speculated that the fort would be their final destination. While at anchor, she observed "many vessels, some bearing the English and some the French flags."

The *Clyde* remained at anchor for two days, until army chief of staff Gen. Henry W. Halleck arrived and the group learned their fate. Francis R. Lubbock, William Preston Johnston, and Joseph Wheeler and his officers were to be sent to Fort Delaware at 6:00 a.m. John H. Reagan departed later for Fort Warren in Massachusetts aboard the *Tuscarora*. Burton N. Harrison was sent to Washington. Jefferson Davis and Clement C. Clay were taken to Fort Monroe. Varina and her family, along with Virginia Clay, remained on the *Clyde* and were sent back to Savannah.[19]

Davis and Clay faced an ordeal that would last almost two years. When the two prisoners arrived at Fort Monroe, they were introduced to the commander, Brig. Gen. Nelson A. Miles, who escorted Davis through a cordon of Union troops. Pritchard took Clay by the arm and followed behind. Fort Monroe was the strongest Federal facility on the East Coast and had been built to protect the entrance to the Chesapeake Bay and the waterway known as Hampton Roads. With walls thirty feet high and fifty feet thick around the casemates, it presented a formidable strongpoint to defend the vital access to the seaports. The road to the fort was guarded, and entry was through three drawbridges that crossed an eight-foot-deep moat. Ironically, Robert E. Lee had supervised construction of the moat in the 1830s. The moat was 125 feet wide below the casemate where Davis was to be held.

After the two prisoners entered the fort, Davis was taken to Casemate No. 2 and Clay was placed in Casemate No. 4. There were guardrooms between the walls of the fort and each cell. Each guardroom was manned by two guards and an officer, who would check on each prisoner every fifteen minutes. Two sentries were posted inside each cell, and a light was kept burning at all times. Guards were also stationed on the opposite bank of the moat and above the cells on the ramparts. Miles ordered that no communication should take place with the prisoners; guards were under orders not to speak to one another in the presence of Davis or to respond to any verbal communication from him. Stanton and Holt were taking no chances with the security of the prisoners, as they may have feared an escape attempt might be made by those still loyal to Davis and the Confederacy.

Stanton's paranoia and obsession with security were demonstrated on May 23, when the officer of the day, Capt. Jerome Titlow, entered Davis's cell with two blacksmiths to put him in leg irons. Davis strongly objected to being shackled and demanded to see Miles. Titlow told him it would be of no use, as Miles had his orders from Stanton. Davis urged him to ask Miles to telegraph Washington to seek relief from what he viewed as outrageous treatment, but Titlow ordered the blacksmith to proceed. Davis struck the blacksmith when he attempted to place the shackle on Davis's ankle, and a struggle ensued with a guard, during which Davis grabbed at the guard's rifle. The guard regained control of the rifle, and Titlow ordered the guard back to his post. Titlow then brought in four other guards, who shoved Davis onto the cot and held him down while the blacksmith riveted the clasp onto the captive president's ankle. Titlow observed that Davis "showed unnatural strength" during the encounter.

While Stanton was behind the order to have Davis placed in irons, Miles had been given discretion to carry out the order. U.S. Assistant Secretary of War Charles Dana wanted the order carried out immediately. He had personally carried the order to Fort Monroe and delivered it to Miles. Halleck overruled Dana and left the matter to Miles to carry out the order at a later time. As soon as Dana and Halleck left the fort, Miles ordered Davis to be shackled. Miles was likely seeking to curry favor with Stanton and Grant, who had selected him for command of the prestigious fort. Only twenty-five years old, Miles had a distinguished war record, and his abilities were greatly respected by Grant. Varina Davis, however, had little regard for his social skills and manners. After her encounters with him, she noted that "he was not respectful, but I thought it was his ignorance of polite usage."[20]

Davis was hardly in any condition to attempt an escape. Dr. John J. Craven, the fort's physician, was called in to check on Davis's poor physical condition. Craven found him to be suffering from a "long established neuralgic disorder" and described his condition as "a mere fascine of raw and tremulous nerves" with "his eyes restless and fevered, his head continually shifting from side to side for a cool spot on the pillow."[21] Apparently, Craven did not provide any medication to Davis; he merely monitored his condition.

Yet Craven proved to be instrumental to Davis's survival at Fort Monroe, because he provided Davis's only meaningful conversation and emotional support while he was in solitary confinement. Craven sought to bolster his morale and spoke with him about various subjects in order to take his mind off his captivity. Accompanied by the officer of the day, Craven was able to break down the rigid barriers between guard and prisoner that had been emplaced by Miles. The men soon conversed with and were fascinated by the knowledge that Davis displayed on a variety of subjects. Craven also asked Miles to remove Davis's leg irons, which Miles denied, but Craven succeeded in obtaining a better mattress to place on Davis's iron cot.

News of Davis's harsh treatment, particularly the shackling, spread quickly throughout the country. While some Northern journalists and others with a deep hatred for Davis likely relished the conditions Davis endured, some Northern politicians, including Thurlow Weed, a friend of President Johnson's, were sensitive to public opinion that was turning against the way the government was treating Davis. In the South, Davis was beginning to be seen in a new light as Southerners sympathized with his sufferings. Weed prevailed upon Stanton to remove the shackles from Davis, arguing that they were not necessary, and Stanton on May 28 ordered Miles to remove the leg irons.

Davis was grateful that the irons had been removed, but Craven remained concerned about the prisoner's overall health. The rations that Davis received were barely able to keep him alive. The bread he received was shredded by soldiers to make sure it didn't conceal any "weapons," and coffee and soup were served in the same dirty, unwashed cup. Davis received a steady diet of heavy beef and bread, which was soon changed when Craven received permission from Miles to allow his wife to cook for Davis.

The degradation of both Davis and Clay, according to Davis, lasted about three months. They were under constant surveillance and in the presence of the guards day and night. With boots squeaking and rifles rattling, sleep was difficult. Sometimes sleep was impossible. The lack of sleep added to both men's overall weak physical condition. Some relief came when Miles finally ordered an end to the pacing of the guards inside the cells. Craven told Miles that keeping the guards in the cells was having an adverse effect on the nerves of the prisoners. In late July, Miles removed the guards from the cells. While this provided some relief, there remained the changing of the guard every two hours in the guardrooms adjacent to the cells.

In addition to the physical privations Davis endured, the mental stresses were equally difficult. As a result of his solitary confinement, Davis was cut off from the outside world for several months. In July 1865, Craven brought him a copy of the *New York Times*. He also supplied Davis with some history books and arranged for an hour's walk each day on the ramparts of the fort. These walks had to be taken with Miles and an armed guard. Craven observed that Miles never failed to say something to Davis that upset him, so the benefit of the exercise was negated by the agitation.

Despite the exercise, Davis's health did not improve. The cell in which Davis was held was continually damp, and this concerned Craven. The matter was finally corrected in October, when Davis was moved to a drier cell on the second floor of Carroll Hall, which served as an officers quarters. Inside the cell were a coal fireplace and a screen to hide the commode, as well as a washbasin. Carroll Hall was a wooden structure, which provided a drier environment, but the noise from the guards was ever present and a light burned intermittently in the cell.

Craven did not believe Davis's condition improved with the change of cells. After nine months of captivity, the former Confederate president was "wasting away" and "not improving" either physically or mentally. He did maintain a will to live, although he was concerned that the mental torture would ultimately impair his ability to defend himself, should he be eventually brought to trial by the government.

While Davis and Clay were enduring the rigors of their confinement, their wives in Savannah were using all of their political and social contacts to help them. The return trip from Fort Monroe was anything but pleasant for the Davis family and Virginia Clay. The *Clyde* remained at anchor off Fort Monroe for two days after Davis and Clay were incarcerated. Finally, in the late afternoon of May 24, the captain received orders to sail to Savannah. Before weighing anchor, about two hundred paroled prisoners were loaded onto the ship, which Virginia Clay described as "a small and stuffy boat at best." Rough seas, hot weather, and overcrowding added to the discomfort of the wives, who were already distraught with worry for their husbands.[22]

Before the *Clyde* steamed toward Savannah, Virginia Clay wasted no time in seeking assistance from influential friends in Washington. Her husband had given her a list of "distinguished public men" to whom she should write on his behalf. The list included the editor of the *New York Daily News* and several judges, as well as Joseph Holt, the judge advocate general. In a May 23 letter to Holt, Virginia Clay asked that Holt provide proper counsel and a fair and impartial trial, and she proclaimed her husband's innocence of any involvement with the "horrid crime" for which the two men had been arrested, that is, complicity in the Lincoln assassination. She wrote thirteen letters, and all but two responded. Only Holt and the archbishop of Bermuda (who was away at the time) failed to answer her pleas for assistance. In her diary, Virginia Clay compared Holt's silence to Judas's betrayal of Jesus, writing, "My list comprised thirteen names, the number that has been accounted unlucky since thirteen sat at the table of our Lord and one betrayed him." She added that, based on the treatment her husband had received from a former friend, "an analogy is unavoidable."[23]

By a stroke of good luck, a sailor provided Virginia and Varina with newspapers, the first they had seen since their arrival at Fort Monroe. The newspaper stories depressed and angered them since they called for Davis's and Clay's executions. After Varina read the papers, "it was such that restoratives were necessary to prevent her from fainting."[24]

As the *Clyde* neared Hilton Head, Virginia pondered as to how she would get her thirteen letters mailed. Someone, possibly the same sailor who had given her the newspapers, placed a note in her cabin that indicated he would mail her letters. Virginia rolled up the letters and put a gold dollar in the package for postage. The stranger mailed the letters at Hilton Head and returned the dollar coin. Later, Virginia Clay learned that the stranger who assisted her was Charles McKim of Philadelphia.

After five days at sea, on May 29, "a bedraggled and travel-stained party" finally arrived at Savannah. The travelers were immediately informed that the Union authorities had forbidden the wives from riding in carriages, and since none of their friends were at the dock to greet them, they concluded that the time of their arrival had been kept secret. Lacking any transportation, the group was forced to walk to the Pulaski House and carry their own luggage. "We were a sad procession," proclaimed Virginia. Several friends recognized the entourage shortly before they reached the hotel and assisted them. Once word spread of their arrival, many other friends arrived at the hotel to greet them. The next day they received flowers and fruit as well as all types of clothing. Many of their former friends from Richmond and Washington were in Savannah, including former Senator David Yulee of Florida and Gen. Hugh Mercer, a friend of Davis.[25]

After settling in at the Pulaski House, Varina Davis, accompanied by Mercer, paid a courtesy call on the Union district commander. There she was informed of her status: she was to remain in Savannah, she could write letters, but they would have to be sent through army channels, and she would have to pay her own expenses. While the people of Savannah provided assistance to her with food and clothes and visited her a number of times, Varina was concerned about the crowded conditions and the impact it would have on the children. There, at the Pulaski House, and later, outside of Augusta, where she was eventually allowed to live, Varina had to content herself with desperate letters to Federal authorities, including President Johnson, urging that she be told about her husband's condition.

In August 1865, Nelson A. Miles allowed Davis to send a letter to Varina, and this opened a channel of communication between the two, although the letters were censored by the military. The letters were a source of strength to Davis, although he and Varina were restricted to discussing only family matters. After hearing rumors of how poorly her husband was being treated and how weak he was, Varina wrote: "My dear, dear Husband, tell me precisely how you are. Do not let my inevitable sorrow be swelled by uncertainties. You do not save me anything. I see in the papers accounts of every pang. Why not tell your poor helpless wife in your own sweet kind way the worst, and thus enable me to defy the penny-a-liners who for an item would wring the last drop of blood out of a broken heart." On a happier note, she remarked "Our little Pie Cake [Winnie] is as well as could be expected as she is cutting several jaw teeth at once. Her eyes look so like yours at times that I thank God for it."[26]

By the fall of 1865, Davis was finally allowed a visitor, the Reverend Charles Minnegerode, the minister at St. Paul's Episcopal Church in Richmond. Minnegerode was preaching the sermon on April 2, 1865, when Davis received Lee's warning of the impending breakthrough at Petersburg. The minister had petitioned President Johnson to visit Davis at Fort Monroe, but for a long time his request was never answered. Richmond friends advised him to take his request to Stanton, an Episcopalian. By going through Stanton's pastor in Washington, Minnegerode finally received permission to visit Davis. While the visits broke the monotony of the former president's isolation, Davis remained in poor mental and physical condition.

Throughout the fall of 1865, Virginia Clay continued to write her influential friends in Washington on behalf of her husband. She sent letters to Horace Greeley and to former President Franklin Pierce, asking them to intervene with President Johnson. She did not hesitate to write directly to

President Johnson, but she never received a reply. Virginia then decided, with the encouragement of friends, to go to Washington. In the capital, on November 26, she was able to arrange a meeting with Ulysses S. Grant. He was sympathetic to her and wrote a note to the president, asking that her husband be released on parole. Virginia went to the White House several times in an attempt to meet with Johnson. Although she finally saw the president, he made no commitments and referred her to Stanton. The secretary of war listened but was also noncommittal.

Shortly before Christmas, Virginia went to New York and again met with friends, including Greeley, editor of the *New York Tribune,* who advised her either to try to get the government to bring her husband to trial or to obtain his release on parole. The meeting with Greeley was in a hotel in which a number of Southerners were staying, including several former Southern generals. When they noticed Virginia and Greeley, they registered their surprise at "Mrs. Clement Clay hobnobbing with that old Abolitionist!" Her lobbying paid off in late December; President Johnson issued a permit that allowed her to visit her husband.[27]

When Virginia Clay saw her husband, she gave him a copy of the charges that were being prepared by Joseph Holt against Davis and him. After reviewing the charges, Clay composed another list of people in Washington whom she should contact on his behalf. Within a month, she secured permission from the president to visit Clement daily. She also asked to see Davis, but this request was denied.

Although she could not see Davis, Virginia was allowed to leave for him a portrait of her and a pot for Davis to make coffee. She sent notes to him on twisted paper, along with cigars, and Davis was able to send her a list of important persons to contact on his behalf. During this time, Virginia kept Varina informed of the visits and of the former president's general condition.

When she arrived at Fort Monroe, Virginia Clay found that Dr. Craven had been reassigned; Dr. George E. Cooper, an army surgeon, had assumed the duties of the fort's physician. Cooper provided the same manner of care to Davis as had Craven, although there were rumors that Cooper was a Radical Republican. Cooper's wife, however, was from Virginia, and her sympathies were with the South and with the two famous prisoners. She and Virginia established a warm relationship during the course of her visits to Clement Clay.

Virginia Clay's incessant lobbying for her husband's release probably had a positive impact on the Davis family. Her letters also had opened a dialogue with the president regarding her husband's parole. Virginia's example no doubt encouraged Varina to seek help from prominent Washington friends as well. Horace Greeley extended his support to the Davises, and Varina hired prominent New York attorney Charles O'Connor to represent the former president. In January 1866, Grant asked the president to allow Varina Davis to travel freely, except to Washington and Fort Monroe. Finally, on January 23, the attorney general allowed her to visit her children in Canada at a time of her choosing.

The following month, Varina Davis left Georgia, accompanied by Burton Harrison, who had been released from Fort Delaware on January 16, 1866. They went first to New Orleans, and their warm reception there led to an outpouring of affection and sympathy for her and her husband. In the defeated South, many Southerners saw her as a symbol of the Lost Cause and the struggle against Radical rule from Washington. After a short stay in the Crescent City, Varina and Harrison traveled to Montreal to visit her mother, her children, and her sister. They had been in Montreal for only a few days when Varina received word that the government had granted her permission to visit her husband. When she arrived at Fort Monroe, she saw that Jefferson's physical condition was very serious. Samuel Cooper agreed with her assessment and told Nelson A. Miles that Davis might die in prison.

The visit to Davis and the realization that his physical condition was deteriorating inspired Varina to drum up support in Washington and throughout the South for his release. She requested an interview with the president and asked for Davis's parole. After writing to other prominent government officials, Davis received better food and Secretary of the Treasury Hugh McCullough inspected the prisoner's conditions at Fort Monroe.

In May 1866, Andrew Johnson agreed to see Varina. Their meeting was cordial, and he suggested that she formally request a parole for her husband. But during this encounter, an incident occurred that gave her an insight into the dynamics of the power struggle occurring in Washington between the president and the Radical Republicans. In the course of their meeting, Senator Thaddeus Stevens strolled into the president's office, berated Johnson, and then stormed out without regard to the meeting with Varina.

The attention focused on the plight of Davis and the treatment afforded him by the Federal government slowly resulted in better conditions for him. In May 1866, Virginia Clay successfully obtained her husband's release, and this sparked Varina's hope that her husband would be freed. When she

returned to Fort Monroe, she was pleased to learn that Davis was finally allowed to roam around the fort freely, from dawn to dusk. Then, after a year
of confinement without any formal charges, Davis was allowed to meet with
his attorneys and to receive visitors other than family members.

Among the former president's early visitors were several Catholic clergy,
including Irish-born Bishop Patrick N. Lynch of Charleston and Father
Matthew O'Keefe, who served in the Army of Northern Virginia. The Rev-
erend Minnigerode continued to visit Davis from Richmond, as did Bishop
Will Mercer Green and Burton N. Harrison's uncle, Dr. William Francis
Brand. The Reverend and former Brig. Gen. William Pendleton came from
Lexington with word of Robert E. Lee's activities at Washington College.

In January 1867, the case against Davis began to unravel. He had been
charged in a district court with murder, cruelty, and treason. The presiding
judge, John C. Underwood, allowed outrageous language to be used in the
indictment, asserting that Davis had "most wickedly, maliciously, and traitor-
ously" waged war against the United States while "not having the fear of God
before his eyes." The indictment further stated that Davis had been "seduced
by the instigation of the devil." The motion for release proffered by Davis's attorneys, O'Connor and George Shea, was denied.

When Shea went to Chief Justice Salmon P. Chase to discuss Davis's
case, he was told that he must file his writ of habeas corpus with Underwood. But Underwood's court would not meet until May.

Finally, due to some political maneuvering and influential friends, it appeared that Davis would finally be released on bail. Varina was able to
arrange for one of Stanton's friends, John W. Garrett, the president of the
Baltimore and Ohio Railroad, to visit the secretary of war. Garrett convinced
Stanton that it would be in the best interests of the United States to have
Davis released on bail. Horace Greeley, Gerrit Smith, and other Northern
businessmen agreed to guarantee the one-hundred-thousand-dollar bond
for his bail. Surprisingly, Underwood granted the writ of habeas corpus, and
the president ordered the new commander of Fort Monroe to have Davis in
Richmond on May 13.[28]

Burton N. Harrison had been released from Fort Delaware on January
16, 1866. Francis R. Lubbock and William Preston Johnston were released from the same prison in November. John H. Reagan was released
from Fort Warren. None of the former cabinet officials were ever charged
with any crime against the Federal government. Attempts were made,

however, to coerce Harrison into confessing that Davis was involved in the Lincoln assassination.

On May 10, Harrison arrived at Fort Monroe and stayed overnight in order to escort Jefferson Davis and Varina to Richmond the next day on the steamer *John Sylvester*. They were accompanied by Gen. Henry S. Burton, Union marshals, Dr. Samuel Cooper, and attorney Robert Ould. Along the riverbank at the various landings, clusters of people gathered to pay their respects to the former president. In Richmond, the couple stayed at the Spotswood Hotel and occupied the same rooms they had in 1861.

Davis appeared in court on Monday morning, May 13. Harrison recalled that there was "a mighty army of counsel here" and that "O'Connor is towering in his supremacy over all lesser personages and looked like a demi-god of antiquity."[29] Davis's supporters held their breath in the courtroom when Judge Underwood spoke, and a sigh of relief was uttered after he pronounced "the case is undoubtedly bailable, and as the Government is not ready to proceed with the trial, and the prisoner is and for a long time has been ready and demanding trial, it seems eminently proper that bail should be allowed."[30]

Upon leaving the courthouse, Davis rode with Minnegerode and Harrison en route to the Spotswood Hotel in an open carriage through streets lined with people. When the former president rose to exit the carriage, someone shouted, "Hats off, Virginians," and five thousand men removed their headgear in homage to Davis. That night, Harrison escorted the Davis family aboard a steamer for New York and then to Montreal.[31]

12

BROTHER AND SISTER

My dear friend, if you will only let me know how I am to find my way over to Staten Island, you know I will with the greatest pleasure come to see you, for I really long to do so.

—James A. Semple to Julia Gardiner Tyler

$\mathcal{T}$HE OTTAWA HOTEL ON St. James Street in Montreal was almost as busy in late August 1865 as it had been during the war. Months before, the lobby would have been filled with men in blue uniforms as the Ottawa was where Northerners tended to congregate when visiting the city. Those with allegiance to the South gathered at St. Lawrence Hall, where patrons could sip mint juleps. Needless to say, spies from opposite camps had lurked around the parlors and bars of both establishments. James A. Semple, for some reason, preferred to stay at the Ottawa, and he would make it his stopping place in Montreal in the months ahead.

Finding William F. Howell in the city was probably not all that difficult. He would not have had time to rent an apartment or a house, so it was a matter of checking hotels and boardinghouses. Exactly how and when Semple caught up to him is not known. What is known is that Howell was not exactly hiding, and he was soon back on good terms with both Varina and her husband. Also, Semple ended up with a money supply in Montreal, which could only mean that he had retrieved the gold, or a portion of it, without hard feelings on the part of either Howell or Semple. In fact, after the Howell family had settled in Chambly—a ferry ride across the St. Lawrence River from the city—Semple spent ten days there.[1]

Howell was definitely in Montreal with his mother and the Davis children the first day they were there.[2] Possibly, he decided that he should help his aging mother on her journey to Canada with the children. At the same time, he undoubtedly saw an opportunity to secret the gold out of the country. While Varina was more or less under the watchful eye of Union authorities, no one was likely to care much about a former commissary agent, so Howell was neither observed nor restricted in his travels. There would be no sense in leaving the gold behind, and once he reached Montreal, the funds could be deposited in a bank there, where it would be safer than in a bank in Augusta or anywhere else in the South. He had no idea where Semple was or when he would be coming back into the country. The last Howell knew, Semple was trying to find passage to Nassau and then to England.

This explanation must have satisfied his pursuer. Semple also realized that his former agent had no personal funds, since he probably had not received any pay from Semple's office for months. The Confederate navy had been able to provide food and clothing, but money was another matter. Semple, of course, knew this—he had received nothing as well—and he probably agreed that Howell had a right to a small amount of the gold. He could have also rationalized that, until Howell found a way to earn a living, funds would be needed for the care and welfare of the president's children, two of whom—ten-year-old Jeff and eight-year-old Maggie—were being entered into school.

For part of 1866, Howell and his wife lived in New York City, where he apparently looked for work. Eventually, he returned to Montreal and made an effort to generate an income by setting up or purchasing a distillery, almost certainly with a contribution from Semple. He also had a partner: his brother-in-law, Jefferson Davis.

With no home and no family, Semple had two loyalties, the president and the South. (Julia Tyler would soon be his third—and most commanding—commitment.) Without question, he was willing to do whatever he could to help Davis. He also agonized over what he could see as disaster for the former

Confederacy. He expected that Andrew Johnson's government would exact heavy penalties before the Southern states would again have a voice in their affairs; the toll on the people would be harder than the deprivations of the war itself. At some point, perhaps in conversation with Davis during the flight south, maybe in conversation with his relatives in Alabama, or in the solitude of his days of hiding in the Okefenokee Swamp, Semple began to formulate a plan through which he could be of some help to the South.

In Semple's mind, and in the minds of some former generals and Southern leaders, the only way that the North would ease up on the states and the people who made up the Confederacy would be if the United States were to be drawn into another war. Should that happen, then the North would need the South to help fight a common enemy. The most logical candidate was England. The two countries were already at loggerheads over what the United States considered to be money owed for the shipping and materials supplied by England to the Confederacy during the war. The United States insisted that England turn over all Confederate vessels remaining in British ports and freeze whatever assets could be found in the bank accounts of the Confederate government and its agents. Fraser, Trenholm and Company in Liverpool was thus put out of business, despite the fact that the firm had customers other than the Confederacy. The situation between the two countries was tense, and Semple wanted to help make it worse. The Fenian Brotherhood might just be the answer.

Semple had no doubt heard of the Fenian Brotherhood, but it may have been John Mitchel who helped him to see the potential benefit for the South. An Irishman by birth, Mitchel had a colorful history, including escaping imprisonment on the island of Tasmania (then called Van Diemen's Land) off the coast of Australia. As editor of the *Richmond Enquirer* and later the *Richmond Examiner* during the war, Mitchel had a dual mission in life: he was an uncompromising advocate of Irish freedom from Great Britain, and he was as fanatical about the right of Southerners to be independent from the North.

Mitchel at times disagreed with Jefferson Davis on government decisions and actions, but he was a friend of the president and a frequent guest at the Confederate White House. His commitment to the South had cost him deeply: two of his sons were killed and a third son lost an arm during the war. At the end of the war, Mitchel was arrested on a vague charge of "aiding the Rebellion" and confined at Fort Monroe, the same prison that held Davis and his friend Clement Clay. He claimed not to be a Fenian, but he was for a time. He also supported the ultimate objective of the Fenian cause (freedom for the Irish people), and like the Fenians, he had a burning hatred for the British government.

Through Mitchel's proselytizing, Davis and anyone who chose to listen knew about the Fenians and their mission in America. The president's roots on his mother's side were Scots Irish, his Scottish ancestors having settled in Northern Ireland. Then, too, Varina's grandfather on her mother's side was Irish and from a county in Northern Ireland as well. No doubt Davis lent a sympathetic ear to Mitchel's views. Semple's roots were Scottish, and he was also probably supportive, not that it mattered that much. What mattered more was the plight of the Southern people.[3]

The Fenian movement actually began as a secret organization of Irish immigrants in New York City. The idea was to train and recruit an army in America to drive the British out of Ireland. John O'Mahoney—a former colonel in the Sixty-ninth New York Infantry of the Irish Brigade—was chosen to lead the American group, while an equivalent faction, known as the Irish Republican Brotherhood (IRB) was set up in Ireland under James Stephens. The IRB was the forerunner of the Irish Republican Army. While the American Civil War had thrown a wrinkle into the plans of the Fenian Brotherhood by siphoning off tens of thousands of Irishmen into the Union and Confederate armies, Fenian leaders ultimately realized that the war provided a superb training ground for the battles to come in Ireland.[4]

The New York City organization spread to other cities in the North and in the South and to Montreal, which became a hotbed of Fenian activity.[5] In each key city, the organization consisted of circles, groups headed by a leader known as a centre, who oversaw recruiting, fund-raising, and caching weapons. The larger cities had more than a single circle; New Orleans, for example, had three.

As might be expected, raising of an army on U.S. soil to overthrow British rule in Ireland was not well received in England—which was what Semple (and Davis) were counting on. They knew that thousands of Irishmen in the United States were sympathetic to the Fenian cause and were ready to join the organization. At the same time, the U.S. government was slow to take any action to contain the Fenian effort, perhaps because England was slow in paying reparations for Union merchant ships sunk by British-built Confederate vessels during the war.[6]

All in all, the United States could well end up in a war with England, and Semple had the time and the money to help push it along. He would be careful, however, to keep his name off the meeting rolls and out of any communications.

During the month of September, Semple must have explored the Fenian movement and may have offered his services at the Fenian headquarters on Broadway in New York. His role in the organization is not clear, but given his constant travels in the postwar years, he may have been a courier between circles. He thus maintained a low profile both because of his connection with the Fenians and because he was an unparoled, unpardoned former Confederate official.

Supporting his travels would be the caches of Confederate gold in Savannah, Montreal, and New York (where he opened an account at the Mechanics National Bank on Wall Street).[7] Also at his disposal *should* have been the gold coins in the possession of Edward M. Tidball. There is evidence, however, that Tidball never parted with the specie and may have refused to do so.

Semple had done a great deal of thinking about Julia and her family, and he regretted that he had not yet contacted her. He had heard nothing of Alex and Gardie, and he worried about them. Were they all right? The last time he saw them was in Richmond, while he was hustling to get his department's records together during the relocation of the Confederate government to Danville. Did they go to Sherwood Forest, assuming it was still standing, or to Staten Island? He doubted they would return to New York, as they were devout "Yankee-haters." But Julia might have insisted on their coming there, so she could collect her family while facing whatever was ahead of them as "Rebels."

He missed his conversations with fifteen-year-old Julie and the joy of her rambunctious five-year-old Birdie. Christened Pearl, Birdie was a nickname that Semple used. Julia and just about everyone else called her Pearlie. Then there were thirteen-year-old Lachlan, eleven-year-old Lyon, and nine-year-old Robert, known as Fitz.

As his mind began to ease somewhat about being caught, Semple allowed himself to wonder how Julia was doing, and he decided to see her. Perhaps she would be glad to see him. In October, he had a chance to find out. Staying at the New York Hotel on Broadway, where he had come for a Fenian meeting, he sent a note to Julia at Castleton Hill.

My dear friend, if you will only let me know how I am to find my way over to Staten Island, you know I will with greatest pleasure come to see you, for I really long to do so. Pray tell me something of Gardie & Alex, they have been constant in my memory since leaving Richmond & I could get no information on them. I have been quite a traveler since I left the Old City—Georgia, Alabama, Florida, Nassau, etc. have been visited & now I have not determined whether to go to Canada on the day after to-morrow or to Philadelphia—I do not wish it known generally that I am here, as I have some particular business to attend to and do not desire to run any risk of being molested until I accomplish my errand—with love to Julie and the children.[8]

On October 16, 1865, the Fenians held a convention in Philadelphia. Attended by six hundred delegates and Semple (assuming he chose not to go to Canada), the meeting exposed a lack of unity in the leadership, and seeds were sown for a major split in the organization. One group, under O'Mahoney, wanted the Fenians to remain committed to raising an army to send to Ireland. The second group, led by William Randall Roberts, a former New York militia colonel, called for an invasion of Canada to be launched from the United States in order to capture Canada and trade it back to England in exchange for Ireland's independence. The split within the brotherhood was never resolved, and the two factions pursued their separate goals with separate headquarters in New York.

In renewing his relationship with Julia, Semple found himself immediately drawn into a family lifestyle he could have only imagined. He had never known his mother and father, never had a brother or sister, and never had children of his own.[9] But here was a family with laughing, boisterous children and a warm acceptance that gave him a general sense of well-being. He and Julia spent hours talking, and he relished the evenings in front of the fireplace. When asked, he advised her much like an older brother or a husband would.

Semple had been captivated by Julia's beauty and vivaciousness for years, but he had no illusions of a closer relationship during that time. As testy as his marriage to Letitia was, he was married, and Julia was the wife of a man he greatly admired, John Tyler. As Semple's marriage had soured, he settled for trying to neutralize Letitia's venom directed at Julia. His efforts did not go unnoticed, and gradually Julia warmed to Semple and came to judge him without painting him with the same brush she used for his wife.

Now, eighteen years later, John Tyler was dead and Semple was estranged from Letitia. He had grown in Julia's mind from a person for whom she had little regard to someone she depended on and was fond of—someone, in fact, she deeply needed in her life. As for Semple, he may not have known the story of the Bogert and Mecamly advertisement and how Julia came to be called the "Rose of Long Island" when she was nineteen. If he had, he would have agreed that the epithet was still appropriate, for even at forty-six, Julia embodied beauty and perfection to him.

His room at Castleton Hill contrasted starkly with the lonely hotel rooms he would be frequenting in New York and other cities. Since Manhattan was twenty miles from Staten Island, with a ferry ride in between, he would need to stay some of the time in a hotel along Broadway in order to get to Fenian headquarters by carriage or afoot. But if he had to be in the city, he would notify Julia, and she would occasionally visit him at his hotel.[10]

Often Semple preferred the Astor House on the lower end of Broadway. He could usually get a room there, and it was close to Sweeney's Hotel, where the Fenians congregated; yet he could separate himself from the noise and confusion and be reasonably comfortable in the aging landmark. Occasionally, the Fenians would use a private parlor at the Astor for a meeting. The hotel was also only a few blocks south of the Fenian headquarters at 22 Duane Street.

When Semple indulged himself, he would take a room farther uptown at the palatial Metropolitan, with its steam heat and speaking tubes, or at the elegant St. Nicholas. The New York Hotel, where he would also stay, was several blocks farther up Broadway. The hotel had always been a favorite with Southerners, though it was outclassed by the newer and larger hotels along the strip.

By mid-November, Semple returned to Augusta, where he visited Varina Davis.[11] She was spending a week with a sister of George Schley, Mrs. Henry McAlpin, who lived near Mill View in Belleville Factory. The Schley brothers, George and William, once owned a large factory there on Butler's Creek that had produced oilcloth, tents, knapsacks, and other items for the Confederacy. The mill itself had been burned in a Union cavalry raid, but the boardinghouse for the former workers remained, with Mrs. McAlpin as an occupant.

Semple's visit was partly social. He asked about how Varina was doing and updated her on events, including where he stood with her brother. He wanted to be able to pass on information to the president as well, and Varina was his only hope. Though she was now allowed to write to her husband, her letters were censored. Coding was a possibility but risky. She had badgered everyone she could think of who had any influence over Davis's imprisonment and care, imploring them to allow her to visit her husband. And she could not jeopardize that with a coded letter about something over which Davis had no control. Still, she may have tried to communicate something to her husband, since censors deleted the beginning and ending paragraphs of her next letter.

In leaving Varina, Semple knew that he had to wait until she was in a position to talk privately with her husband. In the meantime, any decisions regarding Semple's activities had to be made by him. The next day, he wrote to Julia, mentioning that he visited Varina and that he would be back in New York around the end of the month. He would be coming by an inland, underground route through the Galt House in Lexington, Kentucky, and he warned her that she "must be ready" for him. He also expressed relief at hearing from Alex and Gardie and learning firsthand about their schooling overseas.[12]

The next few months for Semple were a blend of travel between Montreal and New York, with occasional respites at Castleton Hill. He grew increasingly drawn to Julia and to the children, and without question, the affection deepened between them. He was also beginning to be plagued with illnesses, no doubt brought on—at least in part—by his lifestyle and the stress of moving around with an assumed name. On Broadway, he was constantly scanning crowds for people who might recognize him, and he lived in fear that someone might innocently call him by name or some constable or soldier might stop him for questioning. Whether the threat of exposure was real or imagined, the physical impact on him was the same.

Thus far, his finances were holding out, as they should have, given the amounts he had deposited in at least three locations and perhaps in New Orleans as well. At the rate he was spending money, though, it could not last indefinitely. Travel and expenses were one thing (and he may have been reimbursed by the Fenians), but the money he provided to Julia was another. Without question, as she was his closest confidant, she knew full well the source of his funds.

Semple's visit to Howell in Chambly occurred in early January 1866.[13] They could have discussed many things, including the gold (which by then was likely deposited in the Montreal Bank), the children (so he could report back to Varina; she seldom received a letter from her mother), and perhaps Howell's business ventures.

Problems within the Fenian Brotherhood were coming to a head, and Semple reported to Julia at the end of January "there has been a great 'blow up' in the Tribe."[14] The two factions were now in different headquarters, each vying to build its membership and an army.

As the end of March approached, Semple was physically and possibly mentally suffering. In a confidential letter to Julia, he wrote:

> Being well aware that I am now often subject to severe attacks of illness, and the probability is that I may die suddenly, I shall leave with you a package of valuable papers, etc., which in case of my death, I give to you. No one but you & myself know of your having it from me. They shall never know it. I have a running account at the Mechanics National Bank, No. 33 Wall Street, N.Y. and whatever amount may be due me at the time of my death, I also give you. For this purpose and to prevent any trouble to you in anyway, I enclose in this a blank check with my signature.

He included for the first time, an expression of his feelings for her:

> Intimate intercourse and close inspection have convinced me of your sincerity, the gentleness surrounding so much pure flame, which you so clearly exhibit daily, is a priceless privilege of nature which adorns you. You are good, I know, and beautiful to my eyes, but you are not mine!! My love you know you have taken.[15]

How Julia was beginning to feel about Semple is unknown. Being the widow of a U.S. president probably tempered anything she wrote to him that could possibly be read by others, including members of her own family. What she said to him in private, however, was never revealed. If nothing else, she trusted him implicitly, even with her own children. Now that Alex and Gardie were settled in school, at least for the time being, she decided that her now sixteen-year-old boy-crazy daughter Julie needed some guidance, a good boarding school perhaps. Julie was as flirtatious as Julia had been twenty years ago. In Julie's case, though, instead of politicians, she was enamored with West Point cadets and young army officers. After learning about the

Convent of the Sacred Heart in Halifax, Nova Scotia, Julia turned to Semple for help.

On March 31, 1866, Julie and Semple left New York for Halifax and arrived there during the evening of April 4.[16] To Julia's surprise, her daughter did not resist being sent away. Perhaps she saw promise in not being under the watchful eye of her mother, even though she was going to a convent. In any case, she was not long in making her first conquest, a West Pointer, whom she soon had in tow during the voyage from Portland, Maine, to St. John, New Brunswick. Apparently, she was not planning to exactly follow the wishes of her mother: "You must write every week to me, telling me everything, and write to very few others—and to no gentlemen."[17]

Semple found Halifax to be a "one-horse" town, but he was happy to spend some time with old Confederate navy friends John Taylor Wood and John Wilkinson, the latter a renowned blockade-runner. Wood, after his flight following Davis's capture, arrived in Halifax from Cuba and was joined there by his family. At the end of the war, Wilkinson relinquished his ship, the *Chameleon,* to James Bulloch, the senior Confederate naval officer in Europe. Deciding not to return to the United States because he probably would have been arrested, Wilkinson ended up in Halifax, where he and Wood ran a successful merchant commission house. Wood never left Halifax, but after several years, Wilkinson returned to his old Virginia home.

As much as Semple grew tired of Halifax, he spent more than a month there, meeting with the convent officials, including the archbishop and lady superior, and making sure Julie was not going to end up wanting to go home. Much of the time, he was sick in bed at the Halifax Hotel. On May 8, he boarded a steamer to return to New York, comfortable that Julie was happy where she was. In writing to Julia before leaving, Semple indicated that he would like to have a couple of photographs of her, "one a profile & the other *low necked.*" He closed by indicating that just seeing her "glorious bright eyes" would do him more good than a surgeon: "I am longing to be with you."[18]

Meanwhile, Julia was having money problems. First, there was a note from a man named Monroe that needed to be paid, which Semple agreed to do if he could get south again to his source of funds. (Semple must have had little in his account at the Mechanics National Bank.) But that was not all she needed. He replied, "As to the amount you say you still require here for your own use, as soon as I can go about, I will raise if for you, if possible—and I feel sure I can. How much is it?"[19] Before 1866 was over, Semple "loaned" Julia around six thousand dollars (equivalent to about seventy-two thousand dollars today).

To say that Julia was extravagant in some respects would be an understatement. While not all of her purchases were for her alone—she was extremely generous in helping others left destitute by the war, including Varina—she was notoriously delinquent in paying her bills and was especially "forgetful" when it came to retail stores.[20] Given her social status as a Gardiner and as the wife of a former U.S. president, she was almost certainly given some leeway and extra courtesy in the bill-collection process. An example of the creative reminders she received was that of A. E. Dean and Co., which made party and wedding cakes. On her bill for $13.18 that had been outstanding for months was the following request: "If Mrs. Tyler thinks this Bill has stood a sufficient length of time perhaps she will oblige us by sending the amt by mail."

Alone in his room at the New York Hotel, Semple wrestled with his feelings for Julia. His infatuation, if that is what it was, had overtaken him to the point where he wrote her the following on May 14:

There is no love like that which springs up in manhood, it is strong, fervent, undying for the one he esteems so highly for the many & varied good qualities which adorn her so admirably, and knows too that the great beauty which she is possessed of, so far from being on the wane, that it is daily increasing in his eyes, her person filling out to the elegant proportions that Raphael delighted to transfer to canvas for the admiration of after ages, as the form of his beloved mistress. Increasingly years are constantly gathering new sweetness & it is this power of accumulation so few are possessed of that makes your life so rich, so full, so beautifully rounded to perfection & must go on until the span of life has passed & you have joined your Mother Earth.

The treasures of the deep sea are not so precious as the concealed joy in my heart, when I could imagine for a moment that my feelings towards you were returned. There can be no love like mine, it is matured & can never grow cold or lukewarm, I love you, yearned to tell you so, but had no great heart-word to tell you how much, all of life or death, heaven or hell hangs on that simple word. I love you with my whole heart & sole, it shall be watered with showers of tender affection, expanded with the kindest attentions &

guarded with the impregnable barrier of unshaken confidence, it shall bloom with fragrance in every season of life. "I ask only to breathe the blessed air you breathe, whether it bears healing or death, it is sweet to me." The stream of love has its giddy billows & cataracts, but there are times when for however brief a space it flows calm & still, yet deep reflecting without a ripple the brightness & the beauty of the external heavens & one can not be deprived of that exquisite feeling.

Among all the gay throng which flits past me as I promenade Broadway not one of them owns a face so lovely, attractive & fascinating as yours, it is beautiful even in repose, & when feeling & thoughts light up and warm your countenance, it is irresistible & what adds to it too, that voice is so full, so sweetly musical & clear, so full of passion, that I am sure the angels must love you. Honor & love shown to the Vice Roy is honor shown to the King, you are my Vice reagent of heaven for this planet, you are my nearest visible representation of the Creator.[21]

While Julia's true feelings can only be surmised, what led Semple to write "the treasures of the deep sea are not so precious as the concealed joy in my heart, when I could imagine for a moment that my feelings towards you were returned"?[22] Did she give him a reason for imagining this? Was she keeping her feelings on a leash because of who she was? Was their relationship only platonic? Were they simply a "brother" and a "sister" helping each other out, or were there deeper feelings on her part as well as his? More was to come between them.

On June 5, Semple returned to New York on business. Choosing to stay at a hotel along Broadway, he let Julia know he was there and she joined him, leaving at some point during the evening. In a relatively long letter to her the next day, he recalled a previous time they had been together:

If you remember the morning, I handed you those letters you had unfortunately left on my pillow, as I went downstairs, you hailed me and said you are "whistling & singing now, I will tell you something which will surprise you & make you sing & whistle another way." I have been patiently awaiting information, would you please tell me at once, do dear."

I know & have done so some time previously, that I suffered myself to loosen the strings of my heart so much, having kept them, for reasons best known to myself, rolled up as it is now in my hand for so many years.[23]

In mid-June Semple headed back to Savannah, probably to replenish his gold supply. On arriving there, he was disappointed to find that the people holding the specie for him were being watched closely by the Federal authorities. No one dared to go near the gold, wherever it had been hidden. Feeling the pressure, Semple went into hiding for a time, assuming a disguise and staying with a German immigrant about six miles outside the city.[24]

He had no idea when he could get at the money in Savannah, so he would need to travel to Montreal and retrieve funds from the cache there, assuming Howell had not yet depleted it. (In New Orleans, Semple apparently had funds, or perhaps someone loaned him money there.) In the Savannah and Augusta area, he had used the name Allen S. James. He decided he should probably continue using the name after he returned to New York and later traveled to Montreal.

At the Astor House on August 3, though he signed the register as Allen S. James, a note reached him from his wife, Letitia, and he assumed she wanted money. (Probably the desk people at the Astor recognized him as James Semple and passed the note on to him.) He would deal with Letitia after he got back from Montreal, where he had to go to retrieve some papers. Now that Varina was allowed to visit the president at Fort Monroe, he had a way to communicate with Davis; he would go to Old Point Comfort (Fort Monroe) after the trip to Montreal in order to update the president. At the same time, he had to admit that not much had been accomplished in terms of helping the South. Of course, the Fenians were still very much a factor to be reckoned with, and their ranks continued to grow daily, even if they were joining competing armies. War with Britain was still a reasonable possibility.

In Montreal, Semple took a room at the Ottawa House and encountered a number of old acquaintances from both the Confederate and British armies and navies. He had not seen some of them for years and enjoyed the relaxing conversation. At night, he felt well enough to attend a ball on the English gunboat *Pylades,* and later a bride he had once dangled on his knee as a child talked him into a boat tour along the river. His long day of relaxation, however, was short-lived; the gunboat was likely a clue to an undercurrent of tension that permeated certain sections of the city.[25]

On May 31, William Randall Robert's branch of the Fenian army invaded Canada. Fenian Col. John O'Neill (a Union officer during the war), commanding some five hundred soldiers, crossed the border from Buffalo to

Fort Erie, Canada. O'Neill's attack was well executed, and the Fenians won the battle of Ridgeway against the first of two Canadian militia units. The border crossing, however, was a neutrality violation that Andrew Johnson could not ignore. He sent Maj. Gen. George Gordon Meade to prevent any crossings of reinforcements and arms and to round up any Fenian soldiers remaining on the U.S. side.

In the meantime, Fenian Brig. Gen. Samuel Spears had marched about twelve hundred troops into Canada, across the Vermont-Quebec border. With British regulars supposedly bearing down on him, Spears returned to the United States and collided with a waiting U.S. army. With no reinforcements and no help coming from Spears, O'Neill had to retreat back into the United States and was also captured.

After placating England by capturing the Fenian army, the Johnson administration then sought to sooth Irish feelings everywhere by quietly releasing the Fenian soldiers and sending them home with railroad tickets. The invasion and its aftermath were over in a matter of days. If Johnson had delayed his action against the Fenians, or if the Fenian army had been able to invade Canada with larger numbers, Semple might have gotten his wish for a war between Britain and the United States. Instead, the result was increased dissention between the two factions of the Fenian Brotherhood. They lacked a common ground and turned to finger pointing and blaming each other for the failed enterprise.

In writing to Julia, Semple is clearly disgusted:

> There is the devil to pay among the "tribe" here, no one speaks to the other & I have heard the most astounding reports & have been questioned by a member of the "tribe" & have no hesitation in at once, answering all the questions in writing, and I tell you now that by my own volition I will never pass another word with one of them. . . . I shall write to Mrs. Davis and inform old Jeff of the circumstances & will at the same time, send a necessary memo of the matters in my charge & decline any further special interest in the matter.

Near the end of the letter, he softened somewhat: "At the same time, I am ready to engage in any matter which will further the interest of the south."[26]

In early September, Semple was back at the Astor House, apparently tired, disgusted, and in pain. For someone no one was supposed to be able to find, he was burdened with problems. He indicated to Julia in a delivered note that he had tried several times to contact her through the "collector" at the Staten Island ferry boat. He was hoping she would be able to come to see him as he was staying at the hotel to "attend to matters." In subsequent letters, Semple commented:

> I have received several letters which recalled me to this place—I hope that I shall get out of the business safely—But to tell you the truth, I shall not be very particular in the matter except to see that I am not imposed on, or my honor impugned—I do so wish I had returned with you. . . .
>
> Letters from Montreal, Baltimore, this city, and Norfolk have disturbed me seriously, but I know it is only because I am sick and my nerves are disturbed for the time being.[27]

Then he asked a revealing question: "Why did you not wake me up the morning you left? I have had some 'dreams' too, which have disturbed my growing equanimity—you will be amused, when I tell you."

Of the letters he received, those from Montreal and New York were Fenian issues, irritations he could deal with. But the communications from Baltimore and Norfolk were different.

13

EXODUS

The past is now past—all is now in the future.

—Burton N. Harrison to fiancée Constance Cary,
May 18, 1867

*A*s 1866 CAME TO a close, most of the Confederate hierarchy—that is, those who chose not to flee to foreign countries (or were caught before they could do so)—had already been allowed to return to their homes. John H. Reagan, Vice President Alexander H. Stephens, and Secretary of the Treasury George A. Trenholm had been released from prison by the end of 1865. Secretary of the Navy Stephen R. Mallory—no doubt incarcerated longer because of the successful operations of Confederate commerce raiders such as the *Alabama* and the *Shenandoah,* which captured or sank millions of dollars' worth of U.S. vessels and goods—was freed in March 1866.[1]

Jefferson Davis's release on bail on May 13, 1867, signaled the beginning of the end of the Federal government's case against the former president and ended the prospect that any former Confederate officials would be prosecuted. After Davis walked out of the courtroom in Richmond a free man, at least for the time being, he left immediately for New York with

Varina, escorted by Burton N. Harrison. There they spent the night at the country estate of his chief counsel, Charles O'Conor; Davis was anxious to leave New York and see his children in Canada.

In Montreal, Davis began a slow recovery process and had the opportunity to visit with a number of former Confederate officials. His physical condition shocked one observer, British army Col. George Denison, who described the "emaciation and weakness" and said that he "looked like a dying man."[2] Besides the physical deterioration, the months of solitary confinement with little or no communication had caused psychological trauma to the point that crowds and loud noises upset Davis.

While Davis was left scarred by the mental and physical torture he had endured at Fort Monroe, he also had to face the fact that he was virtually penniless. Unable to afford to stay at a hotel in Montreal, Davis moved his family into a cheaper hotel with plainer food in Lennoxville. While there, the frail Davis fell down the stairs and broke three ribs. Varina decided that they could not remain in Canada without an income and with her husband having nothing to do.

In July 1868, the Davis family took a steamer to England so he could investigate a job offer from a commission house in Liverpool. In Britain, former Confederates living there in exile—especially Judah P. Benjamin—received Davis warmly. During their time in Liverpool, the Davises resided with Maj. Norman Walker and his wife, Georgiana. Walker had worked for the Confederacy in Bermuda as a purchasing agent and freight forwarder. Although Davis eventually declined the job offer, he used the opportunity to travel in Europe.

Davis nor any other Confederate official was ever brought to trial for treason. On Christmas Day 1868, Andrew Johnson issued a final proclamation of general amnesty, which exempted the former Confederate leadership from prosecution but also disqualified the president and members of his cabinet from holding future public office. Varina did not believe the proclamation went far enough, as "the accusation of complicity in [the Lincoln] assassination was never withdrawn, and the epithet of traitor was hurled at his head by every so-called orator, patrio, or petty penny-a-liner in the North."[3] Federal prosecutors finally dropped the case against Davis in February 1869.

Several months after his arrival in Great Britain, Davis returned to the United States, having been offered a position as the president of the Carolina Insurance Company in Memphis. In 1873 the company failed, and Davis was unemployed. He was then involved in a number of schemes that never materialized, and he declined an offer to become the first president of the Agricultural and Mechanical College of Texas (which later became Texas A&M University).

In 1878, New York publisher Appleton and Company asked Davis to write his memoirs. Needing money, he began *The Rise and Fall of the Confederate Government*. The resulting two-volume tome enabled the former president to present the history of the Confederacy as he and other Southern leaders recalled events. He attacked the project with enthusiasm, because he saw in his writing an opportunity to silence his critics. The book was only mildly received, particularly in the North, but whatever sales he had provided much-needed income.

Davis was assisted in the endeavor by Maj. W. T. Walthall, hired by Davis to collect documents and to contact former generals, cabinet members, etc. for their input about specific events. Also helpful was the offer of a quiet place to write, a small house on the secluded six-hundred-acre plantation of Sarah Anne Ellis Dorsey. Davis had known the wealthy author and widow for many years, and Varina had once attended school with her.

Ultimately the estate, known as Beauvoir, became his. In early 1879, Sarah Dorsey offered to sell the plantation to him for fifty-five hundred dollars, to be paid in three installments. Davis agreed and paid the first installment right away. Apparently knowing she was dying of cancer, Dorsey moved to New Orleans, where she passed away that same year. In her will, Davis discovered that Beauvoir had been left to him, along with three other plantations. He paid the two remaining installments, however, to clear debts on the property.

Davis spent most of his remaining years in seclusion, writing in defense of the Confederacy and venturing out for brief forays into the public. The former president lived only a few months beyond his eightieth birthday, developing acute bronchitis, complicated by malaria, after getting chilled in a sleety November rain while visiting his former home, Brierfield, in Mississippi. Taken to New Orleans for treatment, he died on December 5, 1889.

Varina stayed at Beauvoir for a few years. She then donated the plantation to the state of Mississippi as a Confederate veterans home and moved to New York City, where she supported herself by writing articles for magazines. She also wrote a book in defense of her husband, *Jefferson Davis, A*

Memoir. Her remaining years were relatively peaceful, and she spent much of her time attending operas, theaters, and concerts. She died of pneumonia on October 16, 1905, survived by only one of her six children: Margaret.

WHILE DAVIS had been imprisoned in Fort Monroe, John H. Reagan and Alexander H. Stephens had been incarcerated at Fort Warren in Boston Harbor. The two former leaders were a contrast in appearance: Stephens was of average stature but weighed barely 100 pounds and appeared sickly; Reagan stood over six feet tall and weighed between 250 and 275 pounds.

Initially kept in solitary confinement, by August 1865 the two men were allowed to visit one another, receive mail, and entertain visitors. Neither was accused of a crime, and they anticipated they would be released soon. By early October, Reagan and Stephens dreaded the approaching winter and the conditions they would likely encounter at the prison fort. Fortunately, relief came on October 12, when their release was ordered. The two men left Fort Warren the following day, and after spending a few days in Boston and the surrounding area, they departed for New York City, where they were visited by the mayor of New York and other city officials.

Stephens left New York with his brother and headed south; Reagan remained in New York to consult with Charles O'Conor, Davis's attorney. Reagan also awaited permission to visit Stephen R. Mallory, who had been confined at Fort Hamilton. Afterward, Reagan left for Washington, where he met with Andrew Johnson and Edwin M. Stanton. First, he asked both for an enlargement of the terms of his parole that would permit him to hunt for personal papers and family valuables he had hidden or that had been lost during the escape from Richmond. He also asked that Frank R. Lubbock be released from Fort Delaware and that he be allowed to visit Davis at Fort Monroe. Only the first request was granted, and after discussing many events of the recent war, Reagan left and went to Richmond and then Greensboro, Columbia, and Augusta, where he met with friends and tried to recover his papers and family mementos. From Augusta, he went to New Orleans, arriving there on November 29. After a short visit, Reagan departed for Galveston, arriving there on December 4.

Upon reaching his home in Palestine, Texas, Reagan found barren fields and his house in shambles. In desperate financial straits and alienated from his fellow citizens by a letter he had written to the people of Texas during his stay at Fort Warren, he reached "rock bottom." According to former

Gov. J.W. Henderson, Reagan's letter had been interpreted to mean that "while in prison you weakened in your devotion to the South and had come out for Negro suffrage."[4] Nevertheless, Reagan reversed his fortunes and returned to prominence by being elected to Congress in 1875, serving several terms in the House until he was elected to the Senate in 1887. When he died in 1905, the entire Texas legislature attended his funeral.

Stephens had been a U.S. congressman from Georgia from 1843 until 1859. Before the war, he had been an advocate of the Compromise of 1850 and had hoped that this agreement would end the sectional strife. He viewed the subsequent election of Lincoln as reigniting that conflict, but he attempted to prevent secession as a representative to Georgia's convention in 1861. After the Confederacy was formed, he was chosen as vice president by the Provisional Congress.

There was little need for Stephens's services during the war, but he participated in the ill-fated February 3, 1865, peace conference at Hampton Roads, where he met with Lincoln and Secretary of State William H. Seward. Unable to negotiate an armistice, Stephens returned to Richmond. Convinced the war was lost and disagreeing with Davis's resolve to defend the capital at any cost, he tendered his resignation on February 9,1865, and left for his home in Georgia, where he remained until his arrest on May 11.

Despite his frail and sickly appearance, after twenty-two weeks of imprisonment, Stephens returned to Georgia and ran for office. He was elected to the U.S. Congress in 1873 and served for nine years. In 1882, Stephens was elected governor of Georgia, but he died in office the following year.

While Davis's private secretary Burton N. Harrison provided significant attention and support to the former president and his family and was instrumental in obtaining Davis's release from Fort Monroe, he apparently provided no assistance to other former Confederate officials or to the "cause." Harrison, however, was generous with impoverished Confederate soldiers who sought his help, and he remained loyal to his former chief and stayed in close contact with him.

Harrison had vowed not to marry fiancée Constance Cary of Richmond until Davis was released from prison. But as soon as Davis was freed on bail, Harrison wrote to her, "The past is now the past—all is now in the future."[5] The couple was married in November 1867. As with many other Southern "refugees," the Harrisons settled in New York City, where he became a successful attorney and his wife a noted author and playwright.

The Harrisons traveled widely after the war, primarily as a result of his business with several large corporations. They soon integrated into New York society and spent their summers with the Northern elite at Bar Harbor, Maine. Constance Harrison counted among her friends Theodore Roosevelt's mother. One of the Harrisons' sons, Francis, was appointed as governor general of the Philippines. Their other son, Fairfax, became president of the Southern Railway system. Burton Harrison died on March 29, 1904, in Washington, D.C.

Among the group that left Richmond in April 1865, Treasury Secretary George A. Trenholm endured an especially arduous journey. His wife, Anna, wrote in her diary that he "was so ill and exhausted that I expected to see him drop."[6] By April 26, Trenholm resigned and finally arrived in Columbia, South Carolina, on May 28, stopping along the way to visit with friends and relatives in Abbeville. He was subsequently arrested by Union officials on June 8 in Charleston and was then sent to Fort Pulaski, Georgia. After five days of incarceration, he was paroled, arrested again, and returned to Fort Pulaski. Paroled for the final time on October 11, 1865, Trenholm was never charged, but he strangely received a pardon from the U.S. government on October 25, 1866.

Before Trenholm's first arrest, James Morgan, engaged to one of his daughters, had accompanied Trenholm with two large suitcases filled with gold coins obtained from one of the former treasury secretary's houses in Abbeville. The two had first gone to Columbia, where they had been informed by the commanding officer there that Trenholm was to report to Charleston to surrender himself. Trenholm instructed Morgan to take the gold to Mrs. Henry King, who Morgan described as "a young and beautiful widow; also an authoress of some local renown; but she was more famed for her powers of witty repartee than she was for her beauty, which was great, or her literary efforts."[7]

Morgan was able to locate King's house that night and found that she was entertaining a group of Union army and navy officers. When she greeted Morgan and he informed her of Trenholm's request that she hide the gold, she readily agreed, hiding it under a bed mattress. Morgan did not reveal when Trenholm recovered his gold—or even if he did—but King was known to have visited Trenholm in the Charleston jail before he was transferred to Fort Pulaski. No doubt the subject of the gold came up.[8]

One of the wealthiest men in the South before the war, most of Trenholm's assets were either confiscated or destroyed by the Federal government. Fraser, Trenholm and Company—which once owned and operated a fleet of more than sixty steamers and blockade-runners during the war—was forced to close its doors in Charleston and in Liverpool.

Trenholm returned to Charleston after his release from prison and salvaged his business interests and property. To this end, he formed G. A. Trenholm and Company, a cotton brokerage. While he worked to end the rule of the carpetbaggers in South Carolina and was elected to the state legislature in 1874, he strongly believed in reconciliation of the races during Reconstruction and contributed generously to charities that included churches, hospitals, and orphanages. He died in Charleston on December 9, 1876.

Judah P. Benjamin, the former Confederate secretary of state, was one of the fortunate escapees who never served any time in prison, yet he endured an almost miraculous escape to the Bahamas, Cuba, and ultimately to Great Britain. Arriving there on August 30, 1865, Benjamin was without funds, but he had title to a hundred bales of cotton that he had secured in Great Britain before the evacuation of Richmond. Inflated cotton prices at the end of the war netted him twenty thousand dollars. Benjamin wanted to resume his profession as an attorney, but he needed to study English law. Fortunately, he received an exemption from the required three years of study through influential friends. After clerking with a law firm, he began a successful law practice and became one of the leading attorneys in Great Britain in the late nineteenth century.

One dark cloud hung over Benjamin for several years after the war, and it was the same issue that haunted Davis: Secretary of War Edwin M. Stanton and Judge Adv. Gen. Joseph Holt never relented in asserting that Davis and Benjamin were responsible for the assassination of Abraham Lincoln. U.S. officials pointed out that John Surratt—son of Mary Surratt, who had been executed for her role in the conspiracy—couriered money to Confederate agents in Montreal at the behest of Benjamin. Surratt was ultimately arrested in Europe and tried for his supposed role in the plot, but the jury could not reach a verdict and Surratt was freed. The entire Confederate operation in Montreal and its various schemes were attributed to Benjamin, since his office funded the agents in Canada. As the years passed, the controversy appeared to die a natural death, and so did Benjamin. The *Times* of London, in writing of Benjamin's death in Paris on May 6, 1884, noted, "He had carved out for himself not one, but three histories of great and well-earned distinction."⁹

The other successful escapee was Semple's friend John Taylor Wood, who had ultimately relocated to Halifax, Nova Scotia. His arrival in the Canadian port was marked by dense fog and poor navigation by the ship's crew, which resulted in a delay, but at least he was safe from Union pursuers. Wood had visited Halifax less than a year earlier as captain of the CSS *Tallahassee*, when he had entered the port to take on supplies and coal. Yankee vessels were in pursuit, and the American consul in Halifax had asked British officials to detain Wood's ship. Though he was not detained, he was limited in the amount of coal he could procure. With the assistance of a Canadian pilot, Wood successfully navigated the narrow and hazardous eastern passage into the North Atlantic and then sailed south to Wilmington, where the *Tallahassee* ran the blockade. As commander of the raider, he was responsible for capturing thirty-three Union ships in a five-day period between August 11 and August 15, 1864.

Wood's stay in Halifax was initially short, as he made preparations for a journey to Montreal. Two weeks later, his wife, son, and daughter joined him from Elk Ridge, Maryland. After discussing their options—returning to the United States was apparently not one of them since Wood was not eligible for a parole and the threat of a trial for "piracy" loomed—they decided to return to Halifax. Wood had an affinity for the city, as he enjoyed the climate, the friendliness of the people, and the opportunities for boating.

Wood's successful merchant commission house, formed with John Wilkinson, became a prosperous endeavor, with business being done primarily with firms in Baltimore and Richmond. Wood also entered into the shipping and marine insurance business, and he became a director of the Eastern Company.

Although he rarely visited the United States after the war, when he did, it was in connection with a function or ceremony regarding former Confederates. At the request of Robert E. Lee's family in May 1890, he attended the unveiling of the Lee statue on Monument Avenue in Richmond; in 1892, he visited Norfolk on the thirtieth anniversary of the battle between the CSS *Virginia* and the USS *Monitor* (he had served on the *Virginia* as a second lieutenant during the battle). Despite these visits, Wood did not avail himself of the amnesty proclamations of September 7, 1867, and December 25, 1868. Thirty years after the war, Wood applied to Congress for removal of his political liabilities (being barred from political office), and this was granted by the required two-thirds vote of the House and Senate. Wood, however, remained in Canada, where he died on July 19, 1904, in Halifax and was buried.[10]

Wood's companion on the escape from Florida was Secretary of War John C. Breckinridge. From Havana, Breckinridge went first to the British West Indies and then on to Great Britain. Breckinridge originally believed he would be able to clear up the Confederate accounts that remained in Liverpool, but he found former Confederates there heavily in debt. After Judah P. Benjamin arrived, the two former cabinet officials tried to get Jacob Thompson, who had been in charge of Confederate operations in Montreal, to provide money for Jefferson Davis's defense. Although Thompson contributed a small amount, he apparently kept about one hundred thousand dollars for himself.

While in England, Breckinridge was treated as a celebrity and met with a number of British politicians and notables, including the Archbishop of Canterbury and William Gladstone, British Liberal Party statesman and prime minister. Breckinridge, accompanied by his wife, made a number of friends and gradually recovered his health, which was nearly wrecked by the ordeal of the escape from Florida. Having tired of traveling abroad, Breckinridge moved to Niagara-on-the-Lake, Ontario, which was just across the Niagara River from Fort Niagara, New York.

Breckinridge remained out of the country until after Andrew Johnson signed the general amnesty proclamation in late 1868. He returned to his home in Lexington, Kentucky, in March 1869, where he was welcomed as a hero. Local political leaders urged him to seek public office, but he refused to engage in partisan politics. Likewise, he declined to engage in the numerous quarrels among former Confederate military leaders as they refought battles and attempted to attribute blame and accept praise for the battles in which they participated. Breckinridge spoke out strongly against extremist groups and condemned the activities of the Ku Klux Klan. He resumed his law practice and became the vice president of the Elizabethtown, Lexington, Big Sandy Railroad Company. He died at the early age of fifty-four on May 17, 1875.

Former Attorney General George Davis, perhaps the president's closest friend in the administration, attempted to flee to England but was captured at Key West on October 18, 1865. Imprisoned at Fort Hamilton in Brooklyn, New York, for several months, he was pardoned in 1866. As was the case with many former Confederate leaders, he was impoverished when released, but in his case, he was also the father of six motherless children, his wife having passed away in 1863. Davis resumed his law practice in Wilmington, North Carolina, remarried, and regained a measure of prosperity. He died on February 23, 1896.

When Clement Clay was given his parole in April 1866, his wife was at Fort Monroe to escort him back to Huntsville, Alabama. The rigors of prison had taken a toll on him, and he did not enter politics again. A former U.S. and Confederate senator, Clay was never charged with a crime and yet was pardoned by the U.S. Congress in 1880. He died in 1882 in Huntsville. Virginia, who had strongly lobbied government officials, including Andrew Johnson, for her husband's release, remarried and became an outspoken advocate for women's suffrage before she passed away in 1915.

Secretary of the Navy Stephen R. Mallory was released from confinement at Fort Lafayette in New York Harbor only a month before Clay. Mallory was the last member of the Confederate cabinet to be released from prison. While Mallory was incarcerated, to prevent further loss of property and to show a readiness to support the Union, he agreed to provide information on the itinerary of the Confederate commerce raider CSS *Shenandoah,* which was still operating against U.S. merchant ships in the southwest Pacific. The captain, James Waddell, had been isolated from events in America and was not aware that the war was over. Mallory said that it would be unlikely that any of the heavily armed Union ships could catch the *Shenandoah* and suggested that a propeller-driven ship had the best chance of success. Mallory also gave Union officials information and credentials that would convince Waddell that his mission was over.[11]

The harsh conditions of imprisonment and the dampness of his cell at Fort Lafayette exacerbated the gout that had plagued Mallory through the years. As with most of his compatriots, he was nearly destitute and his law library had been destroyed. After being released from prison, Mallory returned to Pensacola and resumed his law practice. He died there on November 9, 1873.

Mallory's willingness to innovate with new weapons and tactics while operating with scarce resources resulted in major contributions to naval warfare. He developed the first ironclad vessel, the CSS *Virginia,* and twenty-one other ironclads. The Confederate navy also fielded a number of innovations in torpedo and undersea warfare using mines and deployed the

H. L. Hunley, the first submarine to destroy a warship. Confederate commerce raiders had been branded as privateers in the Northern press, and Mallory suffered as a result of the implications that raids on U.S. shipping were acts of piracy. When writing his memoirs, a former crew member of several Confederate warships pointed out that all the cruisers were manned by officers commissioned by the Confederate government who "with rare exceptions were the products of the United States Naval Academy." He added, "A privateersman is a fellow with all the instincts of a pirate, but without the courage to hoist the Jolly Roger."[12]

William Preston Johnston took the oath of allegiance to the United States and was released from Fort Delaware on August 5, 1865. Johnston departed for Montreal with his family and joined the growing group of former Confederates who chose exile in the years immediately following the war. In early 1866, Johnston returned to Louisville, Kentucky, with his family and resumed the practice of law with his former law partner. He reportedly had problems related to the stress of his practice and sought a professorship at Washington College, where Robert E. Lee was the president. By the end of 1866, he had secured a position as a professor of English and history. In 1880, Johnston was selected to be the president of Louisiana State University, and in 1883, he became president of newly established Tulane University in New Orleans. Johnston died in that city on July 16, 1889.

The old leaders ended their days as Confederates, and the Confederate Secret Service, once active in Canada and in the North, was disbanded as the war came to a close and the leadership scattered. Many of those responsible for missions against the U.S. government left for the relative security of Europe. Most welcomed the opportunity to put the war behind them and to rebuild their homes and lives. A few, a very few, carried on with missions they believed would help the South. Semple was one of them.

14

DISILLUSIONMENT
AND
DECEIT

I am getting "skittish" about this matter and think I will have to make myself "scarce" for a month or two down in the "Okeefeenoke Swamp" where I laid so long summer before last.

—James A. Semple to Julia Gardiner Tyler,
January 3, 1867

HE DEFEAT OF THE Fenian army in June had done little to dampen the spirits of the Irish, and both the circles and the membership continued to grow in parts of the United States and, to some extent, in Canada. As 1866 deepened into November, Semple may have been questioning whether or not his efforts on behalf of the Fenians and the South were ever going to bear fruit. A war five years in the future would be of no help to the South, which was suffering now from carpetbaggers, fallow farmlands, and untenable conditions levied on the states by a vengeful North, especially the Radical Republicans.

For the time being, Semple decided to continue as he had been doing, even expanding his travels to other cities that had formed Fenian circles. In late November 1866, he was in Albany, New York. The circle there was growing rapidly, as Irish Catholics in the city rallied to the Fenian cause, frequently holding lectures and sponsoring balls, picnics, and other social gatherings. According to the local newspaper *Argus*, some fifteen hundred people, including state legislators, attended a Fenian ball in January 1866, and in April 1866, some four hundred men enlisted in the Fenian army.

As his belief began to temper that the Fenians could instigate a war between the United States and England, Semple turned toward more personal matters. Robert Tyler, then living in Montgomery, Alabama, was running for the office of adjutant general and inspector general and wanted Semple's help where he had influence in certain sections of the state. He would do what he could in terms of writing letters to acquaintances, including the editors of two newspapers in Mobile and two in the upcountry.[1] For some reason, while following this course of action, he had no qualms about using his own name; he likely expected the communications to be kept private.

A more serious concern was his wife, Letitia. She had moved to Baltimore and opened a school for young ladies called the Eclectic Institute. That alone was enough to upset Semple; for some reason, he objected to her becoming an "educationalist." Apart as they were and had been for so long, what Letitia did was none of his business, just as what he did was none of hers. He knew, however, that she was having a difficult time financially, especially since she had nieces and nephews living with her. Still legally her husband, he felt obligated to help her. Apparently, he put aside his resentment over the school (although he probably expressed his opinion) long enough to send her another thousand dollars. He groused to Julia that eight thousand dollars a year was "'too taut a bowline,' as our sailors say, to haul any tighter on," and indicated that Letitia would receive no more from him for a year. If he did, in fact, give Letitia that amount, she received almost one hundred thousand dollars from Semple in terms of an equivalent amount at the present day's rate of exchange.[2]

The letter Semple had received from Norfolk had to do with an "FM" (Fort Monroe) correspondent who wished Semple to visit Mississippi on a confidential matter. The identity of the person was not disclosed, but Semple wrote to Julia that someone acting on behalf of Jefferson Davis wanted to meet with him. The "correspondent" would not have been Varina but could have been any of a number of people, as Davis was now allowed to have visitors. As to where in Mississippi, the reference might have been to Davis's former plantation, Brierfield, but anyone who met there would not have been alone, since the property was in the hands of U.S. military authorities.[3]

Whoever the correspondent was, and whatever it was that Davis wanted Semple to do, Semple declined. He was sick, worn out, and ready to give up the running around he had been doing for almost two years. To make matters worse, nothing was being accomplished that could in any way help the South. The United States was not going to war against England—at least in the foreseeable future—and he could not hold out indefinitely. Between what he had spent on steamships, trains, and hotel rooms and what he had provided to Julia and to Letitia, the gold that he had been entrusted with was dwindling.

While he may have been wishing he could settle down and resume a normal life, friends in Virginia and in Georgia warned him not to return just yet, as efforts were still being made to find him. In fact, an article in a newspaper near the end of the year made him extremely nervous. He enclosed a copy of it to Julia with the admission, "I am getting 'skittish' about this matter and think I will have to make myself 'scarce' for a month or two down in the 'Okeefeenoke Swamp' where I laid so long summer before last."[4]

Still, he carried on, possibly because he felt he had no alternative, other than to turn himself in, which he was not about to do. On February 5, 1867, Semple registered at the St. Charles Hotel in New Orleans, where Fenian dignitaries would occasionally meet with circle members. In a letter to Julia, he wrote that he had waited at the Waverly Hotel to see her as long as he possibly could. Finally, he had to leave and just made the steamer at the end of Cortlandt Street. (Julia had gone to the Astor looking for him. She was again having money problems, and Semple had left blank notes with his signature at the Astor for her to fill in as she wished. He must have expected, however, that she somehow knew he was staying at the Waverly instead of the Astor, which at times was full.)[5]

Writing to Julia two days later, Semple included a clipping about a steamer, the *R. R. Cuyler.* The news item announced the capture of the vessel, which was suspected of being a Fenian privateer with sixty former Confederates on board. According to the report, "She was heavily armed. The crew was principally obtained from Charleston and Savannah."

Semple had first mounted the clipping in the letter and then, to call attention to it, had written around it, mentioning that when he arrived at the hotel, he was greeted by a warning: "Look out, there is wild work on hand, keep close." Whatever the warning was specifically referring to, Semple was frustrated and angry:

Is nothing ever to be accomplished? I am not disheartened, if anything can be proved, it is more than I think—I shall after I get through here make a break on my own "hook" & let these high dignitaries lay their own plans & carry them out if they can. Had I been in N. Y. all this time, things might have been different. Hereafter, if I can, I mean to be the superior officer. . . . The meeting last night disclosed nothing new to me, although it did to some of them. I do not expect either at any time to be enlightened by the crowd.[6]

Semple's frustrations with what had become his life apparently took a severe toll on his physical and mental health, and he was more than a thousand miles away from the soothing comfort and stability he could count on from Julia during his stays at Castleton Hill. He had collapsed while aboard the steamer to New Orleans, and he was unconscious for more than two hours. Since then, he wavered between euphoria and depression. His letters hinted at the struggle within him: "I have some thousand or so acres in Texas, I have over twelve hundred in Kentucky. I wish these to be given to my birdie Pearl." In the same letter, he asserted, "I must be my own man, go where the wind listeth & come to see my Birdie when I choose. What do I care for their ten or twenty thousand per year, I can make it any time, but I must be a free man." Later he confessed, "I have some money I don't know what to do with it, unless as I did last night lose six hundred at a game of cards, which you know I do not understand. It will be a relief to me to get rid of it."[7]

The extent of his illness can probably best be seen in a February 15, 1867, letter to Julia from New Orleans: "I may never see you again but the love in my heart is as fresh as when I was only aged ten years—regard it dear—I am now the representative of my family and care little what turns up. Except that my dear Sister, don't put your hands on me, for I will resent [it]—my knife is small but I can use it effectively—There is a good deal of anger in me now, and by God, I would strike my Father if he touched me."[8]

It took his wife to straighten him out. Sometime in July 1867, Letitia wrote him a biting letter, criticizing him for fleeing after the war and suggesting that he was having an affair with Julia. Though Letitia and Semple had lived apart for years and never had much of a marriage, Letitia evidently claimed that the reason she was keeping his name was to save it from disgrace. Whatever the truth was in terms of Semple's relationship with Julia, this letter changed Semple. He became focused, he settled his affairs, he gave up the fantasy of helping the South, and his flagrant expressions of love for Julia ended. He responded to Letitia:

> Permit me to write that the charges of your letter are incompatible with what I know to be the fact. Robert, John & Taz [Tazwell] have known me from my boyhood, I am incapable of "fleeing" & they know it. The first 2 . . . knew until the 19th Feb 1866 where I was, could have found me at any moment, as they knew well. I have no complaints to make, nor will I divulge in any way a private life.
>
> Your remarks relative to Mrs. "T" are not worthy of a daughter of John Tyler. No matter what I may think of a lady, I rather think I would keep it to myself—I was suffering & Mrs. "T" offered me a home (. . . I have never had one before) and I accepted it—and passed many pleasant hours there—as to your terms relative to her I throw them back with the scorn which they deserve, a lady she is & always will be.
>
> As to "carrying my name" to save it from disgrace, it is incredulous. I am the custodian of my own honor, nor can I be deprived of it unless by my own acts. . . . You are yet on the sunny side of maidenhood, take your own steps and resume your original name.[9]

In examining Letitia's accusation, she was right in one respect: the Confederate government—which included Semple—had fled Richmond. There is no other way to describe what happened. Then he continued to flee—albeit at a slow pace—once he had the carriage full of gold. Was she right about her husband and Julia as well? Did she have a reason for making the accusation other than rumor? For a time, Julia and Semple were extremely close, and they desperately needed each other. Julia provided a stable family life, a warm and happy home that welcomed him, and people who genuinely cared for him. Semple provided the guidance of an older brother to Julia's children. (In some respects, he was perhaps more like a father in that he made decisions on their behalf, which they accepted.[10]) He offered advice and counsel to Julia on her financial and legal affairs, contributed a significant amount of money, and oversaw the solving of certain domestic problems, such as the need to have her furnace fixed.

Julia occasionally visited Semple in his hotel. At a time when "proper" women walking along Broadway were usually escorted by men, she was at the very least indiscrete. Did she ignore conduct considered to be in good taste because she was an independent person or because she wanted to be with Semple? Also, there is a strong suggestion that at least once she spent the night with him in a hotel on Broadway. Such a liaison certainly gave them freedom they could not have had at Castleton Hill. Also relevant is the fact that, to get there, Julia had to really want to be with him, for she had to cross on a ferry and travel almost twenty miles to reach Broadway.

Soon after he sent his reply to Letitia, Semple returned to Virginia, first to Hampton and then to the burned-out Richmond. Three months later, he wrote to Julia: "The late amnesty takes me in & the oath I have to take is just the same I took so often in the old service & I shall not hesitate."[11] For Semple, the war was finally over.

Julia and Semple remained friends, but from this point on, their lives began to drift apart. Semple settled in the area of Virginia north and east of Williamsburg, where he had been raised as a child. He tried his hand at farming, worked for the York River Railroad for a time, and either considered—or fantasized about—an offer to go to Japan to work for a company that had a New York office. For the rest of his life, he was at somewhat loose ends, and the only pleasure he seemed to have was when he could spend time sailing. With First Family of Virginia (FFV) roots, Semple would have been considered well off in antebellum days, despite having no parents. But whatever he had, he had lost and was only mildly successful in reestablishing himself. When he died in relative obscurity in December 1883, his assets consisted of tracts of land in Kentucky and Texas, a reversionary interest in a farm on the James River, and some stock.[12] Yet he was probably comfortable and better off than many fellow Virginians.

Semple and Letitia never divorced; apparently she chose to continue to protect his name. Then again, maybe his assets, particularly Scotland Neck, the property he had inherited from his family, and the fact that he was entitled to a pension had something to do with her decision. In the end, nothing came of an investigation into Scotland Neck, which Semple had willed to a daughter of a friend. As to his pension, Letitia applied for one based on Semple's service in the U.S. Navy during the Mexican War. In what must have been an act of desperation, she claimed that she "lived with my said husband from the date of my said marriage until the day of his death," a statement that was evidently required in the application process. Her claim was attested to by her brother, John Tyler Jr. They, of course, were *not* telling the truth, but who could blame her? She had nothing else to show for her stormy marriage, not even children of her own. Her efforts were rewarded in 1887 with a pension of eight dollars per month, which she maintained was her sole income. Ten years later, she petitioned the congressional Committee on Pensions for an increase to one hundred dollars a month. She was approved for a monthly stipend of thirty dollars.

Julia spent her years defending herself in lawsuits brought against her by her brother and others and in overseeing the restoration of Sherwood Forest without actually being there. She kept tabs on Alex and Gardie for as long as they were in school, saw to the education of her other children, and made sure that her flirtatious daughter conducted herself properly to the extent she could. Always, always, she worried about paying bills, and she aggressively petitioned the government for a pension she felt was due to her as the wife of a former U.S. president. Mary Lincoln had been awarded three thousand dollars a year while the three other surviving first ladies—including Julia—had yet to be accommodated.

While Alex Tyler found schooling in Germany to his liking, his brother Gardie grew increasingly anxious to return to the South, where he could be in the middle of events and politics. In September 1867, Gardie finally convinced his mother to allow him to complete his education at Washington College, where his strong beliefs were reinforced by a student body of unreconstructed Rebels. Following graduation in 1869 near the top of his class, Gardie read law in the office of Richmond lawyer James Lyons, a longtime family friend, and gained admission to the bar in Virginia. He then moved back to Sherwood Forest and practiced law in Charles City. After a four-year stint as director of the state lunatic asylum, Gardie shifted into politics, his great interest, serving in the Virginia state senate and the U.S. House of Representatives before ending his career as a Virginia circuit court judge. Gardie married late in life (in 1894), taking as his bride Mary Morris Jones, who had four children. He passed away at Sherwood Forest ten years later.

Alex chose a different path. He graduated from both Karlsruhe and Freiburg as a mining engineer. Not content with the military experience gained through his days as an artillerist with the First Rockbridge and Robert E. Lee, Alex enlisted in the Saxon army at the outbreak of the Franco-Prussian War and served as an Uhlan trooper during the occupation of France. As a result, he received a ribbon from the kaiser for "faithful service" in the German army. He finally returned to the United States in

1873, handsome, debonair, and deep in debt. After a series of jobs, interspersed between comparatively long periods of unemployment, Alex was eventually appointed a surveyor in the Department of the Interior. On September 1, 1883, he died unexpectedly in the governor's palace in Santa Fe, New Mexico, where he was serving as government inspector of surveys. While out on a survey, he had run out of fresh water, and though he knew better, he drank contaminated water and contracted dysentery. His wife, Sally Griswold Gardiner, a third cousin whom he had married in 1875, had a long and sad life. She was a widow for forty-four years, outliving all of her children.

Julia Tyler finally moved back to Virginia in 1882 and watched Sherwood Forest slowly return to its former beauty. She would live seven more years, passing away on July 10, 1889, at the Exchange Hotel in Richmond, where she was staying in a room a few doors down and across the hallway from where her husband, John Tyler, had died in 1862. Over the years, Julia and Semple rarely saw each other. They had their time together, a closeness that defies explanation, and neither regretted the relationship.

As to the Confederate treasury, guarded so earnestly by William H. Parker's midshipmen, the bulk of the specie was paid out, including the British sovereigns under the care of Micajah H. Clark and the Van Benthuysens near the Yulee plantation. The notable exception, of course, was the eighty-six thousand dollars in gold carried off by Semple and Edward M. Tidball. Unless an amount remained in his account at the Mechanics National Bank in New York, however, Semple spent what he had, a fair portion of it apparently going to the women in his life: Letitia Tyler Semple and Julia Gardiner Tyler.[13]

There is a cache of the gold unaccounted for: $27,000 dollars in bullion that Tidball brought back to Winchester, an amount worth more than $325,000 today. A letter in the wall of an old farmhouse confirmed the existence of this cache of gold as of February 1866. What eventually happened to it is anybody's guess.

Despite the tendency of historians to discount the possibility, evidence suggests the coins could still be buried in Danville. An analysis of the treasury contents after the government moved on from Danville offers a convincing argument that the coins—except for what was paid out to Joseph E. Johnston's troops—never left town. Certainly, the burial of forty kegs in a field, day or night, would have attracted attention, but not necessarily under the guise of burying soldiers who died in the last battles of the war, such as Sailor's Creek, or during the ongoing fighting between the armies of Lee and Grant after the fall of Richmond.

What if the silver were simply buried in the dirt floor of a warehouse (or the dirt beneath the building, if it sat on blocks)? One possibility could be Semple's store. How unusual would it have been for there to be wagons and activity around the store during the week the Confederate government was setting up offices and the town was overrun with refugees? Discovering the site of the store may be a challenge, but an 1860 map, which was produced from an 1863 map by erasing certain former landmarks and adding changes, reveals a faint outline of the store when the map is backlit and a magnifying glass is used. Then, too, there were other warehouses and other dirt floors where the kegs could have been buried.

Recent events had added to the allure and tend to support the contention that the coins are still in Danville. Certain parts of the city have been investigated with geophysical surveying equipment (pulse-induction radar), and caches of metal have supposedly been identified. Confirmation that the Mexican silver dollars are, or are not, buried in the city apparently rests in the hands of city officials, who to date, have not allowed the digging of an exploratory test hole.

Finding the Mexican silver dollars would definitely be worth the effort, since the modern value of the coins has been estimated to be in excess of sixteen million dollars.

EPILOGUE

𝒜 TALL GRANITE MONUMENT stands noticeably in the graveyard behind Bruton Parish Church in Williamsburg, Virginia. The marker, about twenty feet from the wall of the church, is observed, if only briefly, by thousands of visitors to the colonial village every year. It indicates that James A. Semple, a paymaster in the U.S. and C.S. navies, is buried there, along with the mother and father he never knew and a "devoted" servant, Mammy Sarah. The monument also suggests that Letitia Tyler Semple, his wife, is buried there as well. (She is not.) Letitia is actually buried in an unmarked grave about a mile away, in a cemetery known as Cedar Grove. There are few records of the burials and sites of the graves there, and she rests in obscurity, as unable to be with her husband in death as she was in life.

Today, Sherwood Forest stands as an elegant reminder of a Tidewater lifestyle long gone. The symbiotic relationship between the "Rebel and the Rose" has been buried in fragile letters and other long-forgotten documents, fodder only for historians with a great deal of patience to find it. But it did exist as a powerful force in the lives of two vital personalities who survived a turbulent era.

APPENDIX

ANALYSIS OF CONFEDERATE TREASURY FUNDS

*T*HE FOLLOWING provides a breakdown of the assets in the Confederate treasury at the time the funds left Richmond on the night of April 2, 1865. No accurate count was made during the packing process, so the total cannot be determined. The disbursements, however, are known to have occurred. The conclusions that follow are based on three possible scenarios.

BREAKDOWN OF FUNDS DISBURSED

1. Total funds added up by Micajah H. Clark (silver coins and bullion and gold coins, nuggets, and bullion), reflecting total as of May 3: $288,023*

2. Silver coins used to redeem Confederate money in Danville and left in Greensboro for Joseph E. Johnston: $39,000†

3. Gold coins paid to Maj. Gen. J. F. Gilmer on April 26 for repair of bridges and roads during travel south to Washington, Georgia: $4,000

Total amount in treasury as it left Danville, Virginia, on April 9: $331,023

---

* Actual amount counted = $288,022.90 includes payments made by Breckinridge on May 3.

† Two boxes containing $35,000 in gold sovereigns (British pounds) were left in Greensboro for Jefferson Davis's use, but they were back with Clark by the time he did the totaling on May 4, 1865. In terms of the silver, some amount less than $9,000 was evidently used in Danville to redeem worthless Confederate currency and to pay a purchase order warrant of about $1,200. The rest was left for Johnston.

4. Gold coins known to have been paid out by Clark
   on May 4:   ($92,470)
5. Silver bullion given to Raphael J. Moses by Clark
   on May 4:   ($40,000)
6. Gold coins in meal sack left for Robert Toombs by
   John C. Breckinridge on May 5 (total specie = $5,180):   ($1,780)
7. Gold coins given to John Taylor Wood, William Preston
   Johnston, Francis R. Lubbock, and Charles E. Thorburn
   on May 6 (from $35,000):   ($6,000)†
8. Gold coins given to John H. Reagan on May 6
   (from $35,000):   ($3,500)†
9. Gold coins given to Given Campbell on May 6
   (from $35,000):   ($300)†
10. Gold coins distributed at David Yulee's plantation
    (from $35,000):   ($25,720)
11. Mexican coins known to have been paid out to
    troops by Breckinridge on May 3:   ($4,000)

Possible amount of U.S. silver coins $157,253

ARGUMENT FOR MEXICAN SILVER DOLLARS
BEING LEFT IN DANVILLE

First Scenario

If the money left in Greensboro had been Mexican silver dollars, one can assume that the fifty kegs of Mexican coins were loaded back into a railway car at Danville. Of the $288,023 tallied by Clark, a minimum of $161,000 would have been in reales (since $39,000 was used to redeem worthless Confederate currency in Danville, with the remainder being left

---

† Two boxes containing $35,000 in gold sovereigns (British pounds) were left in Greensboro for Jefferson Davis's use, but they were back with Clark by the time he did the totaling on May 4, 1865. In terms of the silver, some amount less than $9,000 was evidently used in Danville to redeem worthless Confederate currency and to pay a purchase order warrant of about $1,200. The rest was left for Johnston.

for Johnston[‡]). Because $40,000 of the $288,023 was in silver bullion (the amount given to Moses), the gold in Clark's possession would have totaled:

$288,023
- 40,000 (silver bullion)
- 161,000 ($200,000 minus $39,000 paid out and left for Johnston)

$87,023

But at least $103,850 was paid out in gold coins and bullion by Clark and Breckinridge ($92,470 distributed on May 4 plus $1,580 given to Toombs on May 5 plus $9,800 paid out on May 6), and another $25,720 was distributed by Clark's party in Florida. Thus there would not have been enough gold to pay out the total of $129,570 if the Mexican coins were included in the $288,023. In addition, the above scenario assumes the treasury contained no U.S. silver coins. That assumption, of course, is erroneous, because boxes of U.S. coins were loaded in Richmond.

Second Scenario

Assume that Clark did not include the $35,000 in his counting of the specie in the treasury, keeping aside the money originally left for Jefferson Davis. He still would have been short $7,027 ($92,470 + $1,580 = $87,023) in gold. Plus the scenario would need to be based on the fact that the treasury counted by Clark contained no U.S. coins. As indicated in the first scenario, this is simply not true.

Third Scenario

Assume (1) that ten kegs of Mexican silver dollars (4,000 coins per keg) were set aside in Danville, (2) the coins were used to redeem the worthless

---

‡ Exactly how much was redeemed is not significant, because, according to treasury clerk Mann S. Quarles, the coin used to pay out silver in exchange for worthless Confederate currency came from the same cache (probably the kegs of Mexican silver dollars) that was provided to Johnston. Thus the amount received by Johnston totaled around $39,000, less the silver paid out in redeeming the Confederate currency. Quarles reported "something over $30,000 was left after dispersing at Danville and paying a warrant drawn by the P.O. Department of some $1,100 or $1,200." Despite the brisk activity by soldiers and citizens in turning in their useless paper money for silver at a rate of seventy to one; $70,000 in Confederate paper, for example, would require a payout of only $1,000.

Confederate currency, and (3) the kegs were loaded afterward into a railroad car with the rest of the treasury, the cache being earmarked for Johnston in Greensboro. This is a realistic possibility since Clark and another treasury clerk named Addison both recalled that Mexican dollars made up most of the specie delivered to Johnston. If this is true, then thirty-nine kegs of Mexican coins ($156,000 face value) would have been left in Danville.

CONCLUSIONS

1. Other than one keg, the Mexican coins were not part of the treasury when Clark took over responsibility for the money.
2. A minimum of thirty-nine and possibly as many as forty-nine kegs of Mexican silver dollars were left in Danville.
3. The open keg with $4,000 in reale coins was used to pay some of the troops.
4. If the $196,000 in Mexican coins is added to the $331,023 known to have been in Danville ($288,023 + $39,000 + $4,000), and if the $35,000 in gold sovereigns was not added in by Clark when he did the May 4 counting, then the amount in the treasury could have been as high as $562,023 when it left Richmond, exclusive of the foreign exchange (Liverpool Acceptances), the trunk of jewelry, and the keg of copper pennies. Or if Mexican silver dollars made up the cache delivered to Johnston, the total could have been as low as $492,023 ($288,023 + $4,000 + $200,000). Additional unreported expenditures, of course, would have added to each of the totals.

WHAT PROBABLY HAPPENED

The $35,000 in gold sovereigns traveled from Greensboro with the president's baggage, separate from the rest of the treasury. For this reason, the coins were almost certainly not included in the $288,023. Furthermore, given the fact that both Clark and Addison observed that Mexican silver dollars made up most of the specie provided to Johnston, the treasury probably totaled, at a minimum, $527,023 ($288,023 + $4,000 + $35,000 + $200,000) when the treasury train left Richmond. As stated above, additional unreported expenses between Richmond and Washington, Georgia, would have added to the total.

NOTES

Full bibliographic information can be found in the Bibliography

Introduction

1. Seager, *And Tyler Too,* 478.

2. Ibid., 481–82.

3. Ibid., 482.

4. Ibid., 483.

5. James A. Semple to Julia Gardiner Tyler, May 31, 1868, Gardiner-Tyler Family Papers, Yale University, New Haven, Connecticut (hereafter referred to as GTP).

6. Semple to Julia Gardiner Tyler, November 9, 1863, GTP.

Chapter 1: Prologue to Defeat

1. With regard to the military situation and conditions in Richmond prior to the fall of the city, a myriad of accounts are available from participants and observers during and after the war. Of particular note is John B. Jones's *A Rebel War Clerk's Diary.*

2. Jones, *War Clerk's Diary,* 2:373.

3. Tucker, "The Fall of Richmond," 157.

4. Dowdey and Manarin, *Wartime Papers of Robert E. Lee,* 912.

5. Lee, "Reminiscences," 236–37.

6. Davis, *Jefferson Davis,* 2:572.

7. Details on the journey south from Richmond to Charlotte by Varina Davis and her party are taken from an account by Burton Harrison that was originally written for the "entertainment of my children only." The paper was ultimately published as the "Capture of Jefferson Davis" in *Century Magazine* in November 1883, and a galley of the article is archived in the Library of Congress. After accompanying Varina to Charlotte and seeing that she was comfortably situated in what would prove to be temporary quarters, Harrison returned to Danville, where Jefferson Davis was attempting to resurrect operations of the Confederate government while waiting for word from Lee. Days later, the president asked Harrison to rejoin Varina as he had not heard from her since she had decided to continue her travels south from Charlotte and he was nervous about the safety of his family. Harrison caught up to Varina in Abbeville, South Carolina, and remained with the party until it was captured near Irwinville, Georgia, on May 10, 1865.

8. Jones, *War Clerk's Diary,* 2:455.

9. Pvt. James Preston Crowder to his mother, August 9, 1864, James Preston Crowder Papers, Emory University, Atlanta, Georgia. Crowder was killed not long after he wrote the letter.

10. McGuire, *Diary of a Southern Refugee,* 256.

11. Ibid., 329.

12. Edward Pollard, *Richmond Examiner,* April 2, 1865.

13. U. S. Grant to William T. Sherman, April 4, 1864, *Personal Memoirs,* 145.

14. William T. Sherman to Abraham Lincoln, December 22, 1864, Library of Congress, Washington, DC.

15. The Battle of Bentonville: A Bloody Annoyance, March 19–21, 1865, http://civilwar.bluegrass.net/battles-campaigns/1865/650319–21.html.

16. Ibid.

17. Davis, *Long Surrender,* 16.

18. Driver, *1st and 2nd Rockbridge Artillery,* 53.

19. David Gardiner Tyler to Julia Gardiner Tyler, July 24, 1864, GTP.

20. Seager, *And Tyler Too,* 499.

Chapter 2: Final Hours in Richmond

1. Stephen R. Mallory wrote an account of Jefferson Davis and his administration during the flight south from Richmond to Danville, archived under Mallory Recollections, Stephen R. Mallory Papers, Southern Historical Collection. An edited version—entitled "The Last Days of the Confederate Government"—appeared in two installments of *McClure's Magazine* in December 1900 and January 1901. The account also appeared as "The Flight from Richmond" in *Civil War Times Illustrated* in two parts in April 1972 (pp. 25–31) and June 1972 (pp. 28–36). References to Mallory's account come from the *Civil War Times Illustrated* articles.

2. Mary Burrows Fountaine to Marie Burrows Sayre, April 30, 1865, Museum of the Confederacy, Richmond, Virginia.

3. Mallory, "Flight from Richmond," 25.

4. Jones, *War Clerk's Diary,* 2:465.

5. Dowdey and Manarin, *Wartime Papers of Robert E. Lee,* 924.

6. Ibid., 925.

7. Emmeline Allman "Crump" Lightfoot, "Evacuation of Richmond," Manuscript Collection, Virginia Historical Society, Richmond, Virginia.

8. Lankford, *Richmond Burning,* 61.

9. Dowdey and Manarin, *Wartime Papers of Robert E. Lee,* 925.

10. Tucker, "The Fall of Richmond," 156.

11. Hoehling and Hoehling, *Day Richmond Died,* 113.

12. Dowdey and Manarin, *Wartime Papers of Robert E. Lee,* 928.

13. The Copperheads were an organization of Peace Democrats who opposed the war and advocated peace with the Confederacy. Called Copperheads by Republicans, either in reference to the venomous snake or because some wore a copper Liberty-head coin in their shoes or around their necks, they were linked with other secretive (and sometimes militant) groups, such as the Sons of Liberty and the Knights of the Golden Circle. Peace Democrats were most numerous in the midwestern states of Illinois, Indiana, and Ohio; one of their outspoken leaders was Clement L. Vallandigham. New York City was also a center of Copperhead sentiment. Julia and her mother, Juliana, joined a local women's group on Staten Island that distributed pamphlets promoting peace, coordinated relief activities in Southern cities under Union control, and generally supported the Southern cause. Julia also purchased Confederate war bonds and promoted Union Gen. George B. McClellan, the 1864 Democratic presidential candidate against Lincoln. Her Copperhead activities could have resulted in an arrest for disloyalty, as many were, but she was unmolested in this regard, perhaps because she was the widow of a former president of the United States.

14. Why food supplies for the Army of Northern Virginia were so meager during the last months of the war defies reasonable explanation. In a September 1865 report to former Commissary Gen. Isaac M. St. John, former Acting Asst. Commissary Gen. Thomas G. Williams indicated that "during the month of March & up to the 1st of April '65, 300,000 rations of bread and meat were on hand in Richmond warehouses." An additional 2 million rations were stored at Danville, and 180,000 rations were warehoused in Lynchburg. Even tea, coffee, and sugar—items considered scarce in the Confederacy—were available. Most of the supplies in the Richmond warehouses, which were undoubtedly the rations Lee was expecting to find at Amelia Court House, were left to the people roaming the streets after the army evacuated the city. St. John had managed to load a portion of the supplies into wagons and sent them with Gen. Richard S. Ewell, who was trying to join his small command with Lee's. Unfortunately for the Army of Northern Virginia, Union cavalry captured and destroyed the wagons. Although transportation was undoubtedly a problem over the archaic and poorly maintained railroads in Virginia, such an excuse is not relevant in terms of the provisions stored only miles from the lines around Petersburg and Richmond. Incompetence would seem to be the obvious answer. According to Williams, a requisition for rations was never received from the chief commissary of Lee's army. Why the rations were not provided anyway is not clear. As a result, the soldiers subsisted on foods collected from local farmers. Whether or not well-fed soldiers would have meant fewer desertions and a more formidable force against Grant is debatable, but there was no need for the apparent starvation experienced by men and animals.

15. Semple to Julia Gardiner Tyler, March 24, 1865, GTP.

16. Mallory, "Flight from Richmond," 28.

17. Durkin, *Mallory,* 336–37.

18. Semple to Julia Gardiner Tyler, March 25, 1865, GTP.

19. Lightfoot, "Evacuation of Richmond."

20. Capt. Micajah H. Clark, in his report, "The Last Days of the Confederate Treasury and What Became of Its Specie," indicated that he thought the amount was around $230,000 (see *Southern Historical Society Papers,* 9:542–56). Otis Ashmore estimated the bank assets to have been $450,000 or more (see "The Story of the Virginia Bank Funds," *Georgia Historical Quarterly* 2 [September 1918]: 171–97).

21. A few gunboats and three blockade-runners still flew the Stars and Bars after the destruction of the James River Squadron. Unable to find a Confederate port to enter and offload goods, two of the blockade-runners—CSS *Chameleon,* under Lt. John Wilkinson, a friend of James Semple, and CSS *Owl,* under Como. John N. Maffit—put into Liverpool, England. The *Chameleon* docked on April 9, 1865, and the *Owl* docked in mid-July. Both were surrendered to British authorities. Meanwhile, four Confederate ironclads remained in the waters around Mobile, Alabama; two were not yet completed. By the end of April, all four had been either scuttled or captured. On April 12, the city surrendered to Union forces under Maj. Gen. Edward R. S. Canby. The Confederate navy was then down to a single vessel of particular note, CSS *Shenandoah,* and one that saw little action, CSS *Stonewall.* Commissioned in October 1864, the *Shenandoah* was full rigged but had auxiliary steam power, which enabled it to maneuver independent of the wind. With a crew of 130 men, the vessel patrolled the North Pacific and the Bering Strait, capturing Union merchant ships and a large number of whaling boats. Not until August 2, 1865, when it encountered an English ship, did the *Shenandoah*'s captain learn that the war had been over for months. He then disarmed his ship and set sail for England, where he surrendered to British authorities at Liverpool on November 1, 1865. CSS *Stonewall* was an ironclad ram built in Bordeaux, France, in 1863 and eventually secretly sold to the Confederate government. Commissioned at sea in January 1865, *Stonewall* was ordered to attack Union naval and commercial shipping. After making ports in Ferrol, Spain, and Lisbon, Portugal, the ironclad crossed the Atlantic to Havana, Cuba, where it was turned over to Spanish authorities at the end of war.

22. Coski, *Capital Navy,* 217.

23. Semmes, *Memoirs of Service Afloat,* 809.

24. The exact amount of the treasury at the time it was packed in Richmond will never be known. Years later, senior teller Walter Philbrook, who had been ordered by Treasury Secretary George A. Trenholm to take charge of the specie during the trip to Danville, recalled, "Although I have no records of the trip by me, I can say that the amount with which we started was less than $600,000." Calculations of the

disbursements during later events suggest that the total may have been around $527,023 in specie. (See chapter 5 and the appendix for a detailed accounting of the specie.)

25. Quarles, *Memoir,* April 2, 1901, Museum of the Confederacy, Richmond, Virginia.

26. Most of those staying at the American Hotel were full-time residents, as opposed to spending a night or two while visiting the city. Unfortunately, many of the former "guests" had no place to go and had little hope of making it out of the city by boat or train. By leaving the hotel, as later events proved, they escaped death or injury, for the hotel was in the path of the wall of flame that swept the lower part of the city.

27. Semple's relationship with William F. Howell developed as he took over the duties of chief of the Office of Provisions and Clothing from his predecessor, Paymaster John DeBree. Howell's remarkable capabilities and Semple's dependency on the resourceful agent are recounted by William N. Still Jr. (*Confederate Navy,* 29, 81–82).

28. Still, *Confederate Navy,* 82.

29. John Alexander Tyler to Julia Gardiner Tyler, [April 16, 1865?], GTP.

30. Dowdey and Manarin, *Wartime Papers of Robert E. Lee,* 928.

31. John Taylor Wood held two ranks in the Confederacy. As a captain in the navy, he commanded the CSS *Tallahassee.* Prior to that, he was a lieutenant on the ironclad *Virginia.* He was also an aide-de-camp to Jefferson Davis and held the rank of colonel in the cavalry.

32. Davis, *Long Surrender,* 27.

33. White, "Stray Leaves from a Soldier's Journal," 553.

34. Dance, *Lineage of Abraham,* 32.

Chapter 3: The Fugitive and the First Lady

1. Alex had just run the blockade into Wilmington and was living with Semple, while "Brother James" tried to find a midshipman position for him in the navy. But the navy was shrinking with the loss of ports and naval bases, and appointments were essentially nil. Semple arranged interviews with the president and Varina Davis and with Mallory and Trenholm to no avail.

2. Juliana Gardiner (Julia's mother) to Julia Tyler Gardiner, April 1, 1835, GTP.

3. Seager, *And Tyler Too,* 35–37.

4. Ibid., 35.

5. Ibid., 36.

6. Gardiner, "Narrative of the Pequot War," Massachusetts Historical Society.

7. Seager, *And Tyler Too,* 207.

8. The source for the oral history regarding Tyler's relationships with "free blacks" is Dance, *Lineage of Abraham,* 22–23, 98, 106–7. Dance is a professor of

English at the University of Richmond and the author of several books. Ike Ridley, Dance's cousin, stated to the authors in an e-mail: "My grandmother, Elaine Hucles Brown (Tyler's granddaughter), spoke to me about the fact that we were descended from Tyler before her death at the age of 104 in 1999. Unlike Thomas Jefferson's black descendants, my family has little interest in banging on the door of Sherwood Forest, demanding a key. 'We don't talk about those things,' my grandmother would whisper confidentially. She would love to say her uncles chose to go 'white,' 'Negro' or 'Indian,' based on their complexions and preferences." The dates in parentheses for Polly Brown and Martha "Patsy" Boasman Brown are their purported birth years.

9. DeSempill descendants chart showing the ancestral line to James A. Semple.

10. Cedar Hill was identified on maps as a tract of land before a house was built on the property. With the burning of the Semple home during the war, probably by Union soldiers, the land remained unused until recently. Semple had sold the property when he was called to active duty in the U.S. Navy. Reportedly, the only evidence of prior occupants were the remnants of a well. While Semple's parents and a devoted family servant, Mammy Sarah, were buried there in a small family graveyard, evidence suggests their remains were moved at some point to the cemetery next to Bruton Parish Church in Williamsburg, where the marker exists today.

11. Henry Churchill Semple was born on January 18, 1822, and thus was less than a year younger than James A. Semple. After Henry's marriage to Emily Virginia James, they moved to Montgomery, Alabama. During the war, he was major of artillery, and his unit, known as Semple's Battery, fought with distinction in the Army of Tennessee (Henry C. Semple Papers, Southern Historical Collection, University of North Carolina at Chapel Hill).

12. Register of Students in William and Mary College, 1827–81, *William and Mary Quarterly* (July 1923): 159–70.

13. Anne Contesse Tyler, daughter of John Tyler and Mary Armistead Tyler, was born in 1778 and died in 1803, at the young age of twenty-five. The cause of her death is not known, but she may have inherited the delicate physical condition of her mother, who also died young (at age thirty-seven) of a paralytic stroke.

14. Coleman, *Priscilla Cooper Tyler,* 75.

15. U.S. Navy Pension Records and Service Record, James A. Semple, April 28, 1887, National Archives; Dictionary of American Naval Fighting Ships, U.S. Naval Historical Center, Washington, DC.

16. Ibid.

17. Ibid.

18. Ibid.

19. Ibid.

20. Still, *Confederate Navy,* 29.

21. James A. Semple to Stephen R. Mallory, "Report of the Office of Provisions and Clothing," October 1864.

22. The letter has not been corrected for capitalization, spelling, or punctuation. It was written by Semple after a night of conversation with a friend. At the end of the letter, he adds, "I have written as you know hurriedly, for it is very late & [I] leave in the morning." [He was in St. George, Bermuda, a transshipment port for goods from Great Britain being purchased by the Confederacy.] "Tell Stockton to correct all mistakes & if he lets any one find out who is the author, when I return, I will punch his 'cabeza' in fine style for him."

Chapter 4: The New Capital

1. As indicated in chapter 2, note 2, the primary account of Jefferson Davis and his administration during the flight from Richmond to Danville was written by Stephen R. Mallory. Edited versions appeared in *McClure's Magazine* (1900–1901) and *Civil War Times Illustrated* (1972).

2. Mallory, "Flight from Richmond," pt. 1, 29.

3. The *Charles Seddon*, engine no. 14 on the Richmond and Danville Railroad, was known as an "American," which means it had a 4-4-0 wheel arrangement.

4. Mallory, "Flight from Richmond," pt. 1, 29.

5. Still, *Confederate Navy*, 29.

6. Mallory, "Flight from Richmond," pt. 1, 28.

7. Ibid., 28.

8. John Fraser and Company and the company's Liverpool affiliate, Fraser, Trenholm and Company, made significant contributions to the Confederate war effort. A senior partner in both companies, George Trenholm was instrumental in Fraser, Trenholm becoming the exclusive overseas financial agent and banker for the Confederate government. The company was also active in building blockade-runners for the Confederate navy, including CSS *Alabama*, and for operating its own fleet of approximately fifty steamers and sailing vessels between Great Britain and open ports in the South (via Cuba, Bermuda, and the Bahamas). The firm also managed to trade goods through New York City.

9. Known as the Northwest Conspiracy, covert activities were planned and staged using Canada as a base of operations. The intent was to cause uprisings in Illinois, Indiana, and Ohio among antiwar Democrats, most of whom identified themselves as Copperheads. Complementing the uprising were to be the release of Confederate soldiers held in Northern prisons, bank robberies along the Canadian border, and arsons of key hotels in New York City. Except for a raid on St. Albans, Vermont, the missions failed, primarily due to the effectiveness of Northern intelligence, poor timing, defective materials (namely, incendiary Greek Fire), and Confederate ineptness. The full story of Judah P. Benjamin's Secret Service efforts,

to which he had committed more than one million dollars in gold, will never be known as he burned most of his papers before leaving Richmond on April 2, 1865. Further information can be obtained from such sources as Headley, *Confederate Operations,* Oscar Kinchen, *Confederate Operations in Canada and the North,* Horan, *Confederate Agent,* and Miller, "Copperhead Activities."

10. Mallory, "Flight from Richmond," pt. 1, 29.

11. Ibid.

12. Kean, *Inside the Confederate Government,* 156.

13. Hanna, *Flight into Oblivion,* 15.

14. Ibid., 16.

15. Mallory, "Flight from Richmond," pt. 1, 30.

16. Ibid.

17. Carroll (*Confederate Treasure in Danville,* 98) states that, in accordance with Trenholm's instructions, the gold was stored in the Bank of Danville and the Mexican silver dollars were moved to the Benedict house, leaving only the U.S. silver and an opened keg of Mexican coins on the train. Supporting documentation, however, was not referenced, and the authors of this book have been unable to find relevant source material to support Carroll's version of events. Capt. William H. Parker reported: "We did not unpack the treasure from the cars at Danville. Some, I believe, was taken for the use of the government, and, I suspect, was paid out to General Johnston's men after the surrender, but the main portion of the money remained with me." See Parker, "The Gold and Silver in the Confederate Treasury," *Richmond Dispatch,* July 16, 1893.

18. St. John, "Resources of the Confederacy in 1865," 21.

19. Power, *Lee's Miserables,* 275.

20. Wise, *End of an Era,* 415.

21. Mallory, "Flight from Richmond," pt. 1, 30.

22. Ibid.

23. Ibid.

24. Jefferson Davis to the People of the Confederate States of America, April 4, 1865, *OR,* ser. 1, vol. 46, pt. 3, 1382–83.

25. Varina Davis probably read it in the *Charlotte Daily Bulletin.* The proclamation may have also been published, in whole or in part, by other Southern newspapers still able to receive telegrams.

26. Jefferson Davis to Gen. P. G. T. Beauregard, April 4, 1865, in Rowland, *Davis,* vol. 6.

27. Ryan, *Four Days in 1865,* 68–69.

28. Davis, *Long Surrender,* 54; Semmes, *Memoirs of Service Afloat,* 817.

29. Wise, *End of an Era,* 429–45.

30. Jefferson Davis to Varina Davis, April 5, 1865, in Strode, *Davis,* 149.

31. Varina Davis to Jefferson Davis, April 7, 1865, in Strode, *Davis,* 150.

32. According to J. Frank Carroll (*Confederate Treasure in Danville*), sometime during the week prior to the April 2 evacuation of Richmond, Treasurer John C. Hendren smashed the head of one of the kegs of Mexican silver dollars with the intent to use the coins to redeem Confederate paper money held by Richmonders. The problem was that the coins proved to be unpopular, since they were no longer recognized as legal tender by the U.S. government and could not be easily used to purchase goods. The use of the coins was thus abandoned. While the claim is unsubstantiated, the explanation is plausible.

33. See the appendix for a breakdown of the assets in the Confederate treasury and a discussion of the evidence pertaining to the disposition of the Mexican coins.

34. Some books on the flight of the Confederate government—e.g., Davis, *Long Surrender,* and Clark, *Last Train South*—refer to a John Hendera as a treasury clerk. The name also appears in the letter book of President Davis on a note concerning the Bank of Virginia check for $28,244 that the president had wanted cashed. The authors have not been unable to confirm, however, that anyone named Hendera was employed in the Treasury Department. Perhaps Hendera and Hendren were the same person. In any case, John C. Hendren apparently had responsibility as treasurer for the specie when it left Danville.

35. Mallory, "Flight from Richmond," pt. 1, 29.

Chapter 5: Flight South

1. A primary source for events concerning Gens. John C. Breckinridge and Robert E. Lee in the days leading up to the surrender of the Army of Northern Virginia on April 9, 1865, is Davis, *An Honorable Defeat.* Supporting documentation includes Gen. Isaac M. St. John to Jefferson Davis, July 14, 1873, in Rowland, *Davis,* 7:354–55, and Power, *Lee's Miserables,* 275–78.

2. The hamlet of Meherrin is about eighteen miles south of Farmville, Virginia. Lee had passed through Rice, where he previously telegraphed Davis, and was unable to go back there, because the enemy occupied the town. Apparently, however, Lee planned to march south of Farmville, and thus he would pass through Meherrin.

3. *OR,* ser. 1. vol. 46, pt. 3, 1388.

4. David Gardiner Tyler, Diary, April 7, 1865. A portion of the diary was published in *Tyler's Quarterly Magazine* 3 (1948):251–55.

5. In Lee's April 12 report to Jefferson Davis, he stated: "On the morning of the 9th, according to the reports of the ordnance officers, there were seven thousand eight hundred and ninety two (7892) organized infantry with arms, with an average of seventy-five (75) rounds of ammunition per man. The artillery, though re-

duced to sixty-three (63) pieces, with ninety-three (93) rounds of ammunition, was sufficient. These comprised all the supplies of ordnance that could be relied on in the State of Virginia. I have no accurate report of the cavalry, but believe it did not exceed two thousand and one hundred (2100) effective men." According to Union army records, however, 28,231 were paroled April 10–12, 1865. The discrepancy has never been satisfactorily explained.

6. David Gardiner Tyler, Diary, April 11, 1865.

7. Burke Davis (*Long Surrender*) states, "Captain Parker left behind in Greensboro two boxes of gold sovereigns valued at $35,000, for the use of Davis and the Cabinet. In addition, Parker left $39,000 to pay the troops of General Johnston." William H. Parker, however, makes no mention of the circumstances in his memoir, *Recollections of a Naval Officer.* In any case, the $39,000 was undoubtedly in Mexican silver dollars and probably had been reduced somewhat by the amount paid out in Danville in redeeming Confederate paper money.

8. Wise, *End of an Era,* 429.

9. Ibid., 446.

10. Jefferson Davis to Gen. Robert E. Lee, April 9, 1865, *OR,* ser. 1, vol. 46, pt. 3, 1390–91.

11. Dowdey and Manarin, *Wartime Papers of Robert E. Lee,* 934.

12. On the day of Lee's address to his troops, Gardie recorded in his diary that the Army of Northern Virginia was out of ammunition and surrounded by a "vastly superior force." They had received no rations for four days. In referring to Lee's farewell address, he noted, "It is full of feeling and worthy of the man."

13. Mallory, "Flight from Richmond," pt. 1, 31.

14. Some confusion exists as to the actual disposition of the foreign exchange. On the bottom of the order, now in private hands, Lucius Jones wrote, "This was the last order I received in the Confederate War." At a later date he added, "I turned the exchange over to Paymaster Micon at Wilmington, N. C." Yet Postmaster General John H. Reagan indicated in a June 29, 1872, letter to Jefferson Davis that "the acceptances on Liverpool were turned over to me and were taken by federal forces, with my other papers, when we were captured." In a subsequent letter to Davis, dated February 18, 1878, Reagan elaborated: "When we were at Abbeville, South Carolina, the Treasurer [Trenholm], or some officer of the Treasury brought to your attention the fact that there was in the Treasury acceptances on Liverpool and London to the amount of about eighteen thousand pounds sterling. By your direction, I took these bills of exchange into my possession, so that we might afterwards use them when needed. . . . When we were captured the bills of exchange above mentioned were in my saddle bags." If Reagan recalled events correctly, then Lucius Jones must have been wrong about turning over the acceptances to another paymaster after the war was over. Most

likely, at the direction of the president or Mallory, Jones turned them over to Reagan at Abbeville, which is where the Davis party was reunited with the treasury.

15. Jefferson Davis to Gen. Joseph E. Johnston, April 10, 1865, in Rowland, *Davis,* vol. 6.

16. Jefferson Davis to Danville mayor J. M. Walker, April 10, 1865, *OR,* ser. 1, vol. 46, pt. 3, 1391.

17. Ibid., 543.

18. Davis, *Honorable Defeat,* 118.

19. Ibid., 119.

20. Ibid.

21. Ibid., 121.

22. Ibid.

23. Julia could not have known that Robert Tyler, her husband's oldest son, was with the Confederate government during the evacuation of Richmond—though she may have wondered—and was ostensibly in some danger as well. As register, he had an official position with the Treasury Department, but he was probably not subject to arrest by the Union army and could have remained in Richmond. Either because he was uncertain about what might happen when U.S. troops entered the city or because he continued to be an ardent believer in the Confederate cause, he decided to accompany the administration south. Whatever his reason, he left with the Davis party but was released by the president at Charlotte. He then returned to Richmond for a short time before joining his family in Alabama.

Chapter 6: On to Washington

1. John Taylor Wood, Diary, April 11, 1865, John Taylor Wood Papers, Southern Historical Collection.

2. Primary sources for the discussion of events in Greensboro are Davis, *Honorable Defeat,* Davis, *Long Surrender,* Harrison, "Capture of Jefferson Davis," Mallory, *Last Days of the Confederate Government,* and the John Taylor Wood Diary.

3. Headquarters for Gen. William T. Sherman was in Raleigh, some eighty miles to the east of Greensboro. Union cavalry units, however, were raiding in the area, tearing up railroad tracks and telegraph lines and destroying goods and equipment that could be of use to benefit the Confederate war effort.

4. Harrison, "Capture of Jefferson Davis," 132.

5. Gen. John H. Winder died suddenly in February 1865, but his legacy of abusing, insulting, and arresting Greensboro citizens continued to the end of the war and certainly caused bitterness toward the Davis government.

6. Mallory, "Flight from Richmond," pt. 1, 31.

7. Mallory, "Flight from Richmond," pt. 2, 28.

8. Jefferson Davis to Gen. Joseph E. Johnston, April 11, 1865, in Rowland, *Davis,* vol. 6.

9. Dowdey and Manarin, *Wartime Papers of Robert E. Lee,* 935.

10. John Taylor Wood, Diary, April 12, 1865.

11. Davis, *Honorable Defeat,* 133.

12. Ibid., 134.

13. Parker, *Recollections,* 378.

14. Davis, *Long Surrender,* 73.

15. Varina Davis to Jefferson Davis, April 13, 1865, in Strode, *Davis,* 152. The "train" that Varina referrs to in her note to Davis is the train of wagons.

16. Parker, *Recollections,* 382.

17. Ibid.

18. Andrews, *War-Time Journal,* 176.

19. Ibid.

20. Davis, *Long Surrender,* 76.

21. Jefferson Davis to John C. Hendren, April 15, 1865, *OR,* ser. 1, vol. 47, pt. 3, 801.

22. Jefferson Davis to Varina Davis, April 14, 1865, in Strode, *Davis,* 152.

23. Harrison, "Capture of Jefferson Davis," 134.

24. Ibid., 135.

25. Davis, *Long Surrender,* 83.

26. Ibid., 83.

27. Davis, *Honorable Defeat,* 150–51.

28. Parker, *Recollections,* 378–79.

29. Harrison, "Capture of Jefferson Davis," 136.

30. Davis, *Long Surrender,* 85.

31. Mallory, "Flight from Richmond," pt. 2, 33.

32. Davis, *Long Surrender,* 86.

33. Jefferson Davis to Varina Davis, April 23, 1865, in Strode, *Davis,* 156.

34. Ibid., 157.

35. Ibid.

36. Wade Hampton to Jefferson Davis, April 19, 1865, in Strode, *Davis,* 155.

37. Davis, *Honorable Defeat,* 198–99.

38. J. Johnston to J. Schofield, May 8, 1865, *OR,* ser. 1, vol. 47, pt. 3, 443.

39. Capt. M. C. Runyan, Battlefield Report, May 13, 1865.

40. Other smaller forces still existed, namely the District of the Gulf under Maj. Gen. Dabney H. Maury, Georgia state troops under Governor Joseph E. Brown, Brig. Gen. Jeff Thompson's Brigade in Arkansas, forces in North Georgia under Brig. Gen. William T. Wofford, and a battalion of Cherokees, Creeks, Osage, and Seminoles under Brig. Gen. Stand Watie in Indian Territory.

41. John Alexander Tyler to Julia Gardiner Tyler, April 29, 1865, GTP.

Chapter 7: Dispersal of the Treasury

1. Primary sources for the discussion of events as the Davis party made its way out of North Carolina to Washington, Georgia, include Davis, *Honorable Defeat,* Davis, *Long Surrender,* Mallory, *Last Days of the Confederate Government,* and Parker, *Recollections.*

2. Davis, *Long Surrender,* 101.

3. Jefferson Davis to G. A. Trenholm, April 28, 1865, Library of Congress.

4. Davis, *Long Surrender,* 103.

5. Ibid., 112–13.

6. Varina Davis to Jefferson Davis, April 7, 1865, Library of Congress.

7. Ibid.

8. Harrison, "Capture of Jefferson Davis," 138.

9. Lt. George Peck had been the acting master of Parker's midshipmen school ship, CSS *Patrick Henry.* See Andrews, *War-Time Journal,* 187.

10. Andrews, *War-Time Journal,* 191.

11. Harrison, "Capture of Jefferson Davis," 139.

12. Ibid.

13. Burton Harrison to Jefferson Davis, May 2, 1865, Library of Congress.

14. Varina Davis to Jefferson Davis, May 3, 1865, Library of Congress.

15. Harrison, "Capture of Jefferson Davis," 139.

16. Parker, *Recollections,* 385.

17. The bank funds were transported from Augusta to Washington by wagon, under the supervision of Judge William Wood Crump. For some reason, the judge chose to separate the Richmond deposits from the treasury, which returned to Washington by train. In Washington, the bank funds were secured in the vault of the old bank building.

18. Davis, *Long Surrender,* 117.

19. Ibid.

20. Ibid., 118.

21. Ibid., 125.

22. Ibid., 123.

23. Though the $25 and $26 (as well as $26.50) per man have been reported in various sources, the amount is not probable, as that would mean more than four thousand troops were paid; the entire escort supposedly consisted of around a thousand. Also, $108,322.90 is an unusual amount in that it cannot be divided evenly. The most reasonable explanation is that some of the silver was taken by the soldiers and officially recorded in Washington as being paid out.

24. Mallory, "Flight from Richmond," pt. 2, 36. Louis Trezevant Wigfall was a former U.S. senator from Texas before being expelled in July 1861. He was a member of the Provisional Congress of the Confederacy and an aide to Jefferson Davis at the time, which was the probable reason for his dismissal. Wigfall commanded a brigade in the Army of Northern Virginia before taking a seat in the Confederate Congress. Once a close friend of Davis, he became an ardent and outspoken enemy of the president. From Washington, Georgia, Wigfall fled to Texas. Almost a year later he arrived in England, where he attempted to foment a war between England and the United States for the benefit of the South.

Chapter 8: Final Days of Freedom

1. The last days of freedom for the Confederate president and the capture of Jefferson and Varina Davis have been discussed in a variety of reference sources, including Clark, *Last Train South,* Davis, *Honorable Defeat,* Davis, *Long Surrender,* and Hanna, *Flight into Oblivion.* Primary source information is available from a wealth of reports in the *Official Records* and in the private document written by Burton Harrison, as well as the diary of John Taylor Wood.

2. Strode, *Davis,* 162.

3. Davis, *Long Surrender,* 111.

4. Gideon Welles to Rear Adm. Henry K. Thatcher, April 28, 1865.

5. Davis, *Long Surrender,* 126.

6. In the weeks before the collapse of the Confederacy, Edward M. Tidball was involved in a mystery that defies explanation. In the Edward M. Tidball Civil War Papers at Florida State University is a receipt signed by Henry Lillibridger, Quartermaster, Third Brigade, First Division, Twenty-third Corps for Confederate government property consisting of one spring wagon, two mules, and a set of harnesses. The mystery is that Tidball was in Charlotte, North Carolina, at the time, and the date of the receipt is clearly March 15, 1865, almost two weeks before the Davis government fled Richmond. Charlotte was still in Confederate hands, and the closest Union army was that of Sherman, then some one hundred miles to the east, near Raleigh. There had been no attack on Charlotte or a raid in the area by Union cavalry. Why was an official of the Confederate Navy Department relinquishing government property to a Union quartermaster in Confederate territory? Why was the quartermaster not arrested? Also interesting is the fact that, after the war, Tidball received a full pardon, signed by President Andrew Johnson and dated August 29, 1865. Such a pardon would seem unusual in that Confederate government officials were not permitted to apply for a pardon at that time. He also should have been disqualified because of the value of the property he owned in Winchester, Virginia. Was Tidball in collusion with the Union army or some element of the military? While there may be a reasonable explanation for why Tidball turned over the

Confederate property when and where he did and why he apparently received special treatment in terms of a pardon, the circumstances are certainly suspicious. Then, too, the fact that Semple never mentioned chasing down the gold given to Tidball even suggests the intriguing possibility that he learned of Tidball's connections while on the run and decided to avoid contacting him . . . a perfect example of exercising discretion over valor.

7. For details of the payouts made by Capt. Micajah H. Clark and the receipts taken, refer to the appendix.

8. John Taylor Wood, Diary, May 4, 1865.

9. Davis, *Long Surrender,* 136.

10. Clark, "Last Days of the Confederate Treasury," 542–57. Details for analysis are contained on various pages in the report.

11. Davis, *Long Surrender,* 137.

12. Rumors and wild guesses abounded as to the amount in the Confederate treasury and hence at the disposal of Jefferson Davis. Federal columns riding out from Macon, Georgia, were even teased with the possibility of capturing some fifteen million dollars in gold along with the Confederate president.

13. After leaving the Davis camp and escaping from Pritchard, Thorburn rode to Lake City, where he met with Capt. Louis M. Coxetter in an old railroad car. Like Thorburn, Coxetter had been a successful blockade-runner. Thorburn arranged to have Coxetter ready the boat hidden in the Indian River for the president. The plan was abandoned after Davis's capture on May 10.

14. Davis, *Long Surrender,* 144.

15. Midshipman Clifton Breckinridge and Lt. James Clay were both captured eleven miles below Macon on the night of May 10. They were, apparently, on their way to Fort Valley, some sixteen miles farther south. Clifton took his parole and made his way home to Lexington, Kentucky.

Chapter 9: Into the Night

1. Much of the discussion in this chapter is based on letters from Semple to Julia Gardiner Tyler over a period of years in which pieces of information are disclosed. Interactions involving Howell, Semple, Tidball, and Varina Davis played out against a background of known events, personal and historical, as the war drew to a close.

2. Still, *Confederate Navy,* 81–82.

3. Davis, *Long Surrender,* 183–84.

4. Tidball did not qualify for a pardon under the conditions of Johnson's amnesty proclamation of May 29, 1865. He had resigned his U.S. Navy commission to join the Confederacy, which made him ineligible. He may have applied for a special amnesty, which was provided for in the proclamation. In any case, his pardon must have been expedited, because it was issued three months to the day after

the date of the proclamation. With regard to the "farmhouse" that Tidball built, the $31,000 would be equivalent to $430,000 today. Thus Linden Farm was valued considerably more than the surrounding homes, which ranged from $200 to $6,000. Linden Farm exists today, and though the 206 acres purchased by Tidball in 1867 have been reduced to about 4 acres, the property is worth millions of dollars. A few years ago, the farmhouse was being renovated by a new owner. After opening up a wall, the owner discovered a letter that had been hidden for almost 140 years, when the house was being built. Edward M. Tidball had written the letter, which contained a listing of his assets. He stated that, as of February 1866, he still had possession of $27,000 in gold bullion from the Confederate treasury. (The house was built in 1867.)

5. Unfortunately for the new owner, Cedar Hill was burned to the ground, most probably by Union troops during the 1862 Peninsula campaign. Union forces burned other farms and outbuildings and stole furnishings and livestock while encamped in the area.

6. Semple to Julia Gardiner Tyler, June 6, 1866, GTP.

7. Semple to Julia Gardiner Tyler, August 3, 1866, GTP.

8. Semple was both a paymaster and a bureau chief. Paymasters who had more than twelve years of service (all service being considered, U.S. and Confederate) were equal in rank to a commander. As a bureau chief, Semple's rank was the same as that of a commodore, which was equal to a brigadier general in the army. See Still, *Confederate Navy*, 29, for discussion of paymaster equivalency ranks in the Confederate navy.

9. Semple to Julia Gardiner Tyler, January 3, 1867, GTP.

10. Semple to Julia Gardiner Tyler, undated—his first contact with Julia since leaving Richmond on April 2, 1865. His statement that he went to Nassau in combination with the dates of other letters and the locations from which they were written suggest the timing of his journey from Florida through Nassau and back to the United States.

11. Cashin, *First Lady of the Confederacy*, 163–64. Varina Davis to Martha Phillips, August 18, 1865, and Varina Davis to Mrs. Howell Cobb, September 9, 1865, in Rowland, *Varina Howell*, 465–66. Semple to Julia Gardiner Tyler, November 14, 1865, GTP.

12. Levin, *Awful Drama*, 171.

13. Shaw, "My Dearest Friend," 137–40.

14. "Passengers Arrived" (Column), *New York Times*, August 23, 1865.

15. David Gardiner Tyler to Julia Gardiner Tyler, June 26, 1865, GTP. No doubt adding to Gardie's frustration and depression was the absence of a response from his mother to his first letter. The end of the Confederacy and the Southern "way of life," the lack of adequate clothing and money, and the expectation of harassment from victorious Northerners and freed slaves almost certainly tempered the

teenager's normal humor and wit. After the war, the U.S. government prohibited Confederate soldiers from wearing their uniforms and any parts of their uniforms, such as buttons.

16. For a short time, war seemed possible between the United States and France over the continued presence of Emperor Maximilian in Mexico. Gardie may have been drawn to fighting for France for three reasons: (1) the adventure (he was now a "seasoned" soldier), (2) the fact that it could be another way to defeat the North, and (3) the possibility that drawing the United States into a war with France could make it easier for the South to reenter the Union (the North would need the South in any war). Ultimately, the United States would have no part of another devastating war.

17. The Reverend John Fulton and his wife were friends of Julia, and along with her, they had participated in Copperhead activities during the war. The Fultons planned to open a boardinghouse in Carlsruhe for British and American students.

Chapter 10: Gold Rush

1. The primary source for discussion of the events surrounding the president's baggage train is the diary of Tench Tilghman. The fate of the funds belonging to the Virginia banks and the unfortunate destiny of the Chenault family are related by various sources, including Andrews, *War-Time Journal,* Ashmore, "Story of the Confederate Treasure," and Davis, *Long Surrender.*

2. Tench Francisco Tilghman, Diary, May 16, 1865, Florida Historical Society.

3. Ibid., May 17, 1865.

4. Ibid.

5. Ibid., May 18, 1865.

6. Ibid., May 22, 1865.

7. Early in the war, Confederate military authorities wanted to tear up the iron of the Florida Railroad and transfer it to Georgia. Yulee opposed this and was led to believe that Davis was a primary supporter of the plan. Yulee had been falsely told there was a warrant out for his arrest and that Davis sanctioned this action. Only at the end of the war did Yulee learn that the rumor was false.

8. Tench Francisco Tilghman, Diary, May 22, 1865, Florida Historical Society.

9. Davis, *Long Surrender,* 188–89. After his release from Fort Monroe in July 1867, Davis asked Watson Van Benthuysen for the money that he had kept for the Davis family, "$5,000 more or less," which would be used for Davis's legal defense for charges brought against him by the U.S. Government. Van Benthuysen sent Davis a certificate of deposit for only $1,500 without any explanation as to why he did not fulfill his obligation to the Davis family.

10. Clark, "Last Days of the Confederate Treasury," 542–57.

11. Hanna, *Flight into Oblivion,* 118–19.

12. Ibid., 119.

13. *OR,* ser. 1, vol. 47, pt. 3, 653–56. The trunk, when found on the Yulee plan-tation by Union soldiers, contained Davis's personal effects (tobacco, hair brush, comb, toothbrushes, socks, and underwear) as well as the cipher used for "official" and personal communications.

14. Ibid., 653–56.

15. Davis, *Long Surrender,* 185.

16. Ibid., 185.

17. Ibid. Brig. Gen. Edward Porter Alexander was a native of Washington, Geor-gia. He developed a system of signal-flag communication and also saw the potential in viewing enemy positions from the air; he watched the battle of Gaines's Mill in June 1862 from an observation balloon. Alexander commanded Lee's artillery at Gettysburg in July 1863, survived a wound at Petersburg, and surrendered with Lee at Appomattox Court House.

18. Andrews, *War-Time Journal,* 269.

19. Davis, *Long Surrender,* 186.

20. Ibid., 187.

Chapter 11: The Prisoner

1. Various sources were referred to in relating the capture and imprisonment of Jefferson Davis, including letters between the president and his wife, Hanna, *Flight into Oblivion,* Davis, *Long Surrender,* Davis, *Honorable Defeat,* Davis, *Rise and Fall of the Confederate Government,* Harrison, "Capture of Jefferson Davis," the John Taylor Wood Diary, and the *Official Records.*

2. Harrison, "Capture of Jefferson Davis," 145.

3. Ibid.

4. Davis, *Honorable Defeat,* 310.

5. Harrison, "Capture of Jefferson Davis," 145.

6. Ibid.

7. Davis, *Long Surrender,* 153.

8. Clay-Clopton, *Belle of the Fifties,* 257.

9. Ibid.

10. Ibid., 259.

11. Ibid.

12. Ibid.

13. Wheeler, "Effort of Rescue," 88–89.

14. Ibid., 89.

15. Clay-Clopton, *Belle of the Fifties,* 260. USS *Tuscarora* was a screw sloop that tried unsuccessfully to capture the cruiser CSS *Nashville* in 1862 as the Confederate vessel sailed to England and became the first ship to fly the Confederate flag in

British waters. *Tuscarora* served primarily in the North Atlantic as part of the blockading squadron in both the North and South Atlantic before escorting the Confederate prisoners to Hampton Roads.

16. As indicated in chapter 2, note 22, CSS *Stonewall* was an ironclad ram built in Bordeaux, France, and acquired by the Confederacy in 1865. If the warship had succeeded in operating along the East Coast, it would have been a formidable opponent for the *Tuscarora*. Unfortunately for the Confederacy, the *Stonewall* arrived too late in the war to be of any benefit.

17. Clay-Clopton, *Belle of the Fifties,* 260.

18. Wheeler, "Effort of Rescue," 90.

19. Clay-Clopton, *Belle of the Fifties,* 261.

20. Allen, *Davis,* 423–24.

21. Davis, *Long Surrender,* 181.

22. Clay-Clopton, *Belle of the Fifties,* 269.

23. Ibid., 271.

24. Ibid., 270.

25. Ibid., 270–72.

26. Varina Davis to Jefferson Davis, September 14, 1865, in Strode, *Davis,* 174.

27. Clay-Clopton, *Belle of the Fifties,* 330.

28. Davis, *Long Surrender,* 220.

29. Harrison, *Recollections Grave and Gay,* 265–68.

30. Burton Harrison to Constance Cary, May 13, 1867, in Strode, *Davis,* 269.

31. Davis, *Long Surrender,* 223.

Chapter 12: Brother and Sister

1. Semple to Julia Gardiner Tyler, January 3, 1866, GTP.

2. Levin, *Awful Drama,* 171.

3. Sympathy for the Irish ran in the Tyler family and may have rubbed off on Semple. Robert Tyler, John Tyler's oldest son and a close friend of Semple, had been president of the Irish Repeal Association in Philadelphia in the 1840s. Robert's brother, John Tyler Jr., gave himself the rank of "general" after the war and was active in Fenian affairs in the late 1860s.

4. An overview of the Fenian movement can be found online: "The Fenian Raid and Battle of Ridgeway June 1–3, 1866," www.acsu.buffalo.edu/~dbertuca/g/Fenian-Raid.html.

5. In Montreal in 1865, one out of every eight people was Irish.

6. Andrew Johnson and Secretary of War Stanton were slow to act on protests by the British government and were actually sympathetic to the Fenian cause. They even looked the other way in terms of arms, ammunition, and equipment being supplied to the Fenians on U.S. soil. While they may have felt they were intimidating

England as a punishment for supporting the Confederacy, they also were playing into Semple's hands by bringing the two countries closer to war.

7. Semple to Julia Gardiner Tyler, March 28, 1866, GTP.

8. Semple to Julia Gardiner Tyler, possibly early October 1865, GTP. This is his initial contact with her after the war.

9. Julia Gardiner Tyler to Julianna Gardiner, May 2, 1848, GTP.

10. Two letters archived at Yale University are examples of instances in which Semple and Julia Gardiner Tyler almost certainly spent time together in a hotel: Semple to Julia Gardiner Tyler, June 6, 1866; and Semple to Julia Gardiner Tyler, September 6, 1866.

11. Semple to Julia Gardiner Tyler, November 16, 1865, GTP.

12. Ibid.

13. Semple to Julia Gardiner Tyler, January 3, 1866, GTP.

14. Ibid.

15. Semple to Julia Gardiner Tyler, March 28, 1866, GTP.

16. Semple to Julia Gardiner Tyler, April 6, 1866, GTP.

17. Julia Gardiner Tyler to Julia "Julie" Tyler, April 18, 1866, GTP.

18. Semple to Julia Gardiner Tyler, May 7, 1866, GTP.

19. Semple to Julia Gardiner Tyler, May 27, 1866, GTP.

20. Semple to Julia Gardiner Tyler, May 14, 1866, GTP. In fairness to Julia, she was extremely generous in helping friends in the South at the end of the war, and she sent clothing and shoes to those in need. Apparently, her generosity was more timely than payment of the bills. In time, however, all of her bills were paid.

21. Ibid.

22. Semple to Julia Gardiner Tyler, June 6, 1866, GTP. A point to be considered is that Julia was never unaware of who she was. She was definitely indiscrete for the times when it came to visiting a man in his hotel room, and there is evidence she spent the night. But whatever her feelings may have been for Semple, very few of her letters to him are known to have survived, the most notable of which addresses his expression of love for her. "Shall I admit," she wrote, "that it gave me pleasure to read your professions of ardent affection? Perhaps it should have been otherwise, and I shall rather chide you for avowals that do not entirely agree with the abiding friendship I wish should grow up between us—but it is so sweet to be caressed when the heart finds little difficulty in responding that I will forgive you the mere expression of a letter and reproach only myself for suffering their influence to be so agreeable and soothing." The intent is clear; she had taken a public position, but the question remains, was the letter ever sent? It is archived among her effects, and there is no known response from Semple. If this letter was sent and survived, one must then ask, where are the bulk of her letters to Semple? Why would a relative, years later, in commenting on a trunk of Julia's letters,

be reluctant to donate them to a library because of what they contained? In her view, "all the world loves a lover," and they were much too personal for anyone but the family. If Julia actually sought to discourage Semple, why would he have ignored her wishes and continued to write about his feelings for her? Consider, for example, his letter to her on January 13, 1867. He wrote: "Had I ever supposed when I was leaving you at the Hotel that it was to be my [last] affectionate adieu, the kiss I now have given you would have been, as old Chaucer has it 'long, long kiss, a kiss of youth' and could have been ready to enjoy and hear a [] of angels now."

23. Semple to Julia Gardiner Tyler, June 17, 1866, GTP.
24. Semple to Julia Gardiner Tyler, August 13, 1866, GTP.
25. Ibid.
26. Semple to Julia Gardiner Tyler, September 6, 1866, GTP.
27. Ibid.

Chapter 13: Exodus

1. A multitude of sources describe the postwar years for Confederate leaders such as Davis and his cabinet as well as others of importance in his administration. Davis, *Rise and Fall of the Confederate Government,* Davis, *Long Surrender,* and Hanna, *Flight into Oblivion* are notable. See also Nepveaux, *Trenholm and the Company That Went to War,* and Durkin, *Mallory.*

2. Davis was so weakened by his years in prison that city sounds tormented him; he could hardly endure overhearing conversations in a room and the laughter and noise of playing children. Living in a cheap, run-down, and depressing boardinghouse also added to his misery and emotional exhaustion. Davis, then sixty years old, also fell while carrying his daughter Winnie downstairs; he used his body to absorb the fall and protect the child, and his recovery afterward was not quick.

3. Cashin, *First Lady of the Confederacy,* 184.
4. Procter, *Not Without Honor,* 176.
5. Harrison, *Recollections Grave and Gay,* 268.
6. Anna Trenholm Diary.
7. Morgan, *Recollections of a Rebel Reefer,* 248.
8. Ibid., 250.
9. Shingleton, *John Taylor Wood,* 137–38.
10. London *Times,* May 6, 1884. Benjamin had retired the previous year, and after many years of separation from his wife, he returned to Paris and, in the months before his death, to her.
11. Despite the information provided by Mallory, CSS *Shenandoah* continued its cruise in the North Pacific in June 1865, during which time, more than two dozen vessels were captured, most of which were destroyed. The raider then began a

slow voyage toward San Francisco, which the ship's captain believed would be lightly defended. On August 2, 1865, the Confederates encountered an English vessel that had recently departed from San Francisco and learned the war was over. After disarming the ship, they sailed for Liverpool and turned the vessel over to the Royal Navy.

12. Morgan, *Recollections of a Rebel Reefer,* 149.

Chapter 14: Disillusionment and Deceit

1. Semple to Julia Gardiner Tyler, November 27, 1866, GTP.

2. Ibid. In future years, Letitia Semple became destitute. The school failed, and Semple, who had run out of money himself, was evidently unable to help. In the 1870s, the Louise Home was built by Washington DC banker and entrepreneur William W. Corcoran, who invited Letitia to live there with free room and board. The Louise Home was created for elderly women of distinguished backgrounds who found themselves in "genteel poverty." She was often escorted to White House events by Corcoran, and she was a frequent guest of President William McKinley and his wife, Ida, who put the first lady's horse and carriage at Letitia's disposal. She refused, however, to enter the White House after Theodore Roosevelt's "atrocious" renovation in 1902. Letitia lived at the Louise Home until her death on December 28, 1908.

3. Ibid.

4. Semple to Julia Gardiner Tyler, January 3, 1867, GTP.

5. Semple to Julia Gardiner Tyler, February 5, 1867, GTP.

6. Semple to Julia Gardiner Tyler, February 7, 1867, GTP.

7. Semple to Julia Gardiner Tyler, February 26, 1867, GTP. Semple's fascination with Birdie is intriguing. He was especially close to Alex and Gardie, undoubtedly because they lived with him in Richmond and he saw to their comfort and safety. Julie regarded him as an older brother as well, and he often inquired about her. Lachlan, Lyon, and Robert Fitzwalter were younger and within an age range in which they apparently paid less attention to their frequent "visitor." In any case, they are seldom mentioned by Semple in his letters to Julia, and he seems to have no particular advice for them. Birdie, however, is another matter. Semple often closed his letters by mentioning "my Birdie" or by asking Julia to "give Birdie a kiss for me," etc. Certainly, his affection for her can be attributed to the fact that she was a cute five-year-old child, the youngest of Julia's children. That would account for the fawns he bought for Birdie and the dog he also had delivered to Castleton Hill. But why would he intend to give her the land he owned in Texas and Kentucky? Why not Julia or Alex or Gardie or Julie? Was he simply irrational or was there another reason?

8. Semple to Julia Gardiner Tyler, February 15, 1867, GTP.

9. Semple to Letitia Tyler Semple, July 27, 1867, GTP.

10. Semple's advice to Julia and her family members seems to have waned after his July response to Letitia. In moving back to Richmond, he tried to restore some normalcy to his life, apparently, in part, by returning to the neighborhood where he was born and raised, and he again engaged in farming. Cedar Hill was gone, of course, and he either rented property or stayed with friends. Little or nothing of his previous wealth remained.

11. Semple to Julia Gardiner Tyler, October 19, 1867, GTP.

12. Will of James A. Semple, New Kent County, Virginia, Will Book 1, 10–13, probated December 13, 1883.

13. The Mechanics National Bank of New York was founded in 1810, and a vestige of it exists today in that it has gone through fourteen acquisitions, mergers, and name changes, and is now part of the Federal JP Morgan Chase Bank system. Semple's bank account records no longer exist in any of the bank archives.

BIBLIOGRAPHY

PRIMARY REFERENCE SOURCES

Books and Diaries

Allen, Felicity. *Jefferson Davis, Unconquerable Heart*. Columbia: University of Missouri Press, 1999.

Andrews, Eliza Frances. *War-Time Journal of a Georgia Girl 1864–1865*. New York: Appleton, 1908.

Beers, Fannie A. *Memoirs: A Record of Personal Experience and Adventure During Four Years of War*. Philadelphia: Lippincott, 1888.

Carroll, J. Frank. *Confederate Treasure in Danville*. Danville, VA: URE Press, 1996.

Cashin, Joan E. *First Lady of the Confederacy*. Cambridge, MA: Belknap Press of Harvard University Press, 2006.

Clark, James C. *Last Train South: The Flight of the Confederate Government from Richmond*. Jefferson, NC: McFarland, 1984.

Clay-Clopton, Virginia. *A Belle of the Fifties*. New York: Doubleday, 1905.

Coleman, Elizabeth Tyler. *Priscilla Cooper Tyler*. University: University of Alabama Press, 1955.

Corley, Florence Fleming. *Confederate City: Augusta, Georgia, 1860–1865*. Columbia: University of South Carolina Press, 1960.

Coski, John M. *Capital Navy: The Men, Ships and Operations of the James River Squadron*. New York: Savas Beatie, 2005.

Crist, Lynda Lasswell, et al., eds. *The Papers of Jefferson Davis*. 11 vols. Baton Rouge: Louisiana State University Press, 1991–2003.

Dance, Daryl Cumber. *The Lineage of Abraham: The Biography of a Free Black Family in Charles City, VA*. N.p.: Privately published, n.d.

Davis, Burke. *The Long Surrender*. New York: Vintage Books, 1989.

Davis, William C. *An Honorable Defeat: The Last Days of the Confederate Government*. New York: Harcourt Books, 2001.

Davis, Jefferson. *The Rise and Fall of the Confederate Government*. 2 vols. New York: Da Capo, 1990.

Davis, Varina. *Jefferson Davis, A Memoir.* New York: Belford, 1890.

De Leon, T. C. *Four Years in Rebel Capitals: An Inside View of Life in the Southern Confederacy from Birth to Death.* Mobile, AL: Gossip, 1890.

Dowdey, Clifford, and Louis H. Manarin, eds. *The Wartime Papers of Robert E. Lee.* Boston: Little, Brown and Co., 1961.

Driver, Robert J., Jr. *The 1st and 2nd Rockbridge Artillery.* Virginia Regimental Histories Series. Lynchburg, VA: Howard, 1987.

Durkin, Joseph T. *Stephen R. Mallory: Confederate Navy Chief.* Columbia: University of South Carolina Press, 1987.

Freeman, D. S., ed. *A Calendar of Confederate Papers.* New York: Kraus, 1969.

Furgurson, Ernest B. *Ashes of Glory: Richmond at War.* Vintage Civil War Library. New York: Vintage Books, 1996.

Gorgas, Josiah. *Civil War Diary of Josiah Gorgas.* Tuscaloosa: University of Alabama Press, 1947.

Grant, Ulysses S. *Personal Memoirs of U. S. Grant.* 2 vols. New York: Webster, 1885–86.

Hanna, A. J. *Flight into Oblivion.* Richmond: Johnson, 1938.

Harrison, Constance. *Recollections Grave and Gay.* New York: Scribner, 1911.

Hoehling, A. A., and Mary Hoehling. *The Day Richmond Died.* Lanham, MD: Madison Books, 1981.

Jones, John B. *A Rebel War Clerk's Diary.* 2 vols. Philadelphia: Lippincott, 1866.

Kean, Robert. *Inside the Confederate Government.* Baton Rouge: Louisiana State University Press, 1957.

Lankford, Nelson. *Richmond Burning.* New York: Penguin, 2002.

Lee, Richard M. *General Lee's City: An Illustrated Guide to the Historic Sites of Confederate Richmond.* McLean, VA: EPM, 1987.

Levin, Alexandra Lee. *This Awful Drama.* New York: Vantage Press, 1987.

MacDonald, John A. *Troublous Times in Canada: A History of the Fenian Raids of 1866 and 1870.* Toronto: Johnston, 1910.

McCabe, James D., Jr. *Lights and Shadows of New York Life; or the Sights and Sensations of the Great City.* Philadelphia: National Publishing Company, n.d.

McGuire, Judith B. *Diary of a Southern Refugee During the War.* Harrisonburg, VA: Sprinkle, 1996.

Morgan, James M. *Midshipman in Gray.* Boston: Houghton Mifflin, 1917.

Nepveux, Ethel Trenholm Seabrook. *George A. Trenholm: Financial Genius of the Confederacy.* Anderson, SC: Electric City Printing, 1999.

———. *George Alfred Trenholm and the Company That Went to War, 1861–1865.* Anderson, SC: Electric City Printing, 1994.

Parker, William Harwar. *Recollections of a Naval Officer, 1841–1865.* New York: Scribners, 1883.

Pember, Phoebe Yates. *A Southern Woman's Story: Life in Confederate Richmond.* Edited by Bell Wiley. Jackson, TN: McCowat-Mercer Press, 1959.

Procter, Ben. *Not Without Honor.* Austin: University of Texas Press, 1962.

Reagan, John H. *Memoirs, with Special Reference to Secession and the Civil War.* 2 vols. New York: Neale, 1906.

Rowland, Dunbar. *Jefferson Davis, Constitutionalist: His Letters, Papers, and Speeches.* 10 vols. New York: Little and Ives, 1923.

Rowland, Eron. *Varina Howell: Wife of Jefferson Davis.* Gretna, LA: Pelican, 1998.

Ryan, David D. *Four Days in 1865: The Fall of Richmond.* Richmond: Cadmus, 1993.

Semmes, Raphael. *Memoirs of Service Afloat During the War Between the States.* Baton Rouge: Louisiana State University Press, 1996.

Senior, Hereward. *The Last Invasion of Canada: The Fenian Raids, 1866–1870.* Toronto: Dundurn, 1991.

Shaw, Arthur. *William Preston Johnston.* Baton Rouge: Louisiana State University Press, 1943.

Shingleton, Royce. *John Taylor Wood, Sea Ghost of the Confederacy.* Athens: University of Georgia Press, 1979.

Still, William N., Jr., ed. *The Confederate Navy: The Ships, Men and Organization, 1861–65.* London: Conway Maritime Press, 1997.

Strode, Hudson. *Jefferson Davis: Private Letters, 1823–1889.* New York: Da Capo Press, 1995.

Anna Trenholm Diary. University of South Carolina, Columbia, South Carolina.

David Gardiner Tyler Diary (portions). *Tyler Quarterly Magazine* 3 (1948): 251–55.

Tyler, Lyon Gardiner. *Letters and Times of the Tylers.* 3 vols. Richmond: Whittet & Shepperson, 1884.

Waugh, John C. *Sam Bell Maxey and the Confederate Indians.* Fort Worth, TX: Ryan Place, 1995.

John Taylor Wood Diary. Southern Historical Collection, University of North Carolina, Chapel Hill, North Carolina.

Letters and Manuscripts

Campbell, Given. Memorandum of a Journal Kept Daily During the Last March of Jefferson Davis.

Crowder, James. James Preston Crowder Papers, Emory University, Atlanta, Georgia.

W. W. Crump Papers. Virginia Historical Society.

Fenian Brotherhood Collection. The American Catholic History Research Center, Catholic University, Washington DC.

Mary Burrows Fontaine to Marie Burrows Sayre, April 30, 1865. Museum of the Confederacy, Richmond, Virginia.

Gardiner, Lion, Journal (1660). In *History of the Pequot War: The Contemporary Ac-*

counts of Mason, Underhill, Vincent and Gardener. Cleveland: Helman-Taylor Co., 1897. The original document is at the Norfolk Public Library, Norfolk, Virginia.

Gardiner-Tyler Family Papers. Yale University.

Lightfoot, Emmeline Allman Crump. "Evacuation of Richmond." Manuscript Collection. Virginia Historical Society, Richmond, Virginia.

Private documents found in a wall of the Edward M. Tidball farmhouse by current owner T. P. Goodman.

Quarles, Mann S. "Memoirs of Mann S. Quarles, April 2, 1901." Museum of the Confederacy, Richmond, Virginia.

Runyan, M. C. Battlefield Report, May 13, 1865.

Henry C. Semple Papers. Southern Historical Collection, University of North Carolina, Chapel Hill, North Carolina.

Semple, James A. "Report of the Office of Provisions and Clothing, October 1864." Southern Historical Society Papers, University of North Carolina, Chapel Hill, North Carolina.

William T. Sherman to Abraham Lincoln, December 22, 1864. Library of Congress, Washington DC.

Southern Historical Society Letter Collection: Briggs, J. B., to Jefferson Davis, December 26, 1881; Clark, M. H., to Jefferson Davis, December 23, 1881; Davis, Jefferson, to P. G. T. Beauregard, April 5, 1865; Reagan, John H., to Jefferson Davis, June 29, 1872; Reagan, John H., to Jefferson Davis, February 18, 1878; Reagan, John H., to Jefferson Davis, December 12, 1880; Richardson, F. E., to W. T. Walthall, August 26, 1878; Turnstall, G. W., to Jefferson Davis, March 29, 1888; Wheless, John F., to Jefferson Davis, February 10, 1882.

St. John, I. M. "Resources of the Confederacy in 1865." Southern Historical Society Papers, 21. University of North Carolina, Chapel Hill, North Carolina.

Tyler Family Papers. Virginia Historical Society.

Tyler Collection. College of William and Mary.

Articles and Periodicals

Averill, J. H. "Richmond, Virginia. The Evacuation of the City and the Days Preceding It." *Southern Historical Society Papers* 25 (1897): 267–73.

"Britons in the Civil War: John Mitchel and Family." *Crossfire.* The American Civil War Round Table UK. April 1993.

Bruce, H. W. "Some Reminiscences of the Second of April, 1865." *Southern Historical Society Papers* 9 (May 1881): 206–11.

Clark, Micajah H. "The Last Days of the Confederate Treasury and What Became of Its Specie." *Southern Historical Society Papers* 24 (1896): 351–53.

———. "Retreat of the Cabinet from Richmond." *Confederate Veteran* 6 (July 1898): 542–57.

Duke, R. T. W. "Burning of Richmond." *Southern Historical Society Papers* 25 (1897): 134–38.

Gilliam, Robert. "Last of the Confederate Treasury Department." *Confederate Veteran* 37 (November 1929): 110–11.

Gorgas, Amelia. "The Evacuation of Richmond." *Confederate Veteran* 25 (March 1917): 110–11.

Harrison, Burton. "Capture of Jefferson Davis." *Century Magazine,* November 1883, 130–45.

Holcomb, Julie. "Confederate Express Agent James P. Hawkins Got Caught Up in the Evacuation of Richmond." *America's Civil War,* May 2003.

Lee, George T. *South Atlantic Quarterly* (July 1927).

Mallory, Stephen R. "The Last Days of the Confederate Government." *McClure's Magazine,* December 1900, 99–107; January 1901, 239–48. Also published under title "Flight from Richmond." *Civil War Times Illustrated,* April 1972, 25–31; June 1972, 28–36.

Parker, William H. "The Gold and Silver in the Confederate States Treasury." *Southern Historical Society Papers* 21 (1893): 304–13.

Quarles, Garland R. "Some Old Homes in Frederick County, Virginia." Winchester-Frederick Country Historical Society.

"Resources of the Confederacy in 1865: Report of General I. M. St. John, Commissary General." *Southern Historical Society Papers* 3 (March 1877): 97–111.

Shaw, Arthur Marvin. "My Dearest Friend: A Letter from Mrs. Jefferson Davis." *Southwest Review* 33 (Spring 1948): 137–40.

Tucker, Dallas. "The Fall of Richmnond." *Southern Historical Society Papers* 29 (1901): 152–63.

Wheeler, Joseph. "An Effort to Rescue Jefferson Davis." *Century Magazine,* May 1898, 88–89.

Wheless, John F. "The Confederate Treasure: Statement of Paymaster John F. Wheless." *Southern Historical Society Papers* 10 (March 1882): 137–41.

Other Sources

1880 map of Danville, Virginia. City Clerk's Office, Danville, Virginia.

Beers, Henry Putney. *The Confederacy: A Guide to the Archives of the Government of the Confederate States of America.* Washington DC: National Archives Trust Fund Board, 1986.

Certificate of Death: Letitia Tyler Semple.

The City Intelligencer; or Stranger's Guide. University of North Carolina, Chapel Hill, North Carolina.

DeSemple Descendants, Chart. Private papers.

Marriage Records, Winchester, Virginia, 1783–1931.

National Archives and Records Administration. Dictionary of American Fighting Ships. Washington, DC.

———. U.S. Navy Pension Records and Service Records. Washington DC.

New Kent County (VA) Will Book.

Presgraves, Jim (Reprinter). *New Kent Country, Charles City County: Families & History.* Reprinted from *Hardesty's Historical and Geographical Encyclopedia.* Chicago, 1884, Wytheville, VA, 2000.

Register of Students in William and Mary College, 1827–1881. *William and Mary Quarterly* (July 1923): 159–70.

Richmond City Business Directory, 1860.

Tidball, Edward M. Civil War Papers. Florida State University. Tallahassee.

U.S. Census, Frederick County, Virginia, 1870.

U.S. Navy Department. *Official Records of the Union and Confederate Navies in the War of the Rebellion.* 30 vols. Washington DC: Government Printing Office, 1894–1927.

U.S. Navy Historical Center. Ships' History Section. Washington DC.

U.S. War Department. *The War of the Rebellion: A Compilation of the Official Records of the Union and Confederate Armies.* 128 vols. Washington, DC: Government Printing Office, 1880–1901. Cited as *OR* in the notes section.

Wood, John Taylor, Papers (includes diary). University of North Carolina at Chapel Hill (Southern Historical Collection).

SECONDARY REFERENCE SOURCES

Books

Ball, Douglas B. *Financial Failure and Confederate Defeat.* Urbana: University of Illinois Press, 1991.

Bill, Alfred Hoyt. *The Beleaguered City: Richmond 1861–1865.* New York: Knoff, 1946.

Bulloch, James D. *The Secret Service of the Confederate States in Europe.* 2 vols. New York: Sagamore Press, 1959.

Brubaker, John H., III. *The Last Capital.* Danville, VA, 1907.

Chesson, Michael Bedout, and Leslie Jean Roberts, eds. *Exile in Richmond: The Confederate Journal of Henri Garidel.* Charlottesville: University Press of Virginia, 2001.

Chitwood, Oliver Perry. *John Tyler: Champion of the Old South.* Newtown, CT: American Political Biography Press, 2003.

Davis, Burke. *To Appomattox: Nine April Days, 1865.* New York: Rinehart & Co., 1959.

Davis, William C. *Jefferson Davis: The Man and His Hour, a Biography.* New York: HarperCollins, 1991.

Evans, Clement A., ed. *The South After the War and the Confederate Navy.* Confederate Military History, vol. 13. Secaucus, NJ: Blue & Grey Press, n.d.

Evans, Eli N. *Judah P. Benjamin: The Jewish Confederate.* New York: Free Press, 1988.

Gray, Wood. *The Hidden Civil War: The Story of the Copperheads.* New York: Viking, 1942.

Greenberg, Brian. *Worker and Community: Response to Industrialization in a Nineteenth Century American City.* Albany: State University of New York Press, 1865.

Headley, John W. *Confederate Operations in Canada and New York.* New York: Neale, 1906.

Hernon, Joseph M., Jr. *Celts, Catholics, and Copperheads.* Columbus: Ohio State University Press, 1968.

Hoehling, A. A., and Mary Hoehling. *The Last Days of the Confederacy.* New York: Fairfax, 1981.

Hoy, Claire. *Canadians in the Civil War.* Toronto: McArthur & Co., 2004.

Kimball, Gregg D. *American City, Southern Place: A Cultural History of Antebellum Richmond.* Athens: University of Georgia Press, 2000.

Markle, Donald E. *Spies and Spymasters of the Civil War.* New York: Hippocrene, 2004.

Marquis, Greg. *In Armageddon's Shadow: The Civil War and Canada's Maritime Provinces.* Montreal: McGill-Queen's University Press, 1998.

Marvel, William. *Lee's Last Retreat: The Flight to Appomattox.* Chapel Hill: University of North Carolina Press, 2002.

Pollard, Edward A. *Southern History of the War.* New York: Fairfax Press, 1977.

Power, J. Tracy. *Lee's Miserables: Life in the Army of Northern Virginia from the Wilderness to Appomattox.* Chapel Hill: University of North Carolina Press, 1998.

Putnam, Sallie B. *Richmond During the War; Four Years of Personal Observation.* London: Carleton & Co., 1867.

Rattray, Everett T. *The South Fork: The Land and People of Eastern Long Island.* New York: Random House, 1979.

Sharf, J. Thomas. *History of the Confederate States Navy: From its Organization to the Surrender of Its Last Vessel.* New York: Fairfax Press, 1977.

Tidwell, William A. *April '65: Confederate Covert Action in the American Civil War.* Kent, OH: Kent State University Press, 1995.

Trudeau, Noah Andre. *Out of the Storm.* Boston: Little, Brown and Co., 1994.

Varon, Elizabeth R. *Southern Lady, Yankee Spy.* New York: Oxford University Press, 2003.

Winik, Jay. *April 1865: The Month That Saved America.* New York: HarperCollins, 2001.

Winks, Robin W. *Canada and the United States: The Civil War Years.* Montreal: Harvest House, 1971.

Wright, John H., comp. *Compendium of the Confederacy: An Annotated Bibliography.* 2
    vols. Wilmington, NC: Broadfoot, 1989.

Other Sources

Ashmore, Otis. "The Story of the Confederate Treasure." *Georgia Historical Quarterly*
    2 (September 1918): 119–38.
Richmond Dispatch, various 1865 issues.
Richmond Enquirer, various 1865 issues.

INDEX